guitar facts

the essential reference guide

Thunder Bay Press

An imprint of the Advantage Publishers Group
5880 Oberlin Drive, San Diego, CA 92121-4794
www.thunderbaybooks.com

Volume copyright © 2006 Outline Press (Book Publishers) Ltd.
Text © 2006 the authors, as detailed in Acknowledgements, p96.
Music: ℗ and © 2006 the featured composers and performers.
DVD: © 2006 Outline Press (Book Publishers) Ltd.

All notations of errors or omissions should be addressed to Thunder
Bay Press, Editorial Department, at the above address. All other
correspondence (author inquiries, permissions) concerning the content
of this book should be addressed to Outline Press (Book Publishers) Ltd, 2a
Union Court, 20-22 Union Road, London SW4 6JP, England.

ISBN-13: 978-1-59223-673-2
ISBN-10: 1-59223-673-1

1 2 3 4 5 10 09 08 07 06

Origination and print by Colorprint (Hong Kong)

Text editor: **John Morrish**
Music editor: **Rod Fogg**
Design: **Paul Cooper Design, Balley Design Limited**

No responsibility for loss occasioned to any person acting or refraining
from action as a result of the material in this publication can be
accepted by Thunder Bay Press, Outline Press Ltd, or the authors.

The publishers have made strenuous efforts to contact the owners of any
copyright material used in the preparation of this package. Any additional
information will be welcomed by the publishers.

contents

Somewhere down the line, you get hooked. Probably it's someone you see playing one on TV, or maybe a mindblowing gig you experience. But eventually, you can't deny its allure any longer. That beautiful electric guitar!

For me as a child, it was the magical instruments of John Lennon, Paul McCartney, and George Harrison that first fascinated me. I really couldn't put into words then why I loved John, Paul, and George's guitars so much; it seemed so blindingly obvious and elemental that it hardly occurred to me to even try.

Later on, it was Jimi Hendrix's slithery Strats, the custom SGs of Frank Zappa and Todd Rundgren, Jan Akkerman and Jeff Beck's black Les Pauls, the exotic double-necked instruments of John McLaughlin and Jimmy Page – these guitars and a thousand others all held me in their sway for different reasons. Even though my musical training had been on keyboard, my need to play the guitar became overwhelming.

I suspect it's much the same for you – that's why you're reading this book, isn't it? Needless to say, if it's the electric guitar you love, you've assuredly come to the right place.

It's something to do with the ability to bend and sustain a note, I figure, but there's undeniably a singing/crying quality to the guitar, a human sound that most anyone can understand. People who are mortally offended by the sound of squealing, loudly expressive guitar seem likely to have issues with emotionally expressive human behavior in general.

The guitar is your therapist, your biographer, and your armor. Why biographer? Because the guitar reveals things about yourself that few people would ever speak about. But when you can convert your feelings into notes, the guitar protects your secrecy at the same time it tells the world your secrets. Nifty trick, that.

The guitar connotes freedom – from convention, repression, politeness. But it's also a tool of the greatest sensitivity, a means to deliver the most delicate melodic beauty. Sometimes you hear a player who can take you from one extreme to another in the twinkling of a phrase, in a completely natural and uncontrived way, using their own individual vocabulary, their "voice" as a player. This is what style is, and this is what every player can arrive at – as long as they don't give up playing. The electric guitar is a friend for life, and will be as patient with you as you're willing to be with yourself.

Before the advent of synthesizers and computers in music, all the wildest sounds on pop records used to come from the electric guitar, through a variety of sound modification devices, effects pedals, mixing-board alchemy, and endless amplifier-speaker combinations. As you travel through your own journey as a guitarist, you'll discover the secret formulas as to how all those amazing sounds were created – but to the innocent listener, it will all sound like magic, just like The Beatles sounded to me when I was a kid.

There's your job, electric guitarist – bring some magic into the world! And have a fantastic time doing it.

Mike Keneally
Mike is a fine guitarist who has played with Frank Zappa, Steve Vai, Robert Fripp, and many other legendary musicians. He now tours with The Mike Keneally Band.

Airline

White Stripes star Jack White's use of a 1964 "Res-O-Glas" (fiberglass) Airline model has elevated the status of these guitars enormously in recent years, although they have traditionally been of slightly less interest than the somewhat similarly styled National models.

The Airline brandname was used by the Montgomery Ward mail-order company in the 1950s/1960s on instruments supplied by a number of manufacturers. Some were produced by Kay, but others by Valco, the company that made guitars for National and Supro. Most of the Valco-made Airlines are similar to the more basic Supros, though some -- like White's guitar -- have unconventional body shapes with more deluxe appointments.

Aria

Japanese guitar-maker Aria attained a level of quality, player respect, and professional endorsement in the late 1970s and early '80s when the majority of its Asian peers were still struggling with credibility issues in western markets.

Aria was one of the seminal companies in the globalization of guitar-making, with a history that includes major involvement in the 1970s "copy era." Along the way, Aria produced an extraordinary number of guitar models. The sheer magnitude of Aria lines and the worldwide markets in which they have been sold is daunting.

The company was founded in Japan as an importing operation by classical guitarist Shiro Arai in the early 1950s. Arai began manufacturing classical guitars around 1956 and entered the electric market in 1960, developing a mix of solidbodies and hollowbodies (including a "violin"-shape body) bearing the Arai, Aria, Aria Diamond, and Diamond brandnames, as well as manufacturing various instruments for other companies.

The turning point came at the NAMM instrument trade show in the US in 1968 where Gibson was exhibiting its newly reissued Les Pauls. This inspired Arai in 1969 to build the first Japanese-made bolt-on-neck copy of the Gibson classic, formally kicking off the "copy era" of the 1970s. Copies of the Ampeg Dan Armstrong clear Lucite guitar and Fender's Telecaster quickly followed, mushrooming into copies of virtually all popular American guitar models.

In the mid 1970s Aria added another electric-guitar brand, Aria Pro II, including models with fancy inlay. The Aria brandname continued to be used in various markets. Many of the better models were built at the Japanese Matsumoku factory, until it closed in 1987. Copies continued until 1978, the year Aria picked up its first big-name endorser in Herb Ellis, whose PE-175 was a Gibson-inspired archtop electric. Full-body and thinline electrics would be mainstay Aria offerings from this time.

c1964
Airline (Valco made)

1982
Aria Urchin Deluxe

However, 1977 saw the introduction of Aria's first truly original design, the Matsumoku-made PE Prototype series. These were either set-neck or bolt-on-neck single-cutaway guitars with carved tops and a sweeping curve down from the body's upper shoulder into the cutaway opposite. The Japanese PE Prototypes, many with luxurious appointments, some with vibratos and P.J. Marx pickups, were succeeded by Korean-made versions that began to appear in 1988.

More original Aria designs debuted in 1979, including offset-double-cutaway guitars with pointy horns, and a signature hollowbody for British jazzer Ike Isaacs. The first RS Rev Sound series were through-neck guitars made in an Alembic style, with active electronics, and a few double-necks. They lasted until 1982. The TS Thor Sound (also called Tri-Sound) guitars were passive or active, in set-neck, bolt-on-neck and through-neck configurations, and lasted until 1983. Lines offered in Europe included the shortlived YS and NK (Noise Killer) series.

In 1981 Aria added the CS Cardinal Sound series with passive electronics (lots of switches on some models) and either bolt-on or glued-in necks. Most of these were

> ### 1964 Airline Res-O-Glas model
> **BODY:** modernistic semi-solid body made from fiberglass.
>
> **NECK:** bolt-on maple neck with bound rosewood fingerboard; 20 narrow nickel-silver frets; 14th fret neck/body joint; zero fret; 1 ⅝" nut width, 24 ¾" scale length..
>
> **HEADSTOCK:** six-a-side open-gear tuners, plastic nut.
>
> **BRIDGE:** basic bar bridge adjustable for height only; trapeze tailpiece.
>
> **ELECTRONICS:** two wide-topped single coil pickups with individual Volume and Tone controls; three-way selector switch and master Volume.
>
> **SOUND:** wiry, gritty and bright. A classic lo-fi or garage rock sound.

available for a few years. In 1982 Aria helped start a wave of exotic guitar shapes, introducing its B.C.-Rich-inspired Urchin series (to 1984), the mini-Flying-V XX series and the mini-Explorer ZZ series, the latter two with fancy paint jobs and available in one form or another through 1987. From 1982 to 1986 some of the models from different series were rolled into a Black'n'Gold line with appropriate black finishes and gold hardware.

In 1983 Aria introduced a revamped RS Rev Sound line with Strat-like styling and bolt-on necks. In a number of variations, these would dominate Aria's offerings into the 1990s. The earliest of these second-generation Rev Sound guitars came with elegant thin horns and were either active or passive, although after 1985 most were passive, with models such as the Bobcat,

---

1982 Aria Urchin Deluxe

BODY: dual cutaway pointy design made from solid alder with flamed maple top.

NECK: bolt-on neck with 22 medium jumbo frets, unbound rosewood fingerboard, 12" radius, 1 ¹¹⁄₁₆" nut width, 24 ¾" scale length.

HEADSTOCK: back-angled asymmetrical headstock, three-per-side enclosed die-cast tuners, synthetic nut.

BRIDGE: vintage Stratocaster vibrato-style unit, saddles individually adjustable for height and intonation.

ELECTRONICS: two Aria humbucking pickups with individual Volume controls and master Tone control; three-way toggle pickup selector; ¼" output.

SOUND: full fat and heavy, with a degree of snap and edge. A tone aimed at generally heavy rock styles.

Wildcat and Straycat suggesting directions to come.

By the mid 1980s the RS profile would thicken up to take on even more of a Fender style. Other popular mid-1980s models in this long-running series included the Knight Warrior and Road Warrior. In 1985 the definition of RS was changed to Rock Solid, then the Cat series in 1986. Original Aria locking vibratos were joined by Kahlers in 1986. These guitars lasted through 1987 and the end of Matsumoku's Japanese factory.

A number of other Japanese-made offset-double-cutaway lines were also offered during this period, including the MM Mega Metal, IC Interceptor, IG Integra, GT and XR series, many being variations on the superstrat, but none as popular as the Cats.

In 1987 Aria briefly offered a US Custom series of American-made guitars. That same year Aria shifted its general production to Korea, continuing the superstrat theme and beginning with the SL series, followed by a

mind-dizzying list of essentially similar models over the next few years. Mainly these were differentiated by timbers, figured tops, level of appointments and sometimes subtle differences in body contouring.

A few of the better models continued to be made in Japan, but the need to remain at a lower price-point meant that the majority of production was now based in Korea. In 1988-89 came the CT, LB Libra, VA Vanguard, and WR Warrior series, supplanted in 1989 by yet more superstrats including the Polaris, VS, and AW series. These were replaced by the FS, JS, XL Excel, VP Viper, and MA Magna series in 1990, many remaining for a few years. In 1991 the high-end AQ Aquanotes appeared, later evolving into the CR Cobra line. These were followed by the current and decidedly low-end STGs in 1993. Most were gone by the mid 1990s.

During 1991 Aria made a line of Ventures signature models, revived in 1999. In 1994 Aria's US distributor NHF Industries unveiled a single-cutaway model originally called the Nashville 93, styled by British designer Trev Wilkinson and originally made in the US. Gretsch objected to use of the Nashville name and the guitar became the 615 Custom, named for Nashville's telephone area code. Lower-grade 615s were made in Korea until 1998.

Launched at the same time was the more Strat-like Fullerton series, with further Wilkinson input. The top models were made in the US, most others in Korea. At the end of the decade the Aria Pro II line was anchored by PEs (renamed Pro Electrics), Fullerton, and STG solidbodies, plus the long-running TA thinlines and FA "jazzers."

Baldwin

The distinctive shapes and styles of many of Jim Burns's British-made guitars have often been known to players in the US with the Baldwin brand name attached.

In the 1960s this Cincinnati-based specialist maker of pianos and organs briefly dabbled with electric guitars. In 1965 they bid unsuccessfully for Fender but bought the Burns company of England for $250,000. Burns already had some American experience through the distributor Lipsky and by badging some models with the Ampeg brand.

After Baldwin took control there were "transition" examples; a few guitars even carried both Burns and Baldwin brands. In 1966 the existing Nu-Sonic, GB65 and CB66 models were dropped and various changes made. Most significant was a new "flattened-scroll" headstock, replacing the original Burns type on most models. The Baby Bison and Vibraslim were redesigned with a new, short Rezo-tube vibrato.

1965 Baldwin Double Six

BODY: offset double-cutaway body made from solid alder.

NECK: bolt-on maple neck with bound rosewood fingerboard with 21 narrow nickel-silver frets, 7 ¼" radius, 1 ¹¹⁄₁₆" nut width, 25 ½" scale length.

HEADSTOCK: symmetrical headstock with six-a-side tuners; zero fret.

BRIDGE: simple notched steel bar bridge, adjustable via thumbscrews for height only; covered stop-bar type tailpiece.

ELECTRONICS: three single-coil Burns Tri-Sonic pickups, made with ceramic magnets, DC resistance approximately 6.5k to 7.5k; three-way switch to select each pickup individually, controls for master Volume and individual Tone for neck and middle pickups only.

SOUND: bright and twangy, but with some body, depth and sizzle; good power, clarity and sustain.

In 1967 Baldwin introduced the Gibson 335-like 700 series, with Italian-made bodies. By 1968 bar-magnet pickups were being fitted to the Marvin and Bison models. In 1970 Baldwin discontinued Burns production, concentrating their particular management skills on Gretsch, which they had acquired in 1967.

B.C. Rich

The guitars of the B.C. Rich company defined the "pointy rock axe" before such a genre existed, and have remained major players in a corner of the market devoted to heavier sounds and more radical styling.

B.C. Rich founder Bernardo Chavez Rico was a pioneer in through-neck, radically shaped solidbodies with onboard pre-amps and lots of switches. His guitars became favored by heavy players like Tony Iommi, Rick Derringer, Nikki Sixx, Blackie Lawless and Lita Ford. It's ironic to note, therefore, that Rico began as a flamenco and classical guitarist making acoustic guitars in his father's Los Angeles shop in the mid 1950s.

The first guitars branded B.C. Rich were acoustics, beginning around 1966, while the first electrics were fancy Gibson copies in 1969. Rico's first original through-neck, heel-less design was the single-cutaway Seagull, around 1971 – with an extra little point on the upper bout indicating B.C. Rich's future direction. Early pickups were Gibsons and Guilds, followed by DiMarzio humbuckers from 1974-86. Seagulls were endorsed by Dominic Troiano and Dick Wagner.

Then came the studies in graceful angularity for which B.C. Rich is known, including the Mockingbird and novel ten-string Bich (1976), the Warlock (1981), and Ironbird, Wave and Stealth models (1983). Fancy woods and bright paint jobs were

1979 B.C. Rich Mockingbird Standard

BODY: radical dual-offset-cutaway body made from maple with mahogany stripes, maple neck/body core.

NECK: neck-through-body construction with maple neck/body core with unbound rosewood finberboard; 24 jumbo nickel-silver frets, 1 $\frac{11}{16}$" nut width (approximately) and 12" fingerboard radius; 25 $\frac{1}{2}$" scale length.

HEADSTOCK: back-angled headstock, with three-a-side Grover Imperial tuners; bone nut.

BRIDGE: Leo Quan Badass Bridge (modified wrapover style) with six individually adjustable saddles.

ELECTRONICS: two DiMarzio humbucking pickups; controls for master Volume, preamp Volume, and master Tone; large three-way toggle switch for selection of pickups individually or together; mini toggle switches for preamp on/off, pickup phase, and 'Dual Sound' selections for each pickup; six-position rotary control (chickenhead knob) for Veritone-style tonal presets.

SOUND: bright, stinging and hot at its core, with a broad range of passive and active variables.

Brian Moore

While some of the respected new independent makers that emerged in the 1990s might be regarded as offering upgraded examples of classic models, Brain Moore guitars are not easily pinned to being a direct descendant of anything that has gone before. The company has forged a look and vibe that is all its own by achieving a fine balance between conventional wood and newer composite materials, married to sometimes exotic modern styling.

Patrick Cummings, ex-Gibson general manager, teamed up with Brian Moore, ex-Steinberger plastics expert, to produce high-end, exclusive guitars, starting in 1994 and based in Brewster, New York. The first model was the M/C1 (Moore/Cummings). Its composite semi-hollow body had a center-block inside to acoustically "tune" the instrument, and an arched figured-wood top. Recent instruments have been virtually all wooden. The Korean-made iGuitar, a synth-access hybrid instrument, and the more conventional iSeries debuted in 2000. The C90 and DC/1 are popular modles from the Brian Moore Custom Shop, and feature contored and highly figured maple tops.

Burns

Nothing looks, plays or sounds quite like an original Burns (except, briefly, a Baldwin). These British-made guitars have earned a certain revival of status thanks to their use by notable Brit-rock players of the late 1990s and 2000s.

Jim Burns was born in north-east England in 1925. His first production guitar, the Ike Isaacs Short Scale model, appeared on the market in 1958 with the Supersound brandname. Only about 20 were made.

In 1959 Jim joined forces with Henry Weill. Burns-Weill guitars were somewhat crudely constructed and among the earliest British-made production solidbodies. The line included the small-bodied Fenton and the RP (named for British session player Roy Plummer). The angular body shape and Art Deco headstock of the RP soon earned it the nickname "Martian cricket bat." Few Burns-Weill guitars were made; by late 1959 the partnership was over.

In 1960 Jim Burns formed Ormston Burns Ltd (though many guitars were branded "Burns London"). The first guitar was the Artiste, with advanced features for its time including a heel-less set neck and 24 frets. With a Burns vibrato tailpiece it soon became the Vibra Artiste. The Sonic was a popular twin-pickup small-bodied solid aimed at beginners.

The first high-end Burns was the Bison, launched in 1961. The body's long,

sweeping horns curved upwards, inwards and forwards to create a unique sculpture in wood. Originally the Bison appeared as a set-neck, four-pickup guitar liberally adorned with gold-plating, ebony fingerboard, a new bridge/vibrato unit boasting maximum sustain and smooth operation, a patented "gear box" truss-rod system (later adopted by Gretsch), and low-impedance Ultra Sonic pickups linked to new circuitry that included a novel Split Sound effect. Only 50 were built before a revised version was introduced in 1962 with bolt-on neck, rosewood fingerboard, three pickups, simplified vibrato and chrome-plated hardware. While not as eye-catching as its predecessor, it was a more playable, practical guitar, seemingly the epitome of Burns design, character, quality, and innovation.

More new models appeared in 1962 including the Jazz Split Sound and Split Sonic guitars, with Bison-style circuitry linked to three Split Sound pickups. Cheaper partners were the two-pickup Jazz and three-pickup Vista Sonic. In 1963 Burns ventured into semi-acoustics with the twin-pickup TR2. Its on-board "active"

1964 Burns Marvin:

BODY: offset double-cutaway body of solid alder, with ribcage and forearm contours.

NECK: bolt-on maple neck with unbound rosewood fingerboard; with 7 $\frac{1}{4}$" fingerboard radius, 21 nickel-silver frets, 1 $\frac{5}{8}$" nut width; 25 $\frac{1}{2}$" scale length.

HEADSTOCK: symmetrical scroll topped headstock with three-a-side tuners; zero fret.

BRIDGE: Burns Rezo-tube vibrato system.

ELECTRONICS: three Burns Rez-o-matik single coil pickups with six individual alnico slug pole pieces, DC resistance approximately 6k. Three-way switch to select each pickup individually, with three 250k potentiometers for master Volume, and Tone controls for neck and middle pickups.

SOUND: bright and cutting, with a certain openness and depth at its core.

---

typical, and Craig Chaquico of Jefferson Starship was an endorser in 1980. A few bolt-neck B.C. Riches were built in the late 1970s, including the Nighthawk (Eagle-style) and Phoenix (Mockingbird). A number of Strat-style guitars (ST, Gunslinger, Outlaw) debuted in 1987.

B.C. Rich began making guitars outside the US in 1976 with a small number of B.C. Rico-brand Eagles produced in Japan. Asian production resumed in 1984-86 with the Japanese-made NJ Series (for Nagoya, Japan), versions of popular designs as well as some 335-style Standard thinlines, and the US Production Series (US-assembled Korean kits). The Korean-made Rave and Platinum Series followed in 1986, the same year the NJ Series shifted production to the Cort factory in Korea.

Marketing of the non-US guitars was taken over in America in 1987 by Class Axe of New Jersey, who introduced their own design, the Virgin, that year. In 1989 Bernie Rico began a three-year break, licensing to Class Axe the rights to B.C. Rich. During his vacation Rico built handmade Mason Bernard guitars.

In 1994 Rico resumed building B.C. Rich guitars in Hesperia, California, including extra-fancy versions of classics (arched tops, figured woods, abalone trim), variations of other popular guitars (Junior V, Tele-style Blaster), signature models (Jeff Cook, Kerry King), and new designs (super-pointy Ignitor; contoured-top, Tele-style Robert Conti six- and eight-strings). Rico died in 1999; since then his son Bernie Jr continued the company.

transistorized pre-amp, for wider tone colors, was an idea ahead of its time. The TR2 was superseded in 1964 by the similarly-styled but passive Vibraslim line.

The next Burns classic was the Marvin, introduced in 1964, designed in conjunction with Hank Marvin. The Marvin copied the construction, scale-length and circuitry of Hank's famous Fender Strat. But the headstock had a distinctive "scroll" top, and a two-bar handrest and three-piece pickguard completed the visual distinctions. The Marvin's new Rez-o-Matik pickups were modeled on Fender, although unlike the Strat all three were angled. The main innovation was a new Rezo-tube vibrato unit which had

a knife-edge bearing and six tubes to anchor the strings rather than Fender's single metal block. The vibrato was largely responsible for the Marvin's tone, somewhat sweeter and deeper than the Fender. Only about 400 original Marvins were produced.

The Bison was restyled to match the new Marvin, losing much of its distinctive character in the process. Also launched at this time was the Double Six 12-string. Players have included Mike Pender, Chris Britton and Hank Marvin plus, later, Mark Knopfler, Gaz Coombes of Supergrass, Alex Kapranos of Franz Ferdinand, and Phil Solem of The Rembrandts. Further down the line, the Sonics were replaced by the Nu-Sonics; Vista Sonics and Split Sonics were gone by 1965. Additions included the GB65, GB66 and Virginian semis, the latter with the round soundhole of a flat-top acoustic.

In September 1965, the Baldwin Piano & Organ Company bought Burns for $250,000 (see Baldwin). The last Burns to appear prior to the Baldwin takeover was the Baby Bison, coincidentally produced for export only. Baldwin acquired sole rights to the Burns brand, so Jim Burns used his middle name, Ormston, as a brand for his late-1960s instruments, including a semi-solid six-string that prompted the line of Hayman guitars he helped develop in 1969 (see Hayman).

In 1973 the Burns UK company was formed. First and best-known model was the Flyte, endorsed by Dave Hill and Marc Bolan. The body design was apparently based on the Concorde aircraft, and two poor Mach One Humbuster pickups were fitted alongside the Dynamic Tension bridge/tailpiece. The Mirage and Artist followed in 1976, later joined by the final Burns UK model, the LJ24. This better guitar came too late to revive the company, which collapsed later that year.

The new "Jim Burns" company was launched in 1979. Despite commercial pressure to revive the best of the past, the company decided to produce new models. First was the odd Scorpion. The body had two carved Scorpion-like lower horns and a headstock representing the sting in the tail. Next came the Steer, reminiscent of the Virginian, and the budget Magpie.

In 1981 the company finally acknowledged demand for vintage styles and issued revised versions of the Marvin and Bison. But economies were made and the revivals lacked much of the character and quality of the originals. In 1983 the Bandit appeared, a small-bodied solid with unusual multi-angled styling. This last effort was the best, but by 1984 the erratic and misguided Jim Burns operation had ceased trading.

Jim himself returned to inactivity and obscurity, while many of his early creations continued to attract more interest on the "vintage" market. In 1991 a British company, Burns London, began producing authentic reproductions and updates of 1960s classics. These included 30/50 Anniversary editions of the Bison and others in 1994. The following year saw the Nu-Sonic, an old name on a Telecaster-style instrument. In 1999 a new Club series was launched with the Marquee model.

In its heyday of the 1960s, Burns represented the best of British guitar design and construction. While not always equal to some of the competition in terms of sound, Burns quality and playability was rarely in question. Jim Burns died in 1998, but his original designs stand as testimony to the man regarded by many guitar fans as the British Leo Fender.

Carvin

The mail-order-only nature of Carvin's business has meant this guitar and amp maker is often not as readily recognized as other quality American brands, although the company's roots go back nearly as far as those of it's California neighbor, Fender.

Carvin guitars had their roots in the Kiesel-brand Bakelite lap-steels and amps made in Los Angeles by Lowell C. Kiesel, beginning in 1947. A distribution problem led in 1949 to a change of brandname – Carvin was named for Lowell's sons Carson and Gavin – and relocation to Covina, California, plus a switch to mail-order. Since mail-order Carvins are essentially custom-made, a variety of options have been available since the beginning.

Carvin began to re-market Harmony and Kay Spanish guitars outfitted with Carvin pickups in 1954, offering its original, Kiesel-designed SGB solidbody with a distinctive body point from 1955 to 1961. Early endorsers included country stars Joe Maphis and Larry Collins. From 1962-68 a more Fender-style body with a steep lower cutaway was used; Bigsby vibratos became standard-issue in 1963. This model was later played by John Cippolina. German Hofner-made necks were used from 1964-76.

In 1968 Carvin relocated to Escondido, California, changing its model designations to SS, briefly using Japanese Strat-style bodies, then switching to German-made bodies the following year. Gibson-style double-cutaway AS55B and AS51 "Thin Acoustical Guitars" began about this time. In 1976 Carvin moved to a larger factory and began producing its first hex-pole pickups, and CM96 or DC150 Stereo Gibson-style solidbodies, now with Carvin-made necks.

Carvin guitar construction switched to glued-in necks in 1978. The company's distinctive sharp-horned offset-double-cutaway shape appeared on the DC200, designed by Mark Kiesel, in 1980. In 1981 this was offered as the DC200K in koa, marking the beginning of Carvin's use of more exotic timbers, standard on high-end models or as options.

Carvin DC production models continued to proliferate with different pickup configurations. From around 1985-88 a DC160 version of the DC150 appeared in quilted maple. By 1989 the typical Carvin three-tuners-a-side headstock was replaced with a pointy-droopy six-in-line version, and several double-neck options were available. That year the flamed-maple DC400 version of the DC200 also debuted.

F A C T   F I L E

The term **Superstrat** is used to define the updated, hot-rodded Fender Stratocaster-inspired designs popularized in the 1980s, which carried more and fatter frets, deeper cutaways, powerful humbucking pickups in a revised layout, and a high-performance (locking) vibrato system. Many also had pointy or dropped headstocks.

In 1985 Carvin made its first venture into exotic shapes with the four-point V220, similar to a Dean ML and endorsed by Craig Chaquico. This was followed in 1987 by the Ultra V, inspired by the Jackson Randy Rhoads. In 1988 Carvin changed construction again to through-neck style, and this became Carvin's favored form of manufacturing. The original Explorer-style headstocks on these changed to pointy-droopy six-tuners-in-line in 1989. A more pointy X220 replaced the V220 in 1990. Pointy guitars were gone by 1993.

From 1987 to 1990 Carvin offered another thinline electric, the SH225, a double-humbucker guitar with very rounded equal cutaways. In 1989 only a rounded-horn version of the offset-cutaway model was offered, the DC145. By the late 1980s Carvin products were used by a host of pros including Elvin Bishop, Jeff Cook, Larry Coryell, Marshall Crenshaw, Lita Ford, Ray Gomez, Alex Lifeson, Steve Lynch and Rick Nielsen, among many others. Later endorsers would also include Jason Becker and Al DiMeola.

In 1991 Carvin augmented its catalog (and factory showroom) by opening two retail outlets in Hollywood and Santa Ana, California, followed later by several European stores. That year a 12-string version of the DC200, the DC120, appeared.

In 1993, with vintage guitar designs all the rage, Carvin added the classic Telecaster-style shape to its repertoire with the TL60, joined the following year by the f-holed AE185. This trend was "solidified" with the solidbody Tele-like SC90 in 1996, the same year Carvin introduced its flagship Allan Holdsworth signature guitar with a two-and-four headstock and an extra dip on the lower bout.

Charvel

Another early name at the front of the "pointy headstock" brigade, Charvel gained a huge dose of credibility at the hands of Edward Van Halen, who ushered in a new style of rock lead-guitar playing using an early model from this maker.

Charvel grew from a small supplier of guitar parts in the late 1970s to a major producer of rock guitars in the 1980s. In 1974 Wayne Charvel set up a guitar repair business in Azusa, northern Los Angeles, California (and soon moved to nearby San Dimas). Charvel began supplying much-needed hardware replacement parts, and from this humble beginning the line would expand to include bodies, necks, pickups and, ultimately, complete guitar kits.

Financial problems struck in 1977, and late the following year Charvel signed over his name and entire operation to employee Grover Jackson. (Charvel himself went on to run several shortlived companies in the 1980s, and launched his own Wayne brand in 1999.)

Grover Jackson continued to offer a customizing service at Charvel for other instruments, while honing his own ideas on guitar design. The results eventually appeared in limited form in 1979 with the first Charvel-brand guitars, of which included Van Halen's famous instrument.

At the start of the 1980s Jackson added a new line under his own name (see Jackson). The Charvel brand was reserved for bolt-on-neck guitars with essentially Fender-style bodies and necks – as well as Gibson- or Vox-inspired alternatives and an original four-point "star" shape. Options in 1981 also included various DiMarzio pickups and flashy custom paint jobs.

Business grew as Jackson's efforts led to high-profile associations with key emerging guitar heroes. In 1986 a joint venture with distributor IMC of Fort Worth, Texas, resulted in a less-expensive made-in-Japan Charvel line sporting Jackson's by now established drooped "pointy" headstock. Jackson/Charvel relocated a few miles east to Ontario, California, by 1987.

The new Charvel line remained Fender-styled: Models One, Two, Three and Four each employed a bolt-on neck and Strat-like body shape. Models Five and Six featured 24-fret through-neck construction allied to a slimmer-horned body. This and the pointy headstock would become characteristics of the new "superstrat" styling, as would Model Six's sharkfin-shape fingerboard markers.

1991
Charvel Surfcaster

Pickup layouts included a single bridge humbucker, as well as the two-single-coils-plus-bridge-humbucker strongly identified with the new rock-oriented superstrats. Vibratos too were considered as mandatory equipment then.

By 1988 the line had expanded, but the following year saw a major revamp signified by a new Charvel logo in a "script" style as on Jacksons. Models were split into named series including Contemporary, Classic, Fusion and Professional. The market for superstrats was now clearly defined, and the new Charvels – fine examples of high-end Japanese mass-manufacture – were intended to fill every niche.

A Korean-made line, new for 1989, was branded Charvette By Charvel and aimed at entry-level players, though by 1991 all instruments regardless of origin were branded Charvel. Some new 1990 models catered for traditional as well as extreme tastes: the Strat-style STs and Tele-like TE contrasted the Avenger's offset-V shape that echoed Jackson's Randy Rhoads.

One of the first determined moves into retro-flavored original design came in 1991 with the Surfcaster semi-solid, a mutated Jazzmaster/Rickenbacker/Danelectro that began as a custom Jackson. The Charvels initially came in six-string (vibrato or fixed-

bridge) and 12-string models. The CX series took over from the Charvettes, maintaining Charvel's low-end presence. A new overtly Fender-style headstock was soon amended to a design that seemed intended to calm trademark lawyers.

In 1994 Charvel's San Dimas series was introduced, named for the location of the old Charvel facility. This marked a return to US manufacture (though three years earlier there had been a limited-edition remake of the original late-1970s model), while the budget CHS series was launched in 1995. The acquistion of Jackson/Charvel by the Japanese electronic musical instrument company Akai in 1997 marked the end of Charvel-brand instruments.

Coral

Danelectro's association with guitarist Vincent Bell and the release of the first widely available electric 12-string continued later in the decade with the spin-off brand Coral, which remains best known for it's slightly unusual "alternative" instruments.

In 1966 the entertainment conglomerate MCA bought Danelectro. MCA maintained the company's base in Neptune, New Jersey, along with founder Nat Daniel, but one of the changes made was the addition of a new Danelectro-made brand in 1967, Coral. The name came from one of MCA's record labels.

1978
Dean Z

Danelectro Standard 3021

BODY: semi-solid body made with poplar core and side frames (sometimes pine, and later plywood) with Masonite (hardboard) top and back; side joints covered with stick-on wallpaper tape.

NECK: bolt-on, one-piece poplar neck with unbound rosewood fingerboard with 9 ½" fingerboard radius, 21 narrow nickel-silver frets, and 1 ⅝" nut width; 25" scale length.

HEADSTOCK: three-per-side tuners; aluminum nut.

BRIDGE: height-adjustable steel bridge plate with one-piece rosewood saddle.

ELECTRONICS: two single-coil 'lipstick tube' pickups, each with a single alnico bar magnet and DC resistance of approximately 4.25k to 4.75k; one stacked double potentiometer for each pickup, with concentric Volume and Tone controls; three-way switch to select each pickup individually or both in series for a hotter output.

SOUND: fairly light and bright, but with a sweet blend of sparkle and depth and a gently percussive attack. Fatter and warmer in the middle switch position.

guitar facts

The first Corals shared the Jaguar-like shape and short Strat-style head of contemporary Danelectros, but were solidbodies with a Coral logo and the unusual "crackle" finishes of the Dane D series. Models included the two- or three-pickup Hornet and 12-string Scorpion.

Joining these Corals in 1967 was the vaguely US-map shaped Coral Sitar, endorsed by Al Nichol and Tom Dawes. Like the earlier Danelectro Bellzouki 12-string, it was co-designed by session-man Vinnie Bell who had spotted a demand in New York studios in the mid 1960s for trendy sitar sounds, popular since George Harrison used a real sitar on The Beatles' 1965 track 'Norwegian Wood.' Bell prompted Danelectro to devise an electric guitar that would make a sitar-like sound. The secret was the flat plastic "bridge" that gave a buzzy sound – and made intonation almost impossible. There was also a bank of 13 extra "drone" strings tuned in half-steps. A similarly-shaped Coral Bellzouki 12-string was also introduced.

New, too, were the f-hole thinline hollowbody Firefly, flat-top Vincent Bell Combo, and Long Horn Series (f-hole hollow versions of the older Danelectro Long Horns). Coral vanished with Danelectro's demise in 1969.

Danelectro

Despite a propensity for meager materials and simple designs, Danelectro did a lot of things correctly right from the very start. Guitars that were devised to be playable but affordable instruments for beginners and novices caught the attention of a surprising number of professional musicians, and have become minor and enduring classics.

Probably no other instruments so humble have garnered as much reverence as Danelectro guitars of the 1950s and 1960s, thrust into immortality primarily through association with the mail-order catalog of Sears, Roebuck. Before competition from Japanese imports, "Danos" were the beginner guitars of the post-war Baby Boom generation.

A Danelectro is reported to have set Jerry Garcia on the road to eventual stardom, and the guitars are heard on records from The Archies' 'Sugar, Sugar' to The Monkees' 'I'm A Believer' and Simon & Garfunkel's 'Sound of Silence.' They have been played by artists as diverse as Jimi Hendrix, Jimmy Page and Los Lobos.

Danelectro's founder was Nathan I. (Nat) Daniel. He began his career in 1933 building amps for a department store in New York City, and the following year was recruited by Epiphone's Herb Sunshine to build the earliest Epiphone Electar amps. Until 1942 Daniel

---

Late-1950s Danelectro U-2

BODY: solid poplar core and side frames (sometimes pine, and later plywood) with ⅜" masonite top and back; side joints covered with stick-on wallpaper tape.

NECK: bolt-on, one-piece poplar neck and rosewood fingerboard with approximately 9.5" radius, 21 nickel-silver frets, and 1.64" nut width; 25" scale length.

HEADSTOCK: three-per-side Kluson tuners; aluminum nut.

BRIDGE: height-adjustable steel bridge plate with one-piece, non-adjustable rosewood saddle.

ELECTRONICS: two identical single-coil 'lipstick tube' pickups, each with single alnico bar magnet and a DC resistance of approximately 4.25k to 4.75k. Two concentric (stacked) 1 meg/100k potentiometers for Volume and Tone for each pickup; three-way switch to select each pickup individually or both in series for a hotter output (standard both-pickups wiring is in parallel).

SOUND: fairly light and bright, but with a sweet blend of sparkle and depth, and a gently percussive attack.

---

continued to supply Epiphone products.

The Danelectro company was founded in 1946 and began supplying amps for mail-order company Montgomery Ward in 1947, and for Sears in 1948. In 1954 Danelectro expanded into solidbody electric guitars, introducing its own Danelectro-brand models. That same year, in the Fall Sears catalog, Danelectro-made Silvertone-brand guitars replaced solidbodies previously made by Harmony. These were small Les-Paul-shaped guitars with either one or two single-coil pickups concealed under a melamine pickguard: Danelectro-brand

---

F A C T   F I L E

As basic as they might appear, the Danelectro "lipstick tube" pickup has been acknowledged as a clever design and a great-sounding unit by many contemporary makers and professional players respectively. The elongated silver tube – made from the joined pair of lipstick tops that give the device its name – contains a single alnico bar magnet around which a coil has been wound, to create a relatively low-powered pickup. Vintage examples typically have DC resistance readings in the 4.25k to 4.75k range. Although not powerful, lipstick tube pickups have a bright, clear tone that still offers a degree of warmth and depth, along with great definition. It's a classic pickup for jangly or chimey styles of playing.

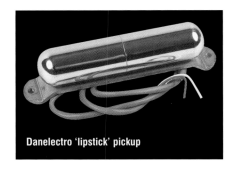

Danelectro 'lipstick' pickup

---

versions were covered in white tweed vinyl (with wide "bell" headstocks); the Silvertones in maroon vinyl (with wide "Coke bottle" headstocks). Most Danelectro guitars sported simple metal bridge/tailpiece assemblies with a moveable rosewood saddle.

In 1955 the small ginger-colored Model C "peanut" appeared with a Coke-bottle headstock. The pickguard had shrunk in size and the pickups were now exposed, first wrapped in brown vinyl tape, followed by unplated and then chrome-plated "lipstick" pickups – the covers for the latter purchased from a lipstick-tube manufacturer.

The similar U-1 and U-2 replaced the Cs in 1956, the main difference being new colors (black, copper, royal blue, coral red, surf green etc). A Danelectro innovation was the six-string bass, introduced as the short-scale UB-2 around 1956. It was effectively a guitar tuned an octave lower than usual. Dano six-string basses of various designs began to appear on records such as Duane Eddy's 'Because They're Young'.

A three-pickup U-3 was added in 1957. By 1957 the U series Danos were also available as Silvertones. In a couple of years the Silvertone line had reduced to a few Danelectro models, replaced largely by Harmony- and Kay-made guitars. Single-pickup Silvertone U models got a new, skinny "dolphin" six-tuners-in-line headstock and lasted through 1961.

In 1958 Danelectro relocated to Neptune, New Jersey, and introduced its legendary semi-hollowbodies, the Standard (one or two pickups, Coke-bottle head), Deluxe (two or three pickups) and Hand Vibrato ("duck foot" head, vibrato). These are known as "short-horns" because of their widely flared double-cutaways. They had laminated masonite tops and backs over wooden frames of either poplar or pine; sides were covered in vinyl. They typified the Dano line through 1966.

Three other classic Danos were introduced in 1959: a "short horn" guitar/bass double-neck in white-brown sunburst; the wood-grained, hollowbody Convertible (with or without pickup); and the white-bronze sunburst Long Horn Bass, with a distinctive lyre shape.

In 1958 studio guitarist Vinnie Bell became associated with Danelectro and in

1961 his Bellzouki was introduced, a 12-string guitar that looked something like a Greek bouzouki. The one-pickup version had a teardrop shape, while the two-pickup model added four extra points. Both had a "mustache" pickguard under the strings and a duck-foot head.

By 1962 the only Dano guitar offered by Sears was the new amp-in-case guitar, a single-pickup short-horn in black metalflake, with three-watt amp and 6" speaker built into the case. This was joined in 1963 by the two-pickup version in red sunburst with five-watt amp, 8" speaker and tremolo. The six-tuners-in-line heads looked like meat cleavers. In 1967 the amp-in-case guitars changed to a new Fender Jaguar-style shape.

In 1963 Danelectro rolled out the little Pro 1 solidbody which, with its asymmetrical, square-ish shape, looked like a poor man's Guild Thunderbird. It did however introduce Daniel's neck-tilt adjustment. It was followed by the exotic Guitarlin with "long-horn" lyre-shaped body and 31-fret neck.

In 1966 the entertainment conglomerate MCA bought Danelectro and, while they kept Daniel in charge, made big changes. The 1967 Slimline guitars were semi-hollowbodies with a Jaguar-style shape, distinctive vinyl side-trim, stubby Strat-like head and two or three pickups, with or without vibrato. A 12-string version was offered. The Hawk line was similar, with one or two pickups but without the vinyl side trim.

Also similar to the Slimlines, the 1967 Dane Series had four basic sub-series: A (one or two pickups); B (two or three pickups); C (crackled two-tone "gator" finish); and D ("gator" finish plus deluxe pickguard in a swirled plastic and brushed-chrome control panel). MCA introduced a new Danelectro-made brand, Coral, in 1967 (see Coral). Finally that year a new Danelectro-brand Electric Sitar debuted, a one-pickup guitar with rounded, sitar-like body shape and matching headstock style.

By 1968 demand for guitars had declined and in 1969 MCA closed the Danelectro factory. Guitar-maker Dan Armstrong obtained some leftover parts and in 1969 sold them with his own pickups as Dan Armstrong Modified Danelectros. Later, Danelectros became collectable cult items, especially when Jimmy Page used a Standard short-horn on stage.

Nat Daniel died in 1994. In 1995 the Evets Corporation obtained rights to the Danelectro name, introducing a line of effects pedals in 1997 followed by guitars in 1998. The new Danelectros were similar in look and construction to the vintage models, with reproduction "lipstick" pickups and similar hardware, although by 1999 the line had begun to expand into retro sparkle finishes and new electronic switching. There were also a number of new designs such as

the Hodad (1999) and Mod (2000), consistent with the spirit if not the letter of the legend that is Danelectro. Following these, Evets withdrew its debutante line of Danelectro reissues and reconfigured the designs somewhat for 2005. Models such as the flagship 56 Pro capture the spirit of the original U2, which updated and improved hardware and construction.

Dean

The "pointy rock guitar" format was approached from a new angle by Dean in the late 1970s. Rather than mining the Superstrat vein that other makers were exploring, Dean produced rock guitars along the lines of Gibson's more radical Moderne Series models of the past – the early versions of which could even be labeled "double-pointy" headstocks, given their unusual broad-V, or "wishbone", headstock designs.

Dean was founded in 1976 by Dean Zelinsky of Evanston, Illinois. Production of the Z (Explorer-like), V (Flying V-style) and a hybrid of the two, the much-emulated ML, began in 1977. Dean's guitars had figured tops and loud DiMarzio pickups.

The Les-Paul-inspired E'Lite and Cadillac appeared in 1979-80, followed by a downsized Baby series in 1982, as favored by Rik Emmett and Sammy Hagar. The 1983 Bel Aire's bolt-on neck came from ESP in Japan and was one of the first guitars (along with the Kramer Pacer) sporting the humbucker/single-coil/single-coil pickup layout that practically defined the coming "superstrat" genre.

Debuting in 1985 were the Hollywood models from ESP in Japan, the Signature series from Korea, and the "heavy metal" Mach V (Japan) and VII (US). Manufacture of Dean's conventional Fender-style guitars shifted to Korea in 1986, including 1987's Eighty-Eight, Jammer and Playmate series.

In 1990 Zelinsky licensed the Dean name to Tropical Music of Miami, Florida, and a year later Korean Strat-style solidbodies debuted. A Reissue Series of early Dean designs was produced in 1993-94 in California, supervised by Zelinsky, becoming American Customs made in Cleveland, Ohio, in 1994.

In 1995 a new Dean factory opened in Plant City, Florida, managed by Armadillo Enterprises, offering US-made American Customs and the US Series with Korean bodies, all variations on classic Dean designs. Models made in the US and Korea (American Spirit) were offered in 1997, including a Korina series, and new Icon models inspired by PRS's designs.

In 1998 Dean continued mining its heritage with the US Custom Shop series, the Flame, Ultima and US Phantom series,

and the European Custom and Premium series, as well as an electric resonator guitar Dimebag Darrell, Michael Schenker, Zakk Wylde and Michael Angelo Batio have been among the many prominent Dean endorsees of the modern era.

Eko

While for a time the Eko brand was anathema to all things tone, the brand has acquired a certain retro chic in recent years, and the look has even been copied.

Among Italy's best-known guitar-makers, and one of the country's biggest exporters, Eko was established in the late 1950s by Oliviero Pigini & Co of Porto Recanati. Pigini at first made accordions, with Eko electric guitars following around 1960. In 1961 Eko teamed up with LoDuca of Milwaukee, Wisconsin, marketing electrics by 1962. They included sparkle- and marble-plastic covered solidbodies and "violin"-shape guitars. During the 1970s Eko sold vaguely Gibson-like guitars primarily in Europe. The brand appeared on a line of Korean-made copies in the late 1980s. During the late 1990s a series of retro-flavor electrics revived Eko's 1960s designs.

Epiphone

Epiphone has evolved into being known as the "budget Gibson brand," and thanks to the consistency and ever-increasing quality of its Asian-

Early 1960s Epiphone Sheraton
BODY: semi-acoustic construction with back, sides, and top of laminated maple, with a pressed arch on the top and solid maple center block; seven-ply top binding and back binding; double cutaway with 20th fret neck/body joint. Blond (natural) finish in nitrocellulose lacquer.

NECK: glued-in, one-piece mahogany neck with multi-bound ebony fingerboard with 12" fingerboard radius, 22 medium nickel-silver frets, and 1 $\frac{11}{16}$" nut width; 24 $\frac{5}{8}$" scale length.

HEADSTOCK: symmetrical back-angled headstock, with three-a-side tuners, multiple binding and vine inlay; bone nut.

BRIDGE: adjustable tune-o-matic bridge and Frequensator trapeze tailpiece.

ELECTRONICS: dual mini-humbucking pickups constructed of single alnico bar magnet beneath, six fixed steel slug pole pieces in one coil and six threaded adjustable pole pieces in the other; DC resistance of approximately 6.5k to 7.5k; nickel-plated steel cover. Three-way toggle switch to select either pickup alone or both together; four 500k potentiometers for individual Volume and Tone for each pickup.

SOUND: a good blend of bright, incisive and warm; not overly aggressive, with a slight woody resonance at its core. Good hum rejection.

Epiphone Casino f

BODY: fully hollow, double-cutaway 'thinline' body made with pressed arched top of laminated maple, laminated maple back and sides; single-bound top and back.

NECK: glued in mahogany neck with bound rosewood fingerboard with 12" radius; neck/body joint at approximately the 16th fret, 22 jumbo nickel-silver frets, and 1 $\frac{11}{16}$" nut width; 24 $\frac{5}{8}$" scale length.

HEADSTOCK: symmetrical headstock with 17 degree back angle, three-a-side Kluson tuners.

BRIDGE: fixed tune-o-matic bridge and Bigsby vibrato tailpiece.

ELECTRONICS: two single-coil P-90 pickups, made with two alnico bar magnets each and six adjustable threaded pole pieces, DC resistance in the range of 7.5k to 8k. Three-way toggle switch for either pickup independently or both together; four controls for individual Volume and Tone for each pickup.

SOUND: deep, rich, a little gritty and fairly hot. Some pronounced midrange emphasis but pretty good balance overall, and an air of openness from the fully hollow body.

made guitars in recent years, has even become an alternative source of a "fully legitimate, genuine Les Paul" model for many players today.

While this is just about all that many younger readers might know the brand for, however, Epiphone has a long and illustrious history. Back when archtops ruled the earth, in the years before and after World War II, Epiphone was one of the most respected guitar companies, making midrange to high-end instruments that were often used in big-band jazz orchestras.

The Epiphone company dates back to the 1870s in Smyrna, Turkey, where Greek-born founder Anastasios Stathopoulo crafted his own-label fiddles, lutes and Greek lioutos. Stathopoulo moved to the United States in 1903 and continued to make instruments, including mandolins, in Long Island City, Queens, New York. Anastasios died in 1915 and his son Epaminondas ("Epi") took over. Two years later the company became known as the House Of Stathopoulo and, following World War I, began making banjos. In 1924 the company's Recording line of banjos was introduced and in 1928 the company name changed to the Epiphone Banjo Company.

Epiphone began producing guitars around 1928, introducing its first round-soundhole Recording archtop guitars, and in the early 1930s the company's famous Masterbilt line of f-hole archtops debuted. By the end of the decade Epiphone was a

major competitor to Gibson, which by now was the leading manufacturer of archtops.

The Epiphone operation was renamed Epiphone Inc in 1935 and introduced a line of electric archtops and amplifiers, initially called Electraphone but quickly changed to Electar. Many of the early Electar amps were made by Nat Daniel who would later found Danelectro. Early Electar guitars were non-cutaway archtops (and lap-steels) that had pickups with large handrests over the strings. By 1939 Epiphone-brand electric archtops included the Century, Coronet and Zephyr (with large oval pickup). In 1939 Epiphone's Herb Sunshine was one of the first to conceive of adjustable polepieces on pickups, and these soon began to appear on Epiphones.

Epi Stathopoulo died in 1943 and control of Epiphone went to his brothers Orphie and Frixo. Pre-war electric archtops continued following World War II, joined by the Kent model in 1949. Epiphone introduced in 1948 its first single-cutaway archtop acoustics, versions of the earlier Emperor and DeLuxe, and added Tone Spectrum pickups to them in 1949. Among the pros who played Epiphones during these early years were George Van Eps, Tony Mottola, Al Caiola and Oscar Moore.

However, Epiphone's challenge to Gibson was about to fall apart. In 1951 a strike shut down Epiphone's New York factory for four months, and Epiphone relocated its factory to Philadelphia, Pennsylvania. During the Philadelphia tenure the company experimented with some solidbody electric prototypes, but none ever made it to production. In 1955 Epiphone introduced an archtop equipped with a DeArmond pickup, endorsed by Harry Volpe. However, in 1957 Frixo Stathopoulo died – and this effectively marked the end of Epiphone's independence.

Gibson purchased Epiphone and relocated it to Kalamazoo, Michigan, turning the brand into its second-tier line. In 1958 Gibson started its new Epiphone line. This included the first solidbody electrics: the equal-double-cutaway, slab-bodied, two-pickup Crestwood and low-end one-pickup Coronet, similar to a Les Paul Special, both with small "New York" pickups and other leftover parts that came from Epiphone with the purchase. All Gibson-made Epiphones had set-necks. Also in 1958 Gibson reworked the old Century electric archtop into a thinline electric with one P-90 pickup.

This was followed by the twin-humbucker, double-cutaway Sheraton thinline in 1959 (a John Lee Hooker signature edition of which would appear just over 40 years later, in 2000).

In 1959 the Epi solidbody line expanded. The Crestwood was renamed the Crestwood Custom, restyled with a trimmer, more

rounded body that sported New York pickups until a change to mini-humbuckers in 1963. The Coronet remained, but now with a P-90 single-coil pickup. New in 1959 was the Wilshire, a Coronet with two P-90s. Both models adopted the new Crestwood body in 1960, the same year seeing the introduction of the single-cutaway Olympic (single pickup), Olympic Double (two pickups) and double-cutaway Olympic Special. Some Epiphones came with a simple flat-spring vibrato, although after 1961 the rosewood-clad Maestro vibrato was also offered, mainly on Crestwood Customs.

Epiphone thinlines continued to expand with the single-pointed-cutaway Sorrento (two mini-humbuckers) in 1960, double-cutaway Professional (mini-humbucker) and Casino (hollow body with two P-90s, essentiallly a Gibson ES-330) in 1961, the non-cutaway Granada (one Melody Maker pickup) and double-cutaway Riviera (two mini-humbuckers) in 1962, and the double-cutaway Al Caiola Custom (two mini-humbuckers) in 1963. The Caiola Standard with two P-90s followed in 1966. In 1964 Epiphone introduced the Howard Roberts Standard with one sharp cutaway, oval soundhole and a mini-humbucker.

Popularity of the thinlines increased in the 1960s when first Paul McCartney acquired a Casino for Beatle studio work, followed by John Lennon and George Harrison, who each used new Casinos on-

1959
Epiphone Emperor

stage in the final fab-four concerts of 1966. The group's new Epis were also all over the *Revolver* LP, and the Beatle connection has ensured the thinlines in general and the Casino in particular a continuing popularity among pop groups keen on reactivating a Merseyside mix.

In 1963 the Epi solidbodies were redesigned to feature a longer upper horn as well as a scalloped "batwing" six-tuners-in-line headstock. A three-pickup Crestwood Deluxe joined the line, and in 1966 a Wilshire 12-string was offered.

Gibson was purchased from Chicago Musical Instruments (CMI) in 1969 by Norlin, an international conglomerate. Kalamazoo-made Epiphone solidbodies continued to be available through 1970, although by that time plans were already underway to transfer production to Japan. The first Japanese-

made Epiphones debuted around 1970. These bolt-on-neck electrics included the 1802 Strat-style solidbody and the 5102T ES-335-style thinline, each with a pair of black-and-white "Art Deco" single-coil pickups. Ironically, Gibson-owned Epiphone thus offered copies similar to those of Aria… the Japanese company that had started the "copy era" by replicating Gibson's Les Paul Custom.

In 1972 Gibson renamed the 1802 as the ET-270 and the 5102T as the EA-250. The company also added two bolt-on-neck "copies" of its venerable Crestwoods, the ET-278 (bound fingerboard) and ET-275, both with two humbuckers, vibratos and Gibson-style headstocks. This Epiphone line-up remained unchanged into the early 1970s. By 1975 the Strat-style guitar was gone and the ET-278 (now stoptail) and ET-275 acquired new finishes and appointments. The EA-250 thinline remained. These were joined by another Crestwood, the ET-290N in natural maple with a maple fingerboard, and a high-end, walnut-topped EA-255 thinline, both with gold hardware.

In 1976 Epiphone added the distinctive Scroll models which had a carved scroll on the upper cutaway horn, as well as the set-neck SC550 (block inlays) and SC450 (dots) and the bolt-on-neck SC350, all with two humbuckers and pre-Gibson-style Epiphone headstocks, differing in finishes and trim. These were available through 1979.

From around 1977-79 Gibson marketed the Epiphone "Rock'n'Roll Star Solid Body Line Up" in Japan, guitars similar to the Scrolls but with equal cutaways and no scrolls, bearing the old Epi names Olympic Custom, Olympic and Wilshire. From 1979-81 Gibson offered the Epiphone Genesis series, again made in Japan. Featuring set-necks, mahogany bodies with carved maple caps, twin humbuckers and the old Epiphone-style headstocks, the Genesis models had various appointments and levels of trim and included the Custom (block inlays, gold hardware), Deluxe (crown inlays, chrome hardware) and Standard (dot inlays).

An even more basic model called simply The Genesis was added in 1981, but the entire series was gone by the end of that year. Following the demise of the Genesis series, in 1982 Gibson briefly offered a number of Japanese-made Epiphone hollowbody electrics: the Emperor, Sheraton, Casino, and Riviera.

Competition had taken its toll on Gibson during the 1970s, particularly the success of Japanese manufacturers. Beginning at this time Gibson began slowly transferring production to a new factory in Nashville, Tennessee, where labor costs were lower than in Kalamazoo. With idle production capability in Kalamazoo, Gibson decided to make Epiphones in America again.

Calling back laid-off workers, in 1982 Gibson unveiled the Kalamazoo-made Epiphone Spirit version of the same-name Gibson model: a set-neck, equal double-cutaway guitar inspired by the Les Paul Special shape. The Gibson featured an Explorer-style headstock, whereas the Epi had a typical Gibson-style "open book" head. The Epiphone Spirit came with either one or two humbuckers. The Spirit was joined by the Epiphone Special, basically an SG with one or two humbuckers. Very few of these were made, and the American-made Epiphones were gone by the end of the year.

As Gibson's Kalamazoo factory wound down to a close, one final Epiphone solidbody was made, a US-map-shaped guitar. This featured a Gibson-style neck glued into a body cut out in the shape of the continental United States. It was intended to be a promotional item but was well received, so Gibson decided to re-brand the map guitars with the Gibson logo. This marked the (temporary) end of Epiphone guitar production, an operation that stretched back to the late 1920s.

In 1984 Gibson closed down its guitar-making at Kalamazoo, selling part of the facility to former employees who formed the Heritage guitar company. During this period Gibson offered a few Japanese-made Epiphone electric thinlines, including the round-cutaway Emperor II and double-cutaway Sheraton, both with two humbuckers. In 1983 a few Epiphone solidbodies had been sourced from the Korean Samick factory.

By the early 1980s Norlin seemed to loose interest in guitar-making altogether. However, in 1984 Gibson was turned over to a broker and at the beginning of 1986 the company was purchased by Henry Juszkiewicz, Dave Berryman and Gary Zebrowski. They promptly revived the Epiphone brand, primarily as a vehicle for Korean-made budget instruments, although a select few Epi models would be made at Gibson's Nashville plant in subsequent years.

The new 1986 Epiphone By Gibson line included versions of both Gibson and Fender stalwarts: copies of Flying V (V-2) and Explorer, plus five S-series Strat-style guitars. By the end of the year these early Korean Epiphones were replaced by a considerably expanded line. Included were three new bolt-on-neck Les Pauls, all now equipped with Steinberger KB locking vibratos. The Les Paul 3 had the popular humbucker/single-coil/single-coil pickup layout. The Les Paul 2 was similar but with two humbuckers, while the Les Paul 1 had a single lead humbucker. Also offered were two Epiphone Firebirds, through-neck guitars with Steinberger KB vibrato and optional layouts of EMG Select pickups.

Six Strat-style guitars were offered in late 1986, including four superstrats with Kramer-style "hockey stick" (or "banana") six-tuners-in-line headstocks plus locking Steinberger KB vibratos. The top-of-the-line X-1000 had through-neck construction, EMG Select pickups in a humbucker/single-coil/single-coil layout, and chevron-shape fingerboard inlays. The X-900 was similar except the body was more like a wide Ibanez Roadstar, with triangular sharktooth inlays. The S-800 was basically a bolt-on-neck version of the X-900.

The S-600 was another similar bolt-neck guitar shaped more like contemporary Kramers. The S-400 (maple fingerboard, humbucker/single-coil/single-coil pickup layout, and locking vibrato) and S-310 (three single-coil pickups and traditional fulcrum vibrato) also had the Kramer body styling. Most of this line-up continued to be available into 1989.

Epiphone tapped a host of celebrities to endorse its new 1986 line, including Les Paul, Chet Atkins (for a new Country Gentleman II thinline) and Howard Roberts (new HR Fusion II and HR Fusion III thinlines), as well as Billy Burnette, Julio Fernandez, Zakk Wylde, Vinnie Zummo and Ed Ott.

guitar facts

Gibson planned a new series of Japanese-made guitars in 1987 to be called the Nouveau By Gibson line, with several new designs including a superstrat similar to the X-1000, an archtop and a model patterned in the style of a PRS solidbody. Whether these ever got beyond the prototype stage is unknown, but in 1988 the PRS-like solidbody provided the Epiphone Spotlight series, sporting through-neck construction, fancy carved maple caps, EMG Select pickups and chevron inlays. A traditional-style vibrato was offered, although some featured the locking Steinberger KB unit. The Spotlights lasted only a year before high costs made them impractical.

While earlier Epiphones had flirted with the idea of copying popular designs, in 1988 Gibson hit on the formula that would bring success to the Epiphone brand in the 1990s. Two new proper set-neck Les Paul copies were introduced, the Custom and the Standard (plus a bolt-on-neck Les Paul 2, now with stoptail).

In 1989 Epiphone revamped the whole line. The Les Paul Custom and Standard, plus the old Strat-style S-310, were joined by the G Series of Gibson SG copies, the G-400 being a set-neck copy of Gibson's SG 62 and the G-310 being a bolt-on-neck version of a 1967 SG. Also new was the Epiphone Flying V, a copy of Gibson's 1967-style V, and the T-310, a Telecaster-style copy with "hockey stick" Explorer-like head.

Though fast becoming passé, three superstrats with Floyd Rose locking vibratos continued to be offered: the bolt-neck 435i and 635i (humbucker/single-coil/single-coil pickup layout) and the neck-through-body 935i (humbucker and one single-coil pickup), all with Explorer-style headstock.

During the 1989 makeover Gibson returned to making a few special Epiphones in Nashville. This time it was the USA Pro, a superstrat replacement for the previous X-1000, though with a bolt-on neck, a locking Floyd Rose vibrato system and a Gibson lead humbucker and neck single-coil pickup.

Another American-made Epiphone was introduced in 1990, the USA Coronet. This presented a clever combination of old and new, reviving the defunct 1960s Epiphone shape and set-neck design, and adding a new reverse-Explorer headstock plus a five-way pickup selector switch, as well as a circuit board that provided humbucker, single-coil, out-of-phase and series/parallel sounds. The USA Coronets came with gold hardware and stoptails or black hardware and Floyd Rose locking vibrato systems.

In 1991 two more new Epiphone "copies" debuted, the EM-2 and EM-1, being Korean-made, bolt-on-neck versions of Gibson's new M-III, slightly offset-cutaway solidbodies with a dramatically extended horn and reverse-Explorer headstock. The

Epiphones were plainer than the Gibson models, but used the same electronic switching system, a combination of a two-way toggle and five-way switch to control the humbucker/single-coil/humbucker pickup layout. This offered either humbucking or single-coil tonalities depending on the position of the two-way switch. The EM-2 featured a locking Floyd Rose vibrato, whereas the EM-1 had a traditional fulcrum vibrato.

Epiphone briefly added to the bottom of its line in 1991 an inexpensive bolt-on-neck Les Paul, the LP-300, and the Strat-style S-300, which would last only a year. Epiphone also continued to add pro endorsers, including Mick Cribbs, Tracii Guns, Dan Toler, Frank Hannon, Pete Pagan, John Ricco and Tom Keifer.

A management change occurred in 1992 when Jim Rosenberg was hired from electronic instrument manufacturer E-Mu Systems to take charge of Epiphone. It was at this time that Epiphone revived the trend of marketing musical instruments through mail-order catalogs. By 1993 a new low-end bolt-neck LP-100 Les Paul had joined the line and the i Series superstrats were gone.

Epiphone added another EM-3 Rebel Custom in 1994 to its line derived from the Gibson M-III (the EMs now also called Rebels). This was still a bolt-on-neck guitar, but appointments such as pick-shape inlays were more like the Gibson original. It also had a new Steinberger Jam-Trem vibrato system. New too in 1994 was the Epiphone Explorer, a copy of the famous Gibson model. By 1995 the EM Rebel models had been dropped and American Epiphone production had ended.

More copies were introduced, including a Firebird, Les Paul Standard Goldtop and Nighthawk Standard and Special. The Les Paul Double Cutaway also debuted in 1995, as did a revised version of the Emperor II thinline, now endorsed by jazz great Joe Pass.

From this point the Epiphone line continued to grow, with more copies of historical Gibson models. These included solidbodies such as the 1958 Explorer, 1958 Korina Flying V, G-400 Custom (three-humbucker SG), Junior SC (single-cutaway Melody Maker), Junior DC (double-cutaway Melody Maker), G-1275 Custom Doubleneck. There were thinline electrics too such as the B.B. King Lucille and Howard Roberts. Reissues of earlier Epis also proliferated, including the Casino, Riviera, Emperor Regent, Sheraton and Sorrento. A signature Supernova model appeared in 1997 for Noel Gallagher, though it lacked the Oasis guitarist's subtle British flag graphic that brightened up the body of his own Sheraton. The release of the limited-edition John Lennon 1965 Casino and Revolution Casino from the Gibson Nashville factory at the end of the 1990s put high-end,

American-made Epiphones in the hands of musicians once again.

The most striking aspect of recent Epiphones has been the veritable explosion of Les Paul variants, with appointments ranging from exotic, transparent and sparkle finishes to flamed-maple and birdseye-maple caps, seven-strings, and even a Metal Edition and a signature model (with snake graphic) for Slash of Guns N'Roses. Given the superb quality of many recent Korean-made Epiphone Les Pauls – such as those in the Japanese-made Elitist line – and the company's growing roster of artists, this historic brand is once again looking very stable and, partially at least, out from under Gibson's shadow.

ESP

Simple, solid, and decidedly rock-minded designs have helped the ESP brand to establish itself as a leading tool of the metal and heavy rock trade. This high-end Japanese maker, established in 1975, at first offered handmade guitars with the Navigator brandname. A move to guitar parts came three years later; ESP-brand instruments soon followed. Many maintained Fender styling, joined during the 1980s by flash graphic-finished superstrats and models aimed at metal players.

Custom and production models emanated from America and Germany as well as Japan. Where original thinking was evident it was restrained rather than radical, as on the Hybrid and 901.

Quality stayed consistently high, as did prices. To reach a wider market the less expensive Edwards line appeared in the late 1980s, followed by the even more affordable Korean-made Grass Roots series. Recent budget-inclined examples from this source carried the large LTD logo.

ESP endorsers range from Ronnie Wood to George Lynch, but the most influential have been Kirk Hammett and James Hetfield, their continued patronage spawning popular signature models.

Fender

By directly addressing working musicians' needs while totally redrawing the blueprint for the electric guitar, the Fender company quickly rose from its upstart status to become the most influential maker of electric guitars. No other instruments of the type have been as widely played, or as widely copied. Fender's solidbody guitars arrived on the scene before there was even such a thing as rock'n'roll. The instruments forever changed not only the way guitars would be manufactured; they also played a huge role in changing the course of popular music.

fender

Mid-1950s Fender Telecaster

BODY: solid swamp ash body (usually two-piece) with single deep cutaway for good access to the 21st fret. Thin, semi-transparent blonde nitrocellulose lacquer finish standard.

NECK: bolt-on, one-piece maple neck and integral maple fingerboard with 7.25" fingerboard radius, 21 nickel-silver frets, and 1 ⅝" nut width; 25 ½" scale length.

HEADSTOCK: asymmetrical headstock with six-in-line Kluson tuners; bone nut; single round steel string tree (later stamped steel 'butterfly' tree).

BRIDGE: through body stringing; semi-suspended bridge with three adjustable brass saddles (later steel).

ELECTRONICS: single-coil bridge pickup with six individual alnico pole magnets and a DC resistance of 7k to 7.5k, with a steel base plate to aid shielding and raise inductance; single-coil neck pickup with six individual alnico pole magnets and a DC resistance of approximately 7.75k. Three-way switch and two 250k potentiometers for Volume and Blend, to select (from 1950-'52) 1) neck pickup with bassy sound and no tone control, 2) neck pickup straight to volume control, 3) neck and bridge pickups with former blended in by second rotary control; or (from 1953-'67) 1) same as above, 2) neck pickup through Tone and Volume controls, 3) bridge pickup along through Tone and Volume controls. After 1967, altered for standard neck, both, bridge switching.

SOUND: bright, snappy, cutting, harmonically rich and – dare I say – twangy, but with a nicely balanced voice, good midrange grunt, and ringing sustain.

guitar facts

1960
Fender Telecaster
Fiesta Red

Jazzmaster pickup

that if you weren't working you were lazy, which was a sin. It seems that Leo would judge himself and everyone else around him by that measure.. and himself hardest of all.

Although he went on to study accountancy and began his working life in the accounts sections of the state highway department and a tire distribution company, Leo's hobby was always electronics, and in his 20s he built amplifiers and PA systems for use at public events such as sports and religious gatherings as well as dances. In about 1939 Leo opened The Fender Radio Service, a radio and record store at Fullerton in the Los Angeles area. Leo had lost his accounting job earlier in that decade of depression. His new shop brought instant introductions to many local musicians including professional violinist and lap-steel guitarist "Doc" Kauffman. Doc had worked

on electric guitar designs for another local company, Rickenbacker.

Lap-steel guitar playing, or Hawaiian guitar playing, had been fashionable in the United States since the 1920s and was still tremendously popular at the time Leo opened his new store. A lap-steel guitar is one that sits horizontally on the player's lap, and its strings are stopped not by the frets, but with a sliding steel bar held in the player's non-picking hand. As the most prevalent type of guitar in America at the time, lap-steels were thus the first guitars to

So successful did Fender become that in 1965 the business was sold to the giant CBS conglomerate for $13 million, an unprecedentedly large figure. Yet the whole affair had started around 20 years earlier when Leo made some electric steel guitars with a few thousand dollars that he'd earned from a record-player design.

From these humble beginnings grew one of the largest, most influential and splendidly original musical instrument manufacturers in the world.

Despite spectacular later successes, during its early years the southern California company came perilously close to failing. It was Leo Fender's sheer determination, combined with his luck in surrounding himself with clever, dedicated people, that helped pull the Fender company through difficult times.

Leo was born in 1909, in a barn near the Anaheim/Fullerton border in the Los Angeles area. His parents ran a "truck farm," growing vegetables and fruit for the market, and had put up the barn first before they could afford to build a house. A friend once recalled that when Leo was small his father had told him that the only thing worthwhile in the world was what you accomplished at work – and

1963
Fender Jazzmaster
Foam Green

guitar facts

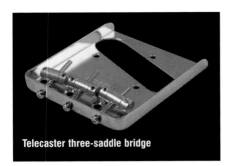
Telecaster three-saddle bridge

Telecaster six-saddle bridge

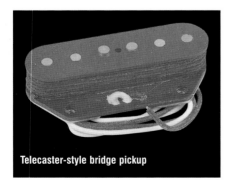
Telecaster-style bridge pickup

"go electric" in the 1930s. Several innovative companies, with Rickenbacker in the lead, had started to experiment with electro-magnetic pickups, attaching them to guitars and connecting them to small amplifiers. During the 1930s (and later) the term "Spanish" was used by players and makers to identify the other (less popular at the time) hold-against-the-body type of guitar.

Leo had by this time already begun to look into the potential for electric guitars and to play around with pickup designs. Leo and Doc built a solidbody guitar in 1943 to test these early pickups, as well as a design for a record-changer good enough to net them $5,000. Some of this money went into starting their shortlived company, K&F (Kauffman & Fender), and the two men began proper production of electric lap-steel guitars and small amplifiers in November 1945.

Another significant person with whom Leo started working at this early stage was Don Randall, general manager of Radio & Television Equipment Co ("Radio-Tel") which was based in Santa Ana, some 15 miles south of Fullerton. Radio-Tel, owned by Francis Hall, became the exclusive distributor of K&F products in 1946 – around the time that Leo and Doc Kauffman decided to split. In 1946 Leo called his new operation Fender Manufacturing (renamed the Fender Electric Instrument Co in December 1947). Leo continued to make lap-steels and amps as he had with K&F, but gradually developed new products. He also expanded into larger premises in Fullerton, separate from the radio store and described by one observer as two plain, unattractive steel buildings.

Yet another important member of the growing Fender team, Dale Hyatt, had joined

the company in January 1946. Hyatt later became a crucial member of the Fender sales team, but one of his early tasks, in late 1947 or early 1948, was to take over the radio store business because Leo was trying to get things started at the new buildings in Pomona Avenue. Next to join Fender's company was George Fullerton, who was to become what one colleague describes as Leo's faithful workhorse. Fullerton started working at Pomona Avenue in February 1948.

Karl Olmsted and his partner Lymon Race had left the services in 1947 and decided to start a much-needed tool-and-die company in Fullerton, making specialist tools, as well as dies that customers could use to stamp out metal parts on punch presses. They were looking for work, and Leo had reached the point where he needed dies to be made for production work. He'd been making parts by hand, cutting out raw metal. But of course Leo now needed to make several identical copies of each component. Race & Olmsted continued to make Fender's tooling and most metal parts for the next 30 years and more, progressing to more complicated, sophisticated and high-production tooling as time went on.

Fender's electric lap-steels enjoyed some local success, and Leo began to think about producing a solidbody electric guitar of normal shape and playing style: an "electric Spanish" guitar. Normal Spanish archtop hollowbody "f-hole" acoustic guitars with built-in electric pickups and associated controls had been produced by makers such as Rickenbacker, National, Gibson and Epiphone at various times since the 1930s, but without much effect on player's habits. And while demand was rising from danceband guitarists who found themselves increasingly unable to compete with the volume of the rest of the band, most of the early electric hollowbody guitars were effectively experimental. They were only partially successful from a technical standpoint, and electric guitars were still some way from becoming a great commercial sensation. Leo's plans would change all that.

A number of guitar makers, musicians and engineers in America were wondering about the possibility of a solidbody instrument. Such a design would curtail the

annoying feedback often produced by amplified hollowbody guitars, at the same time reducing the guitar body's interference with its overall tone and thus more accurately reproducing and sustaining the sound of the strings.

Rickenbacker had launched a relatively solid Bakelite-body electric guitar in the mid 1930s – the type that Leo's friend Doc Kauffman had played – while around 1940 guitarist Les Paul built a personal test-bed electric guitar in New York which used parts from a variety of instruments mounted on a solid central block of pine. In Downey, California, about 15 miles to the west of Fender's operation in Fullerton, Paul Bigsby had a small workshop where he spent a good deal of time fixing motorcycles and, later, making some fine pedal-steel guitars and vibrato units. He also ventured into the solidbody electric guitar and mandolin field, hand-building a limited number of distinctive instruments. He'd started this in 1948 with the historic Merle Travis guitar, an instrument with through-neck construction and hollow body "wings."

It's difficult to judge whether the design of Fender's first solidbody electric guitar was influenced very much by those earlier instruments of Bigsby's. George Fullerton says that he and Leo knew Paul Bigsby and had seen Merle Travis playing his Bigsby guitar. On the other hand, it's possible that Fender and Bigsby just made something similar at the same time.

Leo started work in the summer of 1949 on the instrument which we now know as the Fender Telecaster, effectively the world's first commercially marketed solidbody electric guitar, and still very much alive today. The guitar, originally named the Fender Esquire and then the Fender Broadcaster, first went into production in 1950. Early prototypes borrowed their headstock design from Fender's lap-steels, with three tuners each side, but the production version had a smart new headstock with all six tuners along one side, allowing strings to meet tuners in a straight line and obviating the traditional "angled back" headstock. Fender's new solidbody electric guitar was unadorned, straightforward, potent, and – perhaps most significantly – ahead of its time. As such it did not prove immediately easy for the salesmen at Fender to sell, as Don Randall of Radio-Tel found when he took some prototypes to a musical instrument trade show in Chicago during the summer of 1950. In fact, Randall was aghast to find that competitors generally laughed at the new instrument, calling the prototypes canoe paddles, snow shovels and worse.

A very few pre-production one-pickup Esquire models without truss-rods were made in April 1950, with another tiny production run of two-pickup Esquires two

guitar facts

months later. General production of the better-known single-pickup Esquire with truss-rod did not begin until January 1951.

But in November 1950, a truss-rod was added to the two-pickup model, its name was changed to Broadcaster, and the retail price was fixed at $170. The Broadcaster name was shortlived, halted in early 1951 after Gretsch, a large New York-based instrument manufacturer, indicated its prior use of "Broadkaster" on various drum products. At first, Fender simply used up its "Fender Broadcaster" decals on the guitar's headstock by cutting off the "Broadcaster" and leaving just the "Fender" logo; these no-name guitars are known among collectors today as Nocasters. The new name decided upon for the Fender solid electric was Telecaster, coined by Don Randall. The Telecaster name was on headstocks by April 1951, and at last Fender's new $189.50 solidbody electric had a permanent name.

At Fender, practicality and function ruled. There was no hand-carving of selected timbers as one would find in the workshops of established archtop guitar makers. With the Telecaster, Fender made the electric guitar into a factory product, stripped down to its essential elements, built up from easily assembled parts, and produced at a relatively affordable price. Fender's methods made for easier, more consistent production – and a different sound. Not for Fender the fat, Gibson-style jazz tone, but a clearer, spikier sound, something like a cross between a clean acoustic guitar and a cutting electric lap-steel.

One of the earliest players to appreciate this new sound was Jimmy Bryant, best known for his staggering guitar instrumental duets with pedal-steel virtuoso Speedy West. Bryant soon took to playing the new Fender solidbody. He was respected by professionals in the music business for his session work, including recordings made with Tennessee Ernie Ford and Ella Mae Morse among others.

Bryant also made television appearances on country showcases, and would highlight Fender's exciting new solidbody for the growing TV audience.

It was western swing, a lively dance music that grew up in Texas dancehalls during the 1930s and 1940s, that popularized the electric guitar in the US, at first with steel guitars. Many of its steel players used Fender electrics, notably Noel Boggs and Leon McAuliffe, but there were also some electric-Spanish guitarists in the bands, like Tele-wielding Bill Carson.

Business began to pick up for the Fender company as news of the Telecaster spread, and as Radio-Tel's five salesmen began to persuade instrument store owners to stock the instrument. Early in 1953 Fender's existing sales set-up with Radio-Tel

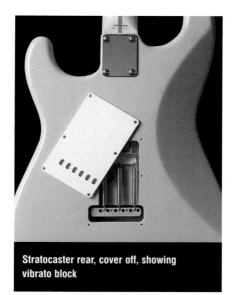

Stratocaster rear, cover off, showing vibrato block

was re-organized into a new Fender Sales distribution company, which was operational by June. Based like Radio-Tel in Santa Ana, Fender Sales had four business partners: Leo, Don Randall, Radio-Tel owner Francis Hall and salesman Charlie Hayes. Hayes was killed in a road accident and in late 1953 Hall bought the Rickenbacker company, so in 1955 Fender Sales became a partnership owned by Leo and Don Randall. It was Randall who actually ran this pivotal part of the Fender business.

The sales side of Fender was, therefore, in capable hands. Another important addition to the Fender team occurred in 1953 when steel guitarist Freddie Tavares, best known for his swooping steel intro over the titles of the Looney Tunes cartoons, joined the California guitar maker, principally to help Leo design new products. Also in 1953 three new buildings at South Raymond Avenue and Valencia Drive were added to the company's manufacturing premises. As well as just two electric guitars, the Telecaster and Esquire, Fender had at this time a line of seven amplifiers (Bandmaster, Bassman, Champ, Deluxe, Princeton, Super, Twin Amp), five electric steel guitars (Custom, Deluxe, Dual, Stringmaster, Student) and its revolutionary electric bass guitar, the Precision, that had been introduced two years earlier.

Another newcomer was Forrest White. He had joined the company after Leo asked if he'd be interested in helping sort out some "management problems" at Fender. White was shocked by the disorganized mess he found at the Fender workshops, and agreed to come in and work for Leo, beginning in May 1954. White soon began to put the manufacturing operations into order.

Now Leo had able men – Forrest White and Don Randall – poised at the head of the production and sales halves of the Fender company. He had a new factory, and a small

but growing reputation. All he needed now, it seemed, was more new products. And along came the stylish Fender Stratocaster, the epitome of tailfin-flash American design of the 1950s.

Leo was listening hard to players' comments about the "plain vanilla" Tele and Esquire, and during the early 1950s he and Freddie Tavares began to formulate the guitar that would become the Stratocaster. Some musicians were complaining that the sharp edge on the Telecaster was uncomfortable, so the team began to fool around with smoothed contouring on the body. The Stratocaster was eventually launched during 1954 – samples around May and June were followed by the first proper production run in October. It was priced at $249.50 (or $229.50 without vibrato) plus $39.50 for a case. The new Fender was the first solidbody electric with three pickups, and also featured a new-design built-in vibrato unit (or "tremolo" as Fender called it) to provide pitch-bending and shimmering chordal effects for the player. It was the first self-contained vibrato

FACT FILE

Tremolo (also tremolo arm, tremolo system, trem) is the erroneous but much-used term for what is actually a vibrato device/system. The musical definition of tremolo is the rapid repetition of a note or notes, whereas vibrato is the rhythmic wavering (sharping and flatting) of the pitch of a note or notes. As if to even the score, Fender dubbed the tremolo channel on many of its amps "Vibrato", although the effect produced was a "repetition of notes." (Even the effects channel on many vintage Tremolux model amps wears the Vibrato tag; some early 1960s Fender models did, however, produce a mild version of true vibrato.)

unit: an adjustable bridge, tailpiece and vibrato system all in one. Not a simple mechanism for the time, but a reasonably effective one. It followed the Fender principle of taking an existing product (in this case the Bigsby vibrato) and improving on it. Fender's new Strat vibrato also had six saddles, one for each string, adjustable for height and length. The complete unit was typical of Fender's constant consideration of musicians' requirements and the consequent application of a mass-producer's solution.

The Strat came with a radically sleek, solid body, based on the shape of the earlier Fender Precision Bass, contoured for the player's comfort and finished in a yellow-to-

Mid-1950s Fender Stratocaster

BODY: from 1954-'56 a solid swamp ash body (usually two-piece) with dual asymmetrical cutaways for good upper fret access. Thin, semi-transparent two-tone sunburst nitrocellulose lacquer finish standard. Post-'56, alder is standard body wood, with ash used only for blond-finished guitars.

NECK: bolt-on, one-piece maple neck and integral maple fingerboard with 7.25" fingerboard radius, 21 nickel-silver frets, and 1 ⅝" nut width (approximately); 25 ½" scale length.

HEADSTOCK: asymmetrical headstock with six-in-line Kluson tuners; bone nut; single round steel string tree (later stamped steel 'butterfly' tree).

BRIDGE: Fender 'Synchronized Tremolo' (vibrato) standard; six individual stamped steel saddles, fully adjustable for height and intonation; steel base plate; steel inertia bar (trem block) for string ball-end anchoring.

ELECTRONICS: three identical single-coil pickups, each with six individual alnico pole magnets and a DC resistance of approximately 6k. Three 250k potentiometers for master Volume, neck pickup Tone and middle pickup Tone, and three-way switch to select each pickup individually only (could be carefully balanced between positions to select neck-plus-middle or bridge-plus-middle.

SOUND: snappy and slightly springing, with a bright, cutting character overall and lots of harmonic sparkle, but good roundness, depth and warmth from the neck pickup. An element of soft compression at all settings.

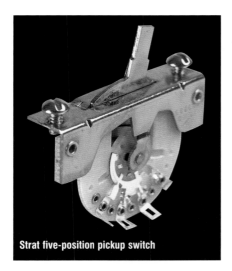

Strat five-position pickup switch

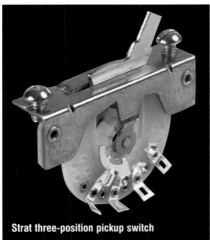

Strat three-position pickup switch

makers. The Stratocaster has appeared in the hands of virtually every great guitarist over the years. Back in the 1950s it was a more specialized market, but nonetheless the Strat fired the music then of players such as Buddy Holly, Carl Perkins and Buddy Guy.

Fender's next model introductions came in 1956 with a pair of new "student" electrics. These had a shorter string-length than was usual for Fender. The "three-quarter size" one-pickup Musicmaster and two-pickup Duo-Sonic were described in the company's literature as "ideal for students and adults with small hands." They were clearly designed for players on a tight budget, for those who were starting out on electric guitar and were flocking to the music-retailer "schools" that were springing up everywhere in the US at the time.

Fender then created a decidedly high-end instrument. The Jazzmaster first appeared on Fender's pricelists in 1958, and at $329 was some $50 more expensive than the Strat. At that sort of price Fender couldn't resist tagging its new Jazzmaster as "America's finest electric guitar... unequaled in performance and design features." Immediately striking to the guitarist of 1958 was the Jazzmaster's unusual offset-waist body shape and, for the first time on a Fender, a separate rosewood fingerboard glued to the customary maple neck. The vibrato system was new, too, with an ill-conceived "lock-off" facility aimed at preventing tuning problems if a string should break.

The sound of the Jazzmaster was richer and warmer than players were used to from Fender. The name Jazzmaster was not chosen at random, for Fender aimed the different tone at jazz players. But jazz guitarists found little appeal in this new,

rather difficult solidbody guitar, and mainstream Fender players largely stayed with their Strats and Teles.

All in all, the Jazzmaster was a distinct change for Fender, and constituted a real effort to extend the scope and appeal of its guitar line. Ironically, and despite significant early success, this has been partly responsible for the guitar's lack of long-term popularity relative to the Strat and Tele, mainly as a result of players' dissatisfaction with the guitar's looks and sounds. Nonetheless, the Jazzmaster remained near the top of the Fender pricelist until withdrawn around 1980.

Most Fender guitars of the 1950s came officially only in sunburst or varieties of the original "blond" (some rare early Esquires were black). But a few guitars, specially made at the factory effectively as one-offs, were finished in solid colors. The rare surviving examples indicate that this practice was underway by 1954, but few players then seemed interested in slinging on a colored guitar, and Fender's main production remained in sunburst and blond instruments.

The company's early production of special-color guitars was certainly casual,

black sunburst finish. Even the jack socket mounting was new, recessed in a stylish plate on the body face. The Strat looked like no other guitar around – and in some ways seemed to owe more to contemporary automobile design than traditional guitar forms, especially in the flowing, sensual curves of that beautifully proportioned, timeless body.

The Stratocaster's new-style pickguard complemented the body lines perfectly. Indeed, the overall impression was of a guitar where all the components ideally suited one another. It's not surprising, therefore, that the Strat is still made today, over 45 years since its birth in the Fender company's functional buildings in Fullerton, California. The exemplary Fender Stratocaster has become the most popular, the most copied, the most desired, and very probably the most played solid electric guitar ever.

On its 40th anniversary in 1994 an official Fender estimate put Stratocaster sales so far at between a million and a million-and-a-half guitars – and that's without the plethora of unsubtle copies or more subtly "influenced" guitars that subsequently appeared from hundreds of other guitar-

---

1962 Fender Jaguar

BODY: body and headstock similar to Jazzmaster, but differences include:

NECK: bolt-on maple neck with unbound rosewood fingerboard with 7.25 radius; 22 narrow nickel-silver frets, 24" scale length.

BRIDGE: same 'floating tremolo' vibrato system as on Jazzmaster, with the addition of a switchable automatic string mute.

ELECTRONICS: two single-coil pickups with 'U' shaped metal brackets to shield the sides of the coils, six individual non-adjustable alnico slug pole pieces; DC resistance of approximately 6.5k. Switching features the same selectable preset rhythm section on the upper horn as the Jazzmaster, but lead circuit comprises slider switches for tone selection and on/off for each pickup, along with master Volume and Tone controls.

SOUND: fairly bright and light overall, but with a roundness and a blurrier edge to the harmonic content, thanks to the 24" scale length. Less midrange thump than a Jazzmaster.

1964
Fender Jaguar
Candy Apple Red

guitar facts

often no doubt the understandable reaction of a small company to lucrative if unusual orders from a handful of customers. But this informal arrangement was given a rather more commercial footing in the company's sales literature of 1956 when "player's choice" colored guitars were noted as an option, at five per cent extra cost. In the following year these Du Pont paint finishes were described in Fender's catalog as "Custom Colors" (a name that has stuck ever since) and in the pricelist as "custom Du Pont Duco finishes," still at five per cent on top of normal prices.

Fender also announced, early in 1957, a Stratocaster in see-through blond finish and with gold-plated hardware. Don Randall says the gold plate was influenced by seeing the new White Falcon model by Gretsch. In fact Fender had trouble getting the gold-plate to stay on the its components. But the gold-hardware blond Strat was in effect Fender's first official Custom Color guitar – although the term has always been more popularly applied since to solid-color varieties. The blond/gold Strat was later known as the "Mary Kaye" model thanks to musician Kaye regularly appearing with such a model in Fender catalogs.

Fender eventually came up with a defined list of its choice of available Custom Colors. In the early 1960s, when many more Custom Color Fenders were being made, the company issued color charts to publicize the various shades. There were three original charts: the first, in about 1960, featured Black, Burgundy Mist Metallic, Dakota Red, Daphne Blue, Fiesta Red, Foam Green, Inca Silver Metallic, Lake Placid Blue Metallic, Olympic White, Shell Pink, Sherwood Green Metallic, Shoreline Gold Metallic, Sonic Blue and Surf Green; the second, around 1963, had lost Shell Pink and gained Candy Apple Red Metallic; and the third, in 1965, lost Burgundy Mist Metallic, Daphne Blue, Inca Silver Metallic, Sherwood Green Metallic, Shoreline Gold Metallic and Surf Green, and gained – all Metallics – Blue Ice, Charcoal Frost, Firemist Gold, Firemist Silver, Ocean Turquoise and Teal Green.

The automobile industry was clearly having a profound effect upon US guitar manufacturers in the 1950s, not least in this ability to enhance the look of an already stylish object with a rich, sparkling paint job. Fender used paints from Du Pont's Duco nitro-cellulose lines, such as Dakota Red or Foam Green, as well as the more color-retentive Lucite acrylics like Lake Placid Blue Metallic or Burgundy Mist Metallic. Decades later the guitars bearing these original Fiesta Reds, Sonic Blues, Shoreline Golds and the like have proved very desirable among collectors, many of whom rate a Custom Color Fender, especially an early one, as a prime catch. This is despite the prevalence

of recent "refinishes" which have become so accurate that even alleged experts can be fooled into declaring some fake finishes as original. Some players find it difficult to understand why collectors can pay a very high premium simply for the promise that a particular layer of paint is "original."

At Fender in the late 1950s a few cosmetic and production adjustments were being made to the company's electric guitars. The Jazzmaster had been the first Fender with a rosewood fingerboard, and this material was adopted for other models around 1959. The company also altered the look of its sunburst finish at the time, adding red to give a three-tone yellow-to-red-to-black effect. By 1959 Fender employed 100 workers in nine buildings occupying some 54,000 square feet.

The last "new" Fender electrics of the 1950s were the bound-body Custom versions of the Esquire and Telecaster, new for 1959. Forrest White got advice on the process of binding from Fred Martin, head of the leading American flat-top acoustic guitar manufacturer Martin. The Customs each listed at just $30 more than the regular unbound versions, but far fewer of these were sold.

As Fender entered the 1960s, the company boasted an extended list of products in addition to its electric guitars. The company's July 1961 pricelist, for example, noted 13 amplifiers (Bandmaster, Bassman, Champ, Concert, Deluxe, Harvard, Princeton, Pro Amp, Super, Tremolux, Twin Amp, Vibrasonic, Vibrolux), five steel guitars (Champ, Deluxe, Dual, Stringmaster, Studio Deluxe), two pedal-steel guitars (400, 1000) and two bass guitars (Jazz, Precision).

The next new electric six-string design to leave Fender's production line was the Jaguar, which first showed up in sales material during 1962. It used a similar offset-waist body shape to the Jazzmaster, and also shared that guitar's separate bridge and vibrato unit, though the Jaguar had the addition of a spring-loaded string mute at the bridge. Fender rather optimistically believed that players of the time were so obsessed with gadgets that they would prefer a mechanical string mute to the natural edge-of-the-hand method. They were wrong. There are many elements of playing technique that simply cannot be replaced by hardware.

Despite the surface similarities, there were some notable differences between the new Jaguar and the now four-year-old Jazzmaster. Visually, the Jaguar had three distinctive chrome-plated control panels, and was the first Fender with 22 frets on the fingerboard. The Jaguar also had a slightly shorter string-length than usual for Fenders, closer to Gibson's standard, making for a different playing feel.

The Jaguar had better pickups than the Jazzmaster. They looked much like Strat units but had metal shielding added at the base and sides, partly as a response to criticisms of the Jazzmaster's tendency to noisiness. The Jag's electrics were even more complex than the Jazzmaster's, using the same rhythm circuit but adding a trio of lead-circuit switches. Like the Jazzmaster, the Jaguar enjoyed a burst of popularity when introduced. But this top-of-the-line guitar, "one of the finest solidbody electric guitars that has ever been offered to the public" in Fender's original sales hyperbole, has never enjoyed sustained success.

As the 1960s got underway it was clear that Fender had become a remarkably successful company. In a relatively short period Fender's brilliantly inventive trio of Telecaster, Precision Bass and Stratocaster had established in the minds of musicians and guitar-makers the idea of the solidbody electric guitar as a viable modern instrument. The company found itself in the midst of the rock'n'roll music revolution of the late 1950s and early 1960s... and were happy to ensure that players had a good supply of affordable guitars available in large numbers.

Fender had captured a huge segment of the new market. Many buildings had been added to cope with increased manufacturing demands, and by 1964 the operation employed some 600 people (of whom 500 were in manufacturing) spread over 29 buildings. Forrest White once said that his guitar production staff were making 1,500 instruments a week at the end of 1964, compared to the 40 a week when he'd joined the company ten years earlier. As well as electric guitars, Fender's pricelist in 1964 offered amplifiers, steel guitars, electric basses, acoustic guitars, electric pianos, effects units and a host of related accessories.

Don Randall remembers writing a million dollars' worth of sales during his first year in the 1950s, which rose to some 10 million dollars' worth in the mid 1960s (translating to some $40 million of retail sales). By that time the beat boom, triggered by The Beatles and the so-called British Invasion of pop groups, was taking the United States by storm. Electric guitars were at their peak of popularity, and Fender was among the biggest and most successful producers. Players as diverse as surf king Dick Dale, bluesman Muddy Waters and pop stylist Hank Marvin – plus thousands of others around and between them – were rarely seen without a Fender in their hands.

Exporting had also become important to Fender's huge success, and had started back in 1960 when sales chief Don Randall first visited the leading European trade show at Frankfurt, Germany. Fenders had become known in Europe, not only through the spread of pop music, but also because of

the many GIs stationed throughout the continent, many of whom played guitars... and Fenders. Britain was an especially important market in the 1960s because of the worldwide success of its pop groups. Up to the start of that deacde it had been virtually impossible for British musicians to buy Fenders, because of a government ban from 1951 to 1959 on the importation of selected American merchandise.

But in 1960 Jennings (see Vox) became the first official British distributor of Fender gear, joined by Selmer in 1962. By summer 1965 both Selmer and Jennings had been replaced as the British Fender distributor by Arbiter which, other than a lapse for a few years in the 1980s, has been Fender's UK agent ever since. Western Europe was clearly the biggest export market, but Fender also did well in Scandinavia, South Africa, Rhodesia (now Zimbabwe), Japan, Australia, Canada and elsewhere.

All in all, Fender was extremely successful. Then, in January 1965, the Fender companies were sold to the mighty Columbia Broadcasting System Inc, better known as CBS. A music-trade magazine reported in somewhat shocked tones: "The purchase price of $13 million is by far the highest ever offered in the history of the [musical instrument] industry for any single manufacturer, and was about two million dollars more than CBS paid recently for the New York Yankees baseball team. The acquisition, a sterling proof of the music industry's growth potential, marks the first time that one of the nation's largest corporations has entered our field. With sales volume in excess of half a billion dollars annually, CBS currently does more business than the entire [musical instrument] industry does at retail. Actual purchase of Fender was made by the Columbia Records Distribution Division of CBS whose outstanding recent feats have included the production of My Fair Lady."

Leo Fender was by all accounts a hypochondriac, and the sale of Fender was prompted by his acute health worries, principally over the sinus complaint that had troubled him since the mid 1950s. Leo was apparently also uncertain about how to finance expansion.

The sale of Fender to CBS has provoked much retrospective consternation among guitarists and collectors, some of whom considered so-called "pre-CBS" instruments – in other words those made prior to the beginning of 1965 – as superior to those made after that date. This was a rather meaningless generalization, and it is a pity that such an assumption became so entrenched.

According to some insiders, the problem with CBS at this time was that they seemed to believe that it was enough simply to pour a great deal of money into Fender. And

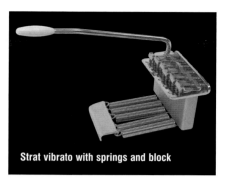

Strat vibrato with springs and block

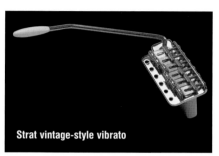

Strat vintage-style vibrato

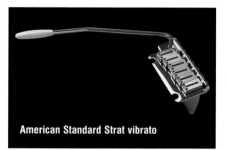

American Standard Strat vibrato

certainly Fender's sales did increase and profits did go up – Randall remembers income almost doubling in the first year that CBS owned Fender. Profit became paramount, said Forrest White, who remained as manager of electric guitar and amplifier production. Clearly there was a significant clash of cultures. The new CBS men, often trained engineers with college degrees, believed in high-volume production, whereas Fender's old guard – the team that had done much to put Fender where it was at the time – were long-serving craft workers without formal qualifications.

Leo's services were retained, CBS grandly naming him a "special consultant in research and development." In fact, he was set up away from the Fender buildings and allowed to tinker as much as he liked – with very little effect on the Fender product lines. A couple of years after the sale to CBS, Leo changed doctors and was given a huge dose of antibiotics which cured his sinus complaint. He completed a few projects for CBS but left when his five-year contract expired in 1970. He went on to design and make instruments for Music Man and G&L.

But Leo was not the first of the old team to leave CBS. White departed in 1967; he died in November 1994. Randall resigned from CBS in April 1969, and formed Randall

Electric Instruments, which he sold in 1987. Fullerton left CBS in 1970, worked at Ernie Ball for a while, and with Leo formed the G&L company in 1979, although Fullerton sold his interest in 1986. Hyatt, who resigned from CBS in 1972, was also part of the G&L set-up, which was sold to BBE Sound Inc after Leo Fender's death in March 1991.

Back at Fender Musical Instruments, the Electric XII – a guitar that had been on the drawing board when the CBS sale took place – finally hit the music stores in the summer of 1965. Electric 12-strings had recently been popularized by The Beatles and The Byrds, who both used Rickenbackers, so Fender joined in the battle with its own rather belated version. An innovation was the Electric XII's 12-saddle bridge which allowed for precise adjustments of individual string heights and intonation, a luxury hitherto unknown on any 12-string guitar. But the 12-string craze of the 1960s was almost over and the Electric XII proved shortlived, lasting in the line only until 1968.

One of Fender's first CBS-era pricelists, dated April 1965, reveals a burgeoning line of products in addition to the company's 11 electric guitar models (namely the Duo-Sonic, Electric XII, Esquire, Esquire Custom, Jaguar, Jazzmaster, Musicmaster, Mustang, Stratocaster, Telecaster and Telecaster Custom).

The other lines included three bass guitars (the Jazz, Precision, and VI), six flat-top acoustic guitars (the Classic, Concert, King, Malibu, Palomino and Newporter) and 15 amplifiers (Bandmaster, Bassman, Champ, Deluxe, Deluxe Reverb, Dual Showman, Princeton, Princeton Reverb, Pro Reverb, Showman, Super Reverb, Tremolux, Twin Reverb, Vibro Champ, Vibrolux Reverb).

1965 Fender Electric XII

BODY: offset waist, double-cutaway solid alder body with rib and forearm contours.

Neck: bolt-on maple neck with unbound rosewood fingerboard with 21 narrow nickel-silver frets, 7 ¼" radius, 1 ⅝" nut width, 25 1/2" scale length.

HEADSTOCK: 'hockey stick' headstock, with six-a-side enclosed Fender tuners; elongated string retainer for middle six strings.

BRIDGE: through-body stringing, fixed bridge with 12 individual saddles adjustable for intonation and overall height.

ELECTRONICS: two split single-coil pickups with fixed alnico magnet pole pieces, DC resistance approximately 9k. Four-way rotary switch to select either pickup individually or both together in series.

SOUND: bright and cutting, but also very thick and edgy, with reasonable note definition. A good blend of jangle and grunt for an electric 12-string.

guitar facts

1977 Fender Telecaster Thinline

BODY: semi-solid single-cutaway ash body with single f-hole; semi-transparent polyester sunburst finish.

NECK: three-bolt 'Tilt Neck' attachment, one-piece maple neck and integral maple fingerboard with 7 ¼" fingerboard radius, 21 nickel-silver frets, and 1 ⅝" nut width; 25 ½" scale length.

HEADSTOCK: asymmetrical headstock with six-in-line sealed Fender tuners; bone nut; single pressed-steel butterfly string tree; bullet truss rod adjustment nut.

BRIDGE: through body stringing; fixed steel bridge plate with six individual saddles, independently adjustable for height and intonation.

ELECTRONICS: two 'Fender Wide Range Humbucking Pickups' with six fixed pole pieces made from cunife magnet slugs, and six adjustable threaded cunife magnet pole pieces (in opposing rows of three); DC resistance of approximately 10k.

SOUND: fat, heavy, hot, and well defined, with a bright edge and decent snap, crackle and pop for a humbucker-loaded guitar.

1971
Fender Mustang

These were accompanied by various Fender-Rhodes keyboards, a number of steel and pedal steel guitars, and a solidbody electric mandolin, as well as reverb and echo units.

Uniquely for Fender, a guitar appeared in its 1965/66 literature that never actually made it into production. Naturally a company makes many designs and prototypes which do not translate to commercial release, but for an instrument to get as far as printed sales material, and then be withdrawn, implies a serious error of judgement somewhere along the line. It was the first sign that CBS might be losing its grip. The guitar was the Marauder, and its obvious distinction was summed up by Fender as follows in the hapless catalog entry: "It appears as though there are no pickups. There are, in reality, however, four newly created pickups mounted underneath the pickguard." The design had been offered to Fender by one Quilla H. Freeman, who had a patent for his idea of hiding powerful pickups under a guitar's pickguard.

Forrest White later remembered that there were problems with weak signals from the pickups, and George Fullerton said he thought there was also a dispute between Freeman and CBS concerning the patent. Whatever the circumstances, we know that Freeman later took the hidden-pickups idea

to another California-based guitar-making company, Rickenbacker, but it seems that their investigations into the idea got no further than prototypes.

A second proposed version of the Marauder was worked on at Fender during 1966. Eight prototypes were built of the new version, this time with three conventional, visible pickups, plus some complex associated control switching. Four of these trial guitars also had slanted frets. It was in this state that the Marauder project was finally laid to rest.

During 1966 CBS completed the construction of a new Fender factory, which had been planned before its purchase of the company. It cost the new owner $1.3million, and was situated next to Fender's buildings on the South Raymond site in Fullerton. Meanwhile, some cosmetic changes were being made to various Fender models. In 1965 the Stratocaster gained a broader headstock, effectively matching that of the Jazzmaster and Jaguar. Also during 1965 the fingerboards of the Electric XII, Jaguar and Jazzmaster were bound, while the following year the same trio was given block-shaped fingerboard inlays rather than the previous dot markers. Generally, CBS seemed to be fiddling for fiddling's sake.

A firm innovation – at least for Fender – came in the shape of a new line of hollowbody electrics. These were the first such electrics from Fender who until this point were clearly identified in the player's mind as a solidbody producer. Evidently the strong success of Gibson's ES line of semi-solidbodies and to a lesser extent models by Gretsch and others must have tempted CBS and its search for wider markets.

German maker Roger Rossmeisl had been brought into the company by Leo Fender in 1962 to design acoustic guitars, and Rossmeisl also became responsible for the new electric hollowbodies. Launched in 1966, the Coronado thinline guitars were the first to appear of Rossmeisl's electric designs for Fender and, despite their conventional, equal-double-cutaway, bound bodies with large, stylized f-holes, they employed the standard Fender bolt-on neck and headstock design. Options included a new vibrato tailpiece, and there was also a 12-string version that borrowed the Electric XII's "hockey-stick" headstock. Rossmeisl was also among the team which came up with a lightweight version of the Tele in 1968. The Thinline Telecaster had three hollowed-out cavities inside the body and a modified pickguard shaped to accommodate the single, token f-hole. It was also around this time – and quite apart from Fender – that Byrds guitarist Clarence White and drummer Gene Parsons came up with their "shoulder strap control" B-string-pull device that fitted into a Telecaster. It was designed to offer string-bends within chords to emulate pedal steel-type sounds.

It was at this time that Rossmeisl was let loose with a couple of guitar designs that were even less like the normal run of Fenders than the Coronado models had been. Rossmeisl's specialty was the so-called "German carve" taught to him by his guitar-making father, Wenzel Rossmeisl. This applies a distinctive "dished" dip around the top edge of the body, following its outline. Rossmeisl adopted this feature for the new hollowbody archtop electric Montego and

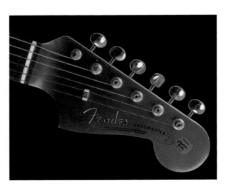

guitar facts

LTD models, all eminently traditional but still obstinately using Fender's customary bolt-on neck. From all reports there were very few of these made, and as a result the models are rarely seen (or played) today.

Toward the end of the 1960s came firm evidence that CBS was trying to wring every last drop of potential income from unused Fender factory stock that would otherwise have been written off. Two shortlived guitars, the Custom and the Swinger, were assembled from these leftovers.

As the close of the 1960s loomed, Fender took a boost when an inspired guitarist by the name of Jimi Hendrix applied the Stratocaster's sensuous curves and glorious tone to his live cavorting and studio experiments. Salesman Dale Hyatt once said – and he was only half-joking, one suspects – that Jimi Hendrix caused more Fender Stratocasters to be sold than all the company's salesmen put together.

One of the few top bands apparently absent from Fender patronage during the 1960s was The Beatles, who at least on-stage contented themselves with a mix of primarily Gretsch, Rickenbacker, Gibson, Epiphone and Hofner guitars. In fact, George Harrison and John Lennon had each acquired a Stratocaster in 1965 for studio use, and Paul McCartney bought an Esquire a year or two later. But the public face of the band remained distinctly Fender-less, which led Don Randall to try to persuade manager Brian Epstein to get his boys into Fender. Probably during 1969, Randall managed to secure a meeting with Lennon and McCartney at the band's Apple headquarters in London. The results were the band's Fender-Rhodes pianos, a Jazz Bass and a VI six-string bass, as well as George Harrison's Rosewood Telecaster – all visible at various times during the Let It Be movie.

The 1970s are believed by many players and collectors to be the poorest years of Fender's production history, and there can be little doubt that quality control slipped and more low-standard Fenders were made during this decade than any other. But some fine Fender guitars were made in the 1970s as well. It's just that there were more average guitars made than good ones – and it often seems as if the good instruments that do turn up were produced in spite rather than because of the company's policies and activities during that decade.

The 1970s would be a time when CBS management cut back on the existing Fender product lines and offered hardly any new models. The last Esquire of the period was made in 1970, the year in which the Duo-Sonic also died. The Jaguar disappeared around 1975, and by 1980 the Bronco, Jazzmaster, Musicmaster and Thinline Tele had all been taken out of production. Elsewhere in Fender's guitar lines, the

original acoustic flat-tops had all gone from the catalog by 1971. Ten years later the steels and pedal-steels had all disappeared, with only amplifiers (some 14 models) offering anything like the previous market coverage. Most of the original Custom Colors had been discontinued during the late 1960s and early 1970s.

So it was that by the start of the 1980s the guitarist who wanted to buy a new Fender electric had little choice beyond the company's ever-reliable Strats and Teles. And apart from a few shortlived exceptions, these came mostly in sunburst, blond, black or natural. It was hard to resist the feeling that the newly-important calculations of the balance sheet had become firmly established at Fender, and had taken precedence over the company's former creativity. A few new electric Fender models did get introduced in the 1970s, but mostly these were variations on familiar themes. Part of Fender's distinction had come from using bright-sounding single-coil pickups; the warmer, fatter-sounding humbucking types were always considered then as a Gibson mainstay. Nonetheless, in keeping with changing market trends, the Telecaster was given a humbucking pickup at the neck position to create the Telecaster Custom in 1972, and similar dabbling led to a sort of Tele-meets-Strat-meets-Gibson: the two-humbucker, Strat-necked Telecaster Deluxe of 1973.

The company made another attempt at thinline hollowbody electrics with the ill-fated Starcaster in 1976, again aimed at competing with Gibson's ever-popular ES line. The Starcaster had left the Fender list by 1980.

By 1976 Fender had a five-acre facility under one roof in Fullerton and employed over 750 workers. Some new "student" models appeared at this time to replace the Musicmaster, Bronco, Duo-Sonic and Mustang. The Lead I and Lead II guitars of 1979 were simple double-cutaway solids, though not especially cheap at $399. They were followed by the single-cutaway Bullet series which began production in 1981. Fender did briefly attempt to have these models produced in Korea, to eliminate tooling costs, but after a number of problems manufacturing resumed in the US.

In the early 1980s the CBS management appears to have decided that Fender needed some new blood to help reverse the decline in the company's fortunes. During 1981 key personnel were recruited from the American musical instrument operation of the giant Japanese company Yamaha, including John McLaren, Bill Schultz and Dan Smith. It appeared that they were brought in to turn around the reputation of Fender, to get the operation on its feet and making a profit once again. One of the new team's recommendations was to start

alternative production of Fenders in Japan. The reason was relatively straightforward: Fender's sales were being hammered by the onslaught of orientally-produced copies. These Japanese copyists made their biggest profits in their own domestic market, so the best place to hit back at them was in Japan – by making and selling guitars there.

So, with the blessing of CBS, negotiations began with two Japanese distributors to establish the Fender Japan company. A joint venture was officially established in March 1982.

In the States the new management team was working on a strategy to return Fender to its former glory. The plan was for Fender in effect to copy itself, by recreating the guitars that many players and collectors were spending large sums of money to acquire: the Fenders made back in the company's glory years in the 1950s and 1960s. The result was the Vintage reissue series, begun in 1982. The guitars consisted of a maple-neck "57" and rosewood-fingerboard "62" Strat, as well as a "52" Telecaster. These Vintage reproductions were not exact enough for some die-hard Fender collectors, but generally the guitars were praised and welcomed. Production of the Vintage reissues was planned to start in 1982 at Fender US (Fullerton) and at Fender Japan (Fujigen). But changes being instituted at the American factory meant that the US versions did not come on-stream until early 1983. Fender Japan's guitars at this stage were being made only for the internal Japanese market, but Fender's European agents were putting pressure on the Fullerton management for a low-end Fender to compete with the multitude of exported models being sold in Europe and elsewhere by other Japanese manufacturers.

So Fender Japan made some less costly versions of the Vintage reissues for European distribution in 1982, with the Squier brand (see Squier). At the end of 1983, with the US Fender factory still not up to the scale of production the team wanted, Fender Japan also built a Squier Stratocaster for the US market. This instrument, together with the earlier Squier Stratocasters and Telecasters, saw the start of the sale of Fender Japan products around the world, and a move by Fender to become an international manufacturer of guitars.

A shortlived pair from the US factory at this time was the Elite Stratocaster and Elite Telecaster, intended as radical new high-end versions of the old faithfuls. Unfortunately the vibrato-equipped Elite Strat came saddled with a terrible bridge, which is what most players recall when the Elites are mentioned. In-fighting at Fender had led to last-minute modifications of the vibrato design and the result was an unwieldy, unworkable piece of hardware. The Elite

Strat also featured three pushbuttons for pickup selection, which were not to the taste of players brought up on the classic Fender pickup switch. There were good points – the new pickups, the effective active circuitry, and an improved truss-rod design – but they tended to be overlooked. The Elites were also dropped by the end of 1984.

Three new-design Fender lines were introduced in 1984, made by Fender Japan and intended to compete with some of Gibson's popular lines. The overall name for the new instruments was the Master Series, encompassing electric archtop D'Aquisto models, with design input from American luthier Jimmy D'Aquisto, and semi-solid Esprit and Flame guitars. Significantly, they were the first Fender Japan products with the Fender rather than Squier headstock logo to be sold officially outside Japan, and the first Fenders with set-necks. Their overtly Gibson image was to be their undoing. Most players wanted recognizable Fenders from Fender. This recurring theme has jarred with all Fender's attempts to introduce new-design guitars.

For a variety of reasons, CBS decided during 1984 that it had finally had enough of this part of the music business, and that it wished to sell Fender Musical Instruments. CBS invited offers and at the end of January 1985, almost exactly 20 years since acquiring it, CBS confirmed that it would sell Fender to an investor group led by Bill Schultz, then president of Fender Musical Instruments. The contract was formalized in February and the sale completed in March 1985 for $12.5million. It's interesting to compare this with the $13million that CBS originally paid for the company back in 1965 (which translates to around $90million at 1985 prices).

The problems facing the new owners were legion, but probably the most immediate was the fact that the Fullerton factories were not included in the deal. So US production of Fenders stopped in February 1985. However, the new team had been stockpiling bodies and necks, and did acquire some existing inventory of completed guitars as well as production machinery. The company went from employing over 800 people in early 1984 down to just over 100 in early 1985.

Fender had been working on a couple of radical guitar designs before CBS sold the company, and these instruments became victims of the crossfire. One was the Performer, which started life intended for US production. But with nowhere to build it in the States, Fender had it manufactured at the Fujigen factory in Japan.

The Performer had a distinctive body shape, twin slanted pickups, 24 frets, and an arrow-shape headstock quite different from the usual Fender Strat derivative, a reaction

to the newly popular "superstrat" design popularized by American guitar makers such as Jackson and including a drooped "pointy" headstock. All in all, Fender's Performer was a thoroughly modern instrument with few nods to the company's illustrious past, but this brave move was killed by the CBS sale. The Japanese operation became Fender's lifeline at this time, providing much-needed product to the company which still had no US factory. All the guitars in Fender's 1985 catalog were made in Japan, including the new Contemporary Stratocasters and Telecasters which were the first Fenders with the increasingly fashionable heavy-duty vibrato units and string-clamps.

One estimate put as much as 80 per cent of the guitars that Fender US sold from around the end of 1984 to the middle of 1986 as Japanese-made.

Fender finally established its new factory at Corona, about 20 miles east of the now defunct Fullerton site. Production started on a very limited scale toward the end of 1985, producing only about five guitars a day for the Vintage reissue series. But Dan Smith and his colleagues wanted to re-establish the US side of Fender's production with some good, basic Strats and Teles that would be seen as a continuation of the best of Fender's American traditions. That plan translated into the American Standard models: the Strat version was launched in 1986; the Tele followed two years later.

The American Standard was an efficacious piece of re-interpretation. It drew from the best of the original Stratocaster but was updated with a flatter-camber 22-fret neck and a revised vibrato unit based on twin stud pivot points. Once the Corona plant's production lines reached full speed, the American Standard Stratocaster proved extremely successful for the revitalized Fender operation. By the early 1990s, the instrument was a best-seller, and was notching up some 25,000 sales annually. In many markets today, including the United States, the American Standard Stratocasters and Telecasters remain the best-selling US-

made Fender models. In 1987 the Fender Custom Shop was officially established at the Corona plant. The Custom Shop was started so that Fender could build one-offs and special orders for players who had the money and the inclination.

While this role remains – and their customers have ranged from Chet Atkins to Lou Reed – the Custom Shop now has a much wider part to play in Fender's expanding business.

The Shop's activities today effectively divide into three. First there are the one-offs, or Master Built guitars as the Custom Shop calls them. These are exactly what most people would understand as the work of a custom shop: instruments made by one person with acute attention to detail and a price to match. The second type is the limited edition, a special numbered run of anything from a handful to several hundred of a specific model. Third, the Custom Shop makes a general line of "catalog" models which it calls Stock Team (or, more personally, Custom Team) items, normally introduced after a style of model has proved popular in one-off requests.

One of the first jobs for the Custom Shop was to make a yellow Vintage reissue Strat for Jeff Beck. At this stage Beck vetoed Fender's wish to produce a Jeff Beck signature edition Strat, and the design intended for that purpose evolved into the Strat Plus. A Jeff Beck signature Strat not dissimilar to the Plus finally appeared in 1991. Signature instruments now form an important part of the Fender line. The first was the Eric Clapton Stratocaster. Clapton had asked Fender to make him a guitar with the distinct V-shape neck of his favorite 1930s Martin acoustic guitar, as well as what he described as a "compressed" pickup sound. Various prototypes were built by George Blanda at Fender, and the final design eventually went on sale to the public in 1988.

Lace Sensor pickups and an active circuit delivered the sound Clapton was after and, curiously, the production model even offers a blocked-off vintage-style vibrato unit, carefully duplicating that feature of Clapton's original. A number of Fender signature models have followed over the years and continue to appear. Some are made in the Custom Shop, others at the Corona factory or further afield, and each one is generally endowed with features favored by the named artist. They range from the posthumous Stevie Ray Vaughan Stratocaster to the Waylon Jennings "tribute series" Telecaster, the Dick Dale surfing Strat to the worn-and-torn Muddy Waters Tele, and the Jerry Donahue Telecaster to the Hendrix Voodoocaster Strat, with many more besides.

In 1988 the Custom Shop produced the 40th Anniversary Telecaster, its first limited-

1997 Fender Jag-Stang

BODY: non-concentric body designed by Kurt Cobain of Nirvana – allegedly rather haphazardly – by dividing the outlines of a Jaguar and a Mustang and splicing them together; made from solid alder.

NECK: bolt-on maple neck with unbound rosewood fingerboard with 7.25" radius; 22 narrow nickel-silver frets, 24" scale length.

BRIDGE: Fender 'Dynamic Vibrato' unit with semi-rocker bridge; bridge is adjustable overall for height, with six individual steel barrel saddles adjustable for intonation.

ELECTRONICS: one humbucking pickup in the bridge position, one single-coil pickup in the neck position; individual three-way slider switches for each pickup to give on/off/reverse-phase-on; master Volume and Tone controls.

SOUND: springy, round and fat in the bridge position, with an air of thick compression; snappy and warm in the neck position; funky and scooped with pickups out of phase.

edition production run. At that time most players and collectors (and Fender itself) believed that the first Broadcaster/Telecaster had been produced in 1948, hence the timing of the anniversary model. John Page, head of Fender's Custom Shop, says that it took some 18 months to build the full edition of 300 guitars – and then many Fender dealers were upset because the company only made 300. So the Shop's next limited run, the HLE Stratocaster (Haynes Limited Edition), was upped to 500 units. Other numbered runs continued to appear from the Custom Shop and became an important

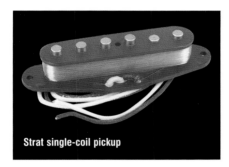

Strat single-coil pickup

part of the Shop's job. A logical extension to the limited editions occurred in 1992 with the Shop's first catalog of standard Custom Shop products – which it now groups together under the general headings of Stock Team and Custom Team guitars.

No production limit is put on these models other than the confines of the Shop's capacity. They include models such as the Carved Top Strat, the Set Neck Strat and the Robben Ford guitars, in series such as Custom Classics, Showmasters, and Time Machines. The expansion of the Custom Shop's business prompted a move in 1993 to new buildings (but still close to the Corona factory) to gain extra space and improve efficiency.

Following the success of the Vintage reissue series, first introduced in 1982, Fender Japan marketed a number of models that re-created many of the guitars from Fender's past. These included reproductions of the Paisley, Blue Flower, Rosewood and Thinline Telecasters, the Jaguar and Jazzmaster, the Mustang, and of course a plethora of Strats recalling various periods.

Fender US came up with a new design in 1991 called the Prodigy, a shortlived attempt to compete with successful guitars from popular makers of the time such as Charvel. It had an offset-waist body with sharper horns than a Strat, two single-coils and a humbucker, and an optional locking vibrato. The Prodigy was among the first Fender guitars to receive attention at the company's new factory in Ensenada, Mexico, which had been established in 1987. Ensenada is some 180 miles south of Los Angeles, just across the

1966
Fender Electric XII
12 string

California/Mexico border. Fender amps started to appear from the Mexico factory in 1989, with guitars following soon after.

By early 1992 the Mexican factory was producing around 175 Fender Standard Stratocasters per day. One estimate in the late 1990s had Mexico assembling around 150,000 Fenders a year, compared to some 85,000 at Corona. The workforce was around 1,000 at the Mexico factory and 700 at Corona. During 1999 Fender launched the first two original-design guitars to be manufactured at its Mexican plant, the Toronado and the Cyclone models.

During the late 1990s Fender put a good deal of effort into offering a greater variety of pickups on some models. The first wave of its own US-made units had begun with the "hotter" Texas Special Strat-type single-coils, first seen on the Stevie Ray Vaughan model in 1992. Also, the company became more inclined to use pickups from popular outside makers, including well-known brands such as DiMarzio and Seymour Duncan. Fender also used the increasingly popular Fishman Powerbridge, with "acoustic"-sounding piezo inserts, on the Power Tele models that it

1965 Fender Electric XII

BODY: offset waist, double-cutaway solid alder body with rib and forearm contours.

Neck: bolt-on maple neck with unbound rosewood fingerboard with 21 narrow nickel-silver frets, 7 ¼" radius, 1 ⅝" nut width, 25 ½" scale length.

HEADSTOCK: 'hockey stick' headstock, with six-a-side enclosed Fender tuners; elongated string retainer for middle six strings.

BRIDGE: through-body stringing, fixed bridge with 12 individual saddles adjustable for intonation and overall height.

ELECTRONICS: two split single-coil hum-cancelling pickups with fixed alnico magnet pole pieces, DC resistance approximately 9k. Four-way rotary switch to select either pickup individually or both together in series.

SOUND: bright and cutting, but also very thick and edgy, with reasonable note definition. A good blend of jangle and grunt for an electric 12-string.

launched in 2000. Fender manufactures some of its own pickups at the Fender Mexico plant for use on guitars assembled there. In addition to the expected single-coil units, there have been humbuckers – and so it seemed to Fender an obvious move to develop and make humbuckers at Corona. The first guitars with the new Fender US-made humbuckers were the California "Fat" models of 1997: the Fat Strat had a bridge humbucker while the Fat Tele came with a neck humbucker.

In the mid 1990s Fender began again to revisit one of its favorite locations: the past. A common request from some artists was for the Custom Shop to make them a replica of a favorite old guitar, usually because the original was too valuable to risk taking on the road. After Keith Richards told the Shop that some replicas made for him for a Stones tour looked too new ("bash 'em up a bit and I'll play 'em") the Shop began to include wear-and-tear distress marks to replicate the overall look of a battered old original. Then Master Builder J.W. Black came up with the idea of offering these aged replicas as standard Custom Shop catalog

Strat wiring layout

items, called Relics. The Shop made two aged 1950s-era samples: a Nocaster (the in-between Broadcaster/Telecaster with no model name) and a "Mary Kaye" Strat (blond body, gold-plated parts). Soon the Custom Shop was reacting to the demand generated from these samples by offering a line of three Relic Strats as well as a Relic Nocaster (a no-decal Broadcaster).

The Relics have proved remarkably successful and the line has expanded. John Page, boss of the Custom Shop, said that the Mary Kaye Relic Strat was the Shop's single best-selling model of the late 1990s, and the general popularity of the Relics was continued into the early 21st century.

At the time of writing, the Custom Shop has reorganized the line to offer three types of "re-creations" in its renamed Time Machine series.

First are the N.O.S. "New Old Stock" guitars, intended as pristine replicas that are produced as closely as possible to original brand new instruments that would have come off the Fender production line during the particular period concerned. Next, there are the Closet Classics, which are meant to be like guitars bought new years ago, played a bit, and shoved under the bed or in a closet. Third is the Relic style, as already discussed, with "aged" knocks and wear added by the Shop.

The Time Machine guitars obviously appeal to a relatively small but growing number of affluent Fender fans keen to acquire a new Fender that has the feel and sound of an oldie and that, in the case of the Relics, is made to look as if decades of wear-and-tear have stained the fingerboard, scuffed the body and tarnished the hardware. The Time Machine series is a brilliant marketing move by Fender, because these guitars are the nearest that the company has got in new instruments to the almost indefinable appeal of vintage guitars, something that most modern manufacturers – and certainly most collectors – had thought was firmly locked away in the past.

Meanwhile there were truly new guitars. Well... almost new guitars. Larry Brooks in the Custom Shop had built a hybrid guitar for grunge supremo Kurt Cobain in 1993 after the guitarist had come up with some ideas for a merged Jaguar and Mustang: the Jag-Stang. A number of also-ran Fender models beyond Stratocasters and Telecasters were proving popular at this time with grunge guitarists: Cobain himself played Jaguars and Mustangs; Steve Turner played a Mustang; J Mascis had a Jazzmaster. And the reason was straightforward. These guitars had the comforting Fender logo on the head, but could be bought more cheaply secondhand than Strats or Teles. The ethics of such deals suited grunge guitarists perfectly.

Cobain, meanwhile, decided to take cut-up photographs of his Jag and Mustang and stick them together this way and that, trying out different combinations to see what they would look like combined. The Custom Shop then took his paste-ups as a basis, assembled the design, and contoured it here and there to improve balance and feel. After Cobain's untimely death in 1994, the guitarist's family collaborated with the Fender company to release a Japan-made production version of the instrument, which was named the Fender Jag-Stang. Cobain's guitar hit the market in 1996.

Fender opened a brand new guitar- and amp-making factory in November 1998, still

in Corona, California. The company described the impressive state-of-the-art factory as arguably the most expensive and automated facility of its type in the world. Since starting production at the original Corona factory back in 1985, Fender had grown to occupy a total of 115,000 square feet of space in ten buildings across the city. Such a rambling spread proved increasingly inefficient, and Fender had begun to plan a new factory during the early 1990s. With this new facility Fender are now clearly geared up for even more expansion, and the new $20million 177,000-square-feet plant affords the continuingly successful Fender a potentially growing production capacity for the future. The new factory, with a staff of 600, also means that Fender's long-standing fight with California's stringent environmental laws are at an end, as the new purpose-built paint section works without toxic emissions.

The new factory may be only 20 miles or so from Fullerton and the site of Leo Fender's original workshops, but it is a universe away from those humble steel shacks that provided the first home for Fender guitar production. However, with his love of gadgetry Leo would undoubtedly have been enthralled by the new plant, not least its automated conveyor system that enables the storage and supply on demand to the production line of a vast inventory of guitar components.

As the 21st century gets underway, the Fender Musical Instruments Corporation is as aware as ever of the value of Leo's

surname. But many musicians, collectors and guitar dealers measure the worth of Fender purely in terms of past achievements – which must be a continuing frustration for a modern company whose new ideas are often resisted for being "un-Fender."

Fender has reached the enviable point today where it dominates the world's electric guitar market. It has achieved its current successes in a variety of ways, not least by trying to provide a model or models that will appeal to every conceivable type of guitar player at every level of skill and affluence.

Fender chairman and CEO Bill Schultz took a moment in 1999 to describe his firm's outlook in simple business-like terms: "Our goal couldn't be more straightforward. Simply put, we're going to be the world's best guitar and guitar-amp company."

The history of Fender and of Fender electric guitars – which continues as you read these words – has been a remarkable mixture of inspiration and invention, of luck and mishap. But the company's best guitars ensure that the Fender name lives on into this new millennium. Players and collectors eager to capture a well-aged slab of yesteryear continue to prize vintage Fenders, and the values of pre-CBS Stratocasters soared with the arrival of that model's 50th anniversary in 2004. Meanwhile, the company continues to launch new models and variations of its own classics that earn it new players every day, and hot young artists from John Mayer to John 5 still make this 60-year-old brand their instrument of choice. Fender guitars will no doubt help further generations of players turn strings and frets and pickups into remarkable music.

Fernandes

Although generally a rung below Japanese makes such as Ibanez and Yamaha in US and European markets, Fernandes is nevertheless a major maker, and one that has earned growing respect in recent years.

At home in Japan, Fernandes has long been one of the biggest brands. Guitar megastar Hotei is a Japanese devotee. Fernandes originated in the early 1970s on copies, but a decade later the catalog had expanded to include flattering imitations not just of Gibsons and Fenders but also Alembic, B.C. Rich and others.

Through the 1980s more players noticed Fernandes, praising accuracy, construction and quality. Name endorsers included Brad Gillis, Steve Stevens, Frank Dunnery, John Mayall and Mick Taylor. Despite Fender's legal successes and its own Japanese-made "copies," Fernandes remained busy in the US and Europe, battling with the likes of Tokai for the role of top copyist.

The 1990s brought a retro flavor to Fernandes, and a new model: the Sustainer.

This was a development of an American electro-magnetic sustain device that had appeared in 1987, refined and incorporated into guitars by Hamer and others. Fernandes developed the system. By the late 1990s it offered regular guitar performance plus controllable, never-ending sustain at any volume. The feature was fitted to numerous Fernandes models from the start of the 1990s, with Billy Gibbons a reported convert. The Fernandes line continues to boast a variety of standard, retro-style and superstrat electrics.

Framus

Occasionally quirky, but usually of high quality, Framus has long been a popular make throughout Europe and in Germany in particular, and made a splash in the US in the 1960s and '70s.
Even though guitars have been made in Germany for centuries, Framus was among the most successful German companies during the fabled guitar boom of the 1960s, when it was known for multi-laminated necks and complex electronics.

Frankische Musikindustrie (Framus) was founded in Erlangen, Germany, by Fred Wilfer in 1946, making acoustic guitars. In 1954 Framus relocated to Bubenreuth, and began adding pickups. Framus soon began making slimline semi-acoustic electric guitars around 1958, the best known being the single-cutaway Billy Lorento hollowbody (for the jazz guitarist later known as Bill Lawrence).

The late 1950s also brought the flat-topped, Les Paul-shaped Hollywood series of semi-solids, which later had single- or double-cutaway styling. They were succeeded in the early 1960s by Strato solidbodies. A great many solids carried this model name, regardless of shape or configuration, and Stratos came with numerous variations of pickups and hardware. By the mid 1960s the shape had changed to a more Fender Jazzmaster-like style, both for solidbody Strato and hollowbody Television models.

By 1965, high-end Framus models had Organtone, a spring-loaded volume control with a hook (or "spigot") operated by the little finger. For the exceptionally coordinated player it could simulate an organ swell effect. Better models often had mutes, plus many switches for questionable circuitry tricks.

Double-cutaway thinline hollowbodies offered in the mid 1960s included the Fret Jet and New Sound, both with multiple switches on the upper horn. Exotic examples from this era included the nine-string Melody, and the Electronica with "18 different string outputs" and onboard pre-amp.

Around 1969 Framus collaborated with Bill Lawrence on the BL series of offset-double-cutaway solidbodies with thick waist and chunky upper horn. In the early 1970s Framus also built Fender and Gibson copies, returning to original thinking around 1974 with the Jan Akkerman semi-hollowbody and the broad, solidbody Nashville series.

In 1977 Framus introduced the Memphis, a sort of anthropomorphic wedge-shape solidbody, and several other distinctive models. Framus limped on into the early 1980s before becoming Warwick, a brand more successful with bass guitars. Warwick revived the Framus brandname in 1995 for a line of high-end German-made regular six-strings.

The line currently includes funky updates of backward-looking designs – such as the Hollywood Custom and Tennessee Pro – and contemporary rock guitars such as the Panthera and Diablo models.

Futurama

Despite its roots as a beginner's instrument, the Futurama brand earned a place in history in the hands of a number of soon-to-be guitar stars.
These cheap import guitars for early British would-be rockers were first made by Neoton – based in Prague, Czech Republic (then Czechoslovakia). The Fender-style Neoton Grazioso arrived in Britain in 1957, marketed by Selmer. At around £55 ($90) it proved popular with many soon-famous players such as George Harrison, Albert Lee and Gerry Marsden. Selmer soon changed the uncommercial Grazioso name to the more evocative Futurama. During 1963 Selmer switched sources, using the new brand on guitars made by Hagstrom of Sweden. The Futurama Coronado model represented the best in Futurama quality, but Selmer dropped the brandname in 1965.

G&L

This California makers is a respected but perhaps underappreciated brand. For three decades, the company has turned out very well-made instruments that address the needs of hardworking professional musicians and enthusiastic amateurs alike ... much like the guitars of its co-founder's first company.
G&L provided the final vehicle for Leo Fender's ideas on guitar design, continuing the tradition established by one of the industry's most famous names. Leo sold Fender to CBS in 1965. After leaving his Music Man operation, he started G&L in Fullerton, California, in 1979.

The first F-100 model appeared a year later. G&L was an abbreviation of "George and Leo", partner George Fullerton having worked with Leo at Fender. Fullerton sold his interest in G&L in 1986.

The two-humbucker F-100 displayed design touches that were distinctly Leo Fender. G&L addressed the less expensive

> ### G&L ASAT Z-3
> **BODY:** single-cutaway solid alder 'slab' body.
>
> **NECK:** bolt-on, one-piece maple neck and rosewood fingerboard with 12" radius, 22 medium-jumbo nickel-silver frets, and 1 ⅝" nut width; 25 ½" scale length.
>
> **HEADSTOCK:** asymmetrical headstock with six-in-line sealed G&L tuners; bone nut; single friction-reducing string tree.
>
> **BRIDGE:** tune-o-matic style bridge with Bigsby B-5 vibrato tailpiece, both partially routed into the body to increase break angle (and therefore tone and sustain).
>
> **ELECTRONICS:** three G&L Z-Coil single-coil pickups, made with two individual 'half length' coils wound to opposite polarity for hum rejection; ceramic magnets with adjustable threaded steel pole pieces; DC resistance approximately 4.5k (although output is deceptively high, given the unusual design); five-way selector switch to give each pickup individually plus bridge-and-middle, neck-and-middle; 250k potentiometers for Volume and Tone.
>
> **SOUND:** snappy, cutting and well-defined, with a full, round voice and relatively high output for a single-coil guitar. Good hum rejection.

end of the market with its first SC series, debuting in 1982 with a body reminiscent of Fender's Mustang. High-end models continued to appear, many being variations on a now-established G&L template. Most striking of these was the limited-edition Interceptor with unusual X-shaped body.

In 1985 Leo refined his original Telecaster for the G&L Broadcaster. Body shape and control plate were familiar; other aspects remained staunchly G&L. Fender objected, so in 1986 G&L's Broadcaster became the ASAT, which went on to be a popular model.

During the late 1980s all-new rock machines included the Invader, Rampage and Superhawk. The Interceptor was modified with extended body horns and a Kahler vibrato, but in 1988 became a more conventional superstrat. In the same year the Comanche appeared, one of Leo's last designs. Signature versions of some models bore Leo's autograph logo on the body. The limited-edition Commemorative marked Leo's death in March 1991.

In late 1991 G&L was sold to BBE Sound of Huntington Beach, California. A Japan-only Tribute series of Japanese-made G&Ls appeared in 1998, including an ASAT, and Korean-made Tributes were soon introduced in other markets. In the US the Comanche model was revived the same year, reintroducing for this as well as other models Leo's distinctive split-coil pickups, now called Z-coils. Toward the late 1990s G&L phased out two of Leo's favored design points: the three-bolt neck joint and "bullet"

1964 Gibson ES-175D

BODY: 16 ¼" wide, 3 ½" deep fully hollow single-cutaway body with laminated maple top, back and sides; pressed-arch top with parallel bracing; bound top and back.

NECK: glued in three-piece maple neck with bound rosewood fingerboard with 12" radius; 14th fret neck/body joint, 19 narrow nickel-silver frets, and 1 ¹¹⁄₁₆" nut width; 24 ⅝" scale length.

HEADSTOCK: symmetrical back-angled headstock with three-a-side replacement Grover tuners (originally Klusons); bone nut.

BRIDGE: a floating two-piece rosewood bridge with thumb wheels for height adjustment would be original, but a tune-o-matic has been added here; also a replacement trapeze tailpiece.

ELECTRONICS: two humbucking pickups, three-way toggle switch for either pickup or both together, four 500k potentiometers for independent Volume and Tone controls for each pickup.

SOUND: warm, full, thick and round, with a slight natural softness in the attack.

NOTE: the guitar pictured belongs to Steve Howe of the band Yes.

guitar facts

style headstock truss-rod adjustment nut. But this was not the result of any failure in their function: it was more that they were often misinterpreted by players.

Gibson

Orville H. Gibson invented the archtop guitar. The namesake company that followed after offered the first commercially available electric guitar from a major maker in the late 1930s, set the standard for the amplified jazz guitar in the 1940s, and a decade later introduced what would become one of the most highly prized solidbody electric guitars of all time – all of which carried substantial design elements established by Orville at the end of the previous century.

Gibson is one of the greatest and most significant fretted instrument manufacturers, and has been in existence for more than 110 years. Orville H. Gibson was born in 1856 in upstate New York, near the Canadian border. He began making stringed musical instruments in Kalamazoo, Michigan, probably by the 1880s, and set himself up as a manufacturer of musical instruments there around 1894.

Orville Gibson had a refreshingly unconventional mixture of ideas about how to construct his mandolin-family instruments and oval-soundhole guitars. He would hand-carve the tops and backs, but would cut sides from solid wood rather than using the usual heating-and-bending method. Also unusual was the lack of internal bracing, which he thought degraded volume and tone. Gibson would often have his instrument's bodies decorated with beautiful inlaid pickguards and a distinctive crescent-and-star logo on the headstock. The only patent that Orville ever received – which was granted in 1898 – was for his mandolin design that featured the distinctive one-piece carved sides, as well as a similarly one-piece neck.

In 1902 a group of businessmen joined Orville Gibson to form the Gibson Mandolin-Guitar Manufacturing company. The instruments that the new operation produced illustrated the diverse range of fretted stringed instruments available in the United States during the early decades of the 20th century. The mandolin was clearly the most popular, and Gibson would soon find itself among the most celebrated of mandolin makers, thanks in no small part to the enormously influential F-5 model that would appear in 1922. Gibson also instigated a successful teacher-agent system to sell its mandolins. This was in contrast to the normal distribution operated by most instrument companies that would be based on a network of retailers.

Orville had left the Gibson company in

1953
Gibson Super 400CES

> **1953 Gibson Super 400CES**
>
> **BODY:** 18" wide single-cutaway fully hollow body with arched maple back, maple sides, and parallel-braced arched solid spruce top. Bound top and back
>
> **NECK:** glued-in one-piece mahogany neck with multi-bound ebony fingerboard with 12" radius; 14th fret neck/body joint, 20 narrow gauge nickel-silver frets, and 1 ¹¹⁄₁₆" nut width; 25 ½" scale length.
>
> **HEADSTOCK:** symmetrical 17 degree back-angled headstock with three-a-side Grover tuners; bone nut.
>
> **BRIDGE:** floating two-piece ebony bridge with thumb wheels for height adjustment; trapeze tailpiece.
>
> **ELECTRONICS:** two P-90 pickups, DC resistance approximately 8k. Independent controls for Volume and Tone and three-way selector switch.
>
> **SOUND:** deep and full-throated, but with decent brightness and definition; plenty of woody resonance. Slightly gritty edge when hit hard.

1903, receiving a regular royalty from the company for the following five years and then a monthly income until his death in 1918. A year earlier the company had moved to new premises on Parsons Street, Kalamazoo (which it occupied until 1984).

Once Orville left Gibson, changes began to be made to his original construction methods, apparently for reasons of efficiency, for ease of production and, indeed, for improvement. Orville's sawed solid-wood sides were replaced with conventional heated-and-bent parts, and his inlaid, integral pickguard was replaced around 1908 with a unit elevated from the instrument's surface: the "floating pickguard." It was devised by Gibson man Lewis Williams, and the general design is still in use today by many producers of archtop guitars.

The guitar began to grow in importance during the late 1920s and into the 1930s, largely replacing the previously prominent tenor banjo. It became essential that any company demanding attention among guitarists should be seen as inventive and forward-thinking in this vital new area. Gibson obliged with many six-string innovations, including Ted McHugh's adjustable truss-rod that did an excellent job of strengthening the instrument's neck. Truss-rods are virtually obligatory on today's guitars.

Thanks to the creativity of gifted employees such as Lloyd Loar, Gibson also established individual landmarks like the L-5 guitar of the early 1920s. With its novel f-holes and "floating" pickguard, this model virtually defined the look and sound of the early archtop acoustic guitar. It soon established itself and was played in a variety of musical styles, none more appealing than the "parlor jazz" music epitomized by the

incomparable guitarist Eddie Lang.

Lloyd Loar was an experienced musician who had started to work at Gibson in 1919 as a designer, and his best-known achievements were the Master Models series that included that ground-breaking L-5 guitar. Loar left Gibson in 1924 and around 1933 formed a company with ex-Gibson man Lewis Williams, primarily to manufacture electric instruments, which they called Vivi Tone or Acousti-Lectric.

The still barely understood potential of electric instruments fascinated Loar, who had devised an early experimental electric pickup while at Gibson in the 1920s. But Loar and Williams's offerings appear to have been too radical and ahead of their time to make any commercial impact, and within a

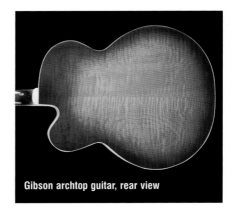

Gibson archtop guitar, rear view

few years of its inception their company had closed. Loar died in the early 1940s at the age of 57.

As players demanded more volume from their guitars, Gibson dutifully increased the size of its acoustic instruments, introducing the superb, huge archtop Super 400 model in 1934. Later in the decade came Gibson's "jumbo" J-series flat-tops. It was around this time that Gibson introduced its first electric guitars, the Electric Hawaiian E-150 cast aluminum steel guitar in 1935, and the following year the EH-150 steel plus an f-hole hollowbody, the ES-150, Gibson's first archtop electric.

The non-cutaway ES-150 electric guitar was a very significant addition to the catalog for Gibson. It effectively marked the start of the company's long-running ES series – the initial letters standing for "Electric Spanish." It's worth noting that, in this context, the term "Spanish" of course had nothing at all to do with nylon-string round-soundhole guitars. Instead, it was being used to distinguish this type of guitar from its Hawaiian-style cousin, the one generally played on the lap.

The ES-150 was famously taken up by Charlie Christian, the genius who showed jazz players what an electric guitar was for. Playing clear, single-note runs as if he were a horn player, Christian virtually invented the idea of the electric guitar solo. The "bar" pickup of the earliest ES-150 models, which was designed by Walt Fuller at Gibson, has subsequently become known as the "Charlie Christian" pickup as the guitarist was by far its best-known user, even though Christian's career was cut tragically short by his early death in 1942 at the age of just 25. Gibson tentatively built on these low-key electric experiments, adding the budget ES-100 archtop in 1938, and following this with its most expensive pre-war electric model, the ES-300, in 1940. When America entered the war two years later Gibson effectively put a halt to its guitar production. As instrument manufacturing gradually recommenced afterwards, Gibson rightly concluded that the electric guitar was set to become an important part of its reactivated business.

Around this time Gibson also manufactured instruments with a number of brandnames in addition to the most famous one. A good deal of the instruments bearing these names were acoustics, but electrics did appear with the following brands: Capital (made for Jenkins mail-order); Cromwell (for a variety of mail-order houses); Kalamazoo (a low-end in-house brand); Old Kraftsman (made for Spiegel mail-order); and Recording King (for Montgomery-Ward mail-order).

A controlling interest in Gibson was purchased in 1944 by the Chicago Musical Instrument Company (CMI), founded some 25 years earlier in Chicago, Illinois, by Maurice Berlin. Gibson's manufacturing base remained at its original factory, purpose-built in 1917 at Kalamazoo, which was roughly equidistant between Detroit and Chicago. The latter city was the location for Gibson's new sales and administration headquarters at CMI. It was at this time that Gibson began to pioneer electric guitars with cutaways. A cutaway offered easier access to the now audible and musically useful area of the upper fingerboard, previously of little use to quiet acoustic players who tended to limit their fret-based ramblings primarily to the headstock end of the neck. Talented and imaginative guitarists openly welcomed the artistic potential of the cutaway ... and now they began to investigate the dusty end of the fingerboard.

Significant new archtop electric guitars debuted in the late 1940s. The ES-350 of 1947 and two years later the ES-5 and sharp-cutaway ES-175 were all aimed at players who were prepared to commit themselves to fully integrated electric instruments that were designed and built as such by Gibson.

Gibson's ES-350 of 1947 was the first of the company's new-style cutaway electrics (and at first it bore the "Premier" tag of the pre-war cutaway acoustics). The 350 was followed in 1949 by the new single-pickup ES-175, Gibson's first electric with a "pointed" cutaway style and a pressed, laminated top. This construction contributed a distinctively bright, cutting tone color to the 175. A two-pickup version, the ES-175D, was added in 1953.

The ES-175 became a popular instrument and was Gibson's first really successful electric guitar. It has made a particular impact among electric jazz musicians, including such luminaries as Joe Pass, while also attracting eclectic modern players like Steve Howe and Pat Metheny.

The ES-5 also debuted in 1949 and was the first electric guitar with three pickups – it was effectively a three-pickup ES-350. However, before long, players found that it was less controllable than they wanted. As with all Gibson's immediate post-war electric guitars, the ES-5 had no pickup switching. Instead, each pickup had a separate volume control, which meant that the only way to achieve a balance between the pickups was to set the three volume knobs at the required positions.

So it was that in 1956 Gibson issued the ES-5 model with redesigned electronics, this time with a new name: the ES-5 Switchmaster. Three individual tone knobs were added alongside the three volume controls, and near the cutaway a four-way pickup selector switch was added, hence the new model name. The switch, explained a Gibson catalog of the time, "activates each of the three pickups separately, a combination of any two, or all three simultaneously."

At a time when Fender had just launched its stylish three-pickup Stratocaster, and Epiphone was offering models with a six-button "color tone" switching system, Gibson probably felt the ES-5 Switchmaster was a potential market leader. But it never caught on. And anyway, by now Gibson had produced proper electric versions of its great archtop acoustics, the L-5 and the Super 400.

In 1951 Gibson became serious about the electric guitar, launching the Super 400CES and the L-5CES (the initials stand for Cutaway, Electric, Spanish). For the 400CES, Gibson built on its existing Super 400C acoustic model, and for the L-5CES combined elements of its acoustic L-5C and electric ES-5 guitars. The new electric models had modified and stronger internal "bracing" to make them less prone to feedback when amplified.

The generally large proportions of the 18″-wide acoustic bodies of the earlier models were retained for these impressive new electrics in the Gibson line. For the 400CES model, the acoustic 400's high-end appointments remained – such as split-block-shape fingerboard inlays, a "marbleized" tortoiseshell pickguard, and a fancy "split-diamond" headstock inlay.

At first the electric 400 and L-5 came with a pair of Gibson's standard single-coil P-90 pickups, but in 1954 changed to more powerful "Alnico" types with distinctive rectangular polepieces. The Alnico nickname comes from the magnet type used in these pickups. A "rounded"-cutaway body style lasted from the launch of the two electrics in 1951 until 1960, when a new "pointed" cutaway was introduced. Gibson reverted to the original rounded design in 1969.

An immense variety of players has at different times been drawn to the power and versatility of Gibson's two leading archtop electrics. The Super 400CES has attracted bluesman Robben Ford, country players like Hank Thompson and Merle Travis (whose custom 400 was described in 1952 as Gibson's "most expensive guitar ever"), rock'n'roller Scotty Moore, and a number of fine jazz guitarists including George Benson and Kenny Burrell. The L-5CES has also had its fans and adherents over the subsequent years, including jazzmen such as Wes Montgomery and John Collins, as well as the fine country-jazzer Hank Garland.

Ted McCarty had joined Gibson back in March 1948, having worked at the Wurlitzer organ company for the previous 12 years. In 1950 he was made president of Gibson. Gibson was finding it hard in the post-war years to get back into full-scale guitar production, and McCarty's first managerial tasks were to increase the effectiveness of supervision, to bolster efficiency, and to improve internal communication.

guitar facts

Gibson began to work on a solidbody design soon after Fender's original Telecaster-style model had appeared in 1950. McCarty had a good team working on the project, including production head John Huis, as well as employees Julius Bellson and Wilbur Marker, while the sales people were regularly consulted through manager Clarence Havenga. It took them all about a year to come up with satisfactory prototypes for a new Gibson solidbody – at which point McCarty began to think about guitarist Les Paul, who was just about the most famous guitar player in America.

In the 1940s Les Paul had been a member of the supergroup Jazz At The Philharmonic, and had played prominent guitar on Bing Crosby's hit 'It's Been A Long Long Time.' Crosby encouraged Paul to build a studio into the garage of the guitarist's home in Hollywood, California, and it was here that he hit upon his effective "multiple" recording techniques. These early overdubbing routines allowed Paul to create huge, magical orchestras of massed guitars, arranged by the guitarist to play catchy instrumental tunes. Les Paul and his New Sound was signed to Capitol Records, with the first release 'Lover' a hit in 1948.

Paul found even greater popularity when he added vocalist Mary Ford to the act. They had married in 1949, and the following year the duo released their first joint record. Guitars and now voices too were given the multiple recording treatment, and big hits followed for Les Paul & Mary Ford including 'The Tennessee Waltz' (1950) and 'How High The Moon' (1951). The duo performed hundreds of personal appearances and concerts, and were heard on NBC Radio's *Les Paul Show* every week for six months during 1949 and 1950. Their networked TV series *The Les Paul & Mary Ford Show* began in 1953, beamed from their extravagant new home in Mahwah, New Jersey. As the 1950s got underway, Les Paul & Mary Ford – "America's Musical Sweethearts" – were huge stars.

Les Paul's obsessive tinkering with gadgetry was not restricted to the recording studio. The teenage Lester, drawn to the guitar, had soon become interested in the idea of amplification. In the late 1930s his new jazz-based trio was broadcasting out of New York on the Fred Waring radio show, with Paul at first playing a Gibson L-5 archtop acoustic, and later a similar Epiphone. The guitarist exercised his curiosity for electric instruments and his flair for technical experimentation by adapting and modifying the Epiphone guitar.

Around 1940, Les Paul used to go at weekends into the empty Epiphone factory in New York in order to fiddle with what he would call his "log" guitar. The nickname was derived from the 4″ by 4″ solid block of pine which the guitarist had inserted between the sawed halves of the body that he'd just dismembered. He then carefully re-joined the neck to the pine log, using some metal brackets, and mounted on the top a couple of crude pickups he'd made for himself.

Later he modified a second and third Epiphone, which he called his "clunkers," this time chopping up the bodies to add metal strengthening braces, and again topped off with Paul's own pickups. Despite their makeshift origins, the semi-solid "log" and the modified "clunker" Epiphones often accompanied Les Paul and Mary Ford on stage and in recording studios throughout the 1940s and into the early 1950s.

Paul was not alone in his investigations. Several unconnected explorations into the possibility of a solidbody electric guitar were being undertaken elsewhere in America at this time, not least at the California workshops of Rickenbacker, National, Bigsby and Fender. A solidbody electric was appealing because it would dispose of the involved construction of an acoustic guitar, and instead use a body or section of the body made of solid wood (or some other rigid material) to support the strings and pickups. Also, it would curtail the annoying feedback produced by amplified acoustic guitars, and reduce the body's interference with the guitar's overall tone, thus more accurately reproducing and sustaining the sound of the strings.

During the 1940s, Paul had decided that he would take his "log" idea to a major guitar manufacturing company in order to try to generate some real interest in its commercial potential. He decided – accurately, as it turned out – that Epiphone would not continue in its present form as a strong force in the guitar world. So around 1946 Paul took his crude log guitar to Gibson's parent company, CMI in Chicago, with the intention of convincing them to market such a semi-solid guitar. No doubt with all the courtesy that a pressurised city businessman could muster, the boss of CMI showed Les Paul the door. A startled Paul recalls that they laughed at his guitar, dismissing him as "the guy with the broomstick." But some years later, as we've seen, Gibson was developing ideas for a solidbody electric guitar in the wake of Fender's new instrument, and Gibson president Ted McCarty decided to contact the now hugely popular Les Paul.

A meeting took place, probably in 1951. McCarty's intention was to interest Paul in publicly playing Gibson's newly designed guitar in return for a royalty on sales – an arrangement generally referred to now as an "endorsement" deal.

It was certainly not a new arrangement for Gibson: the company's Nick Lucas flat-top acoustic model of 1928 had exploited the popularity of Lucas, known as "the crooning troubadour," to produce the contemporary guitar industry's first "signature" instrument.

Gibson's meeting with Les Paul around 1951 was the first opportunity the guitarist had to see the prototype of what would soon become the Gibson Les Paul solidbody electric. A deal was struck: Paul's royalty on

Les Paul models would be five per cent, and the term of the contract was set at five years. Paul's respected playing and commercial success added to Gibson's weighty experience in manufacturing and marketing guitars made for a strong and impressive combination.

The new Les Paul guitar was launched by Gibson in 1952, probably in the spring of that year, and was priced at $210 (this being around $20 more than Fender's Telecaster). Today, this first style of Les Paul model is nearly always called the "gold-top" because of its distinctive gold-finished body face. The

1952 & '59 Gibson Les Pauls

BODY: solid mahogany body with carved, arched maple top (usually of two pieces); top binding; single cutaway. Semi-transparent cherry-to-amber sunburst finish in nitrocellulose lacquer (gold finish on '52 model).

NECK: glued-in, one-piece mahogany neck with rosewood fingerboard with 12" fingerboard radius, 22 jumbo nickel-silver frets, and 1 1⁄16" nut width; 25 5⁄8" scale length. In 1958 and '59 neck profile was chunky, but became much thinner in 1960.

HEADSTOCK: symmetrical headstock at 17 degree back angle, with three-a-side tulip-button Kluson tuners; bone nut.

BRIDGE: adjustable tune-o-matic bridge and stop-bar tailpiece (fixed bar bridge with trapeze attachment on '52 model).

ELECTRONICS: dual humbucking pickups constructed of single alnico bar magnet beneath, six fixed steel slug pole pieces in one coil and six threaded adjustable pole pieces in the other; DC resistance of 7.5k to 8k; nickel-plated steel cover. Three-way toggle switch to select either pickup alone or both together; four 500k potentiometers for individual Volume and Tone for each pickup. (Dual P-90s on '52 model, for a grittier, more cutting sound.)

SOUND: thick, warm, flutey and vocal from the neck pickup, punchy and cutting from the bridge; muscular punch and singing sustain. Good hum rejection.

guitar facts

1952
Gibson Les Paul

length as the new Les Paul. The model came with a new height-adjustable combined bridge/tailpiece which was bar-shaped, joined to long metal rods that anchored it to the bottom edge of the guitar. This was designed by Les Paul, intended for use on archtop guitars (and Gibson also sold it as a separate replacement accessory). It proved unsuitable for the new solidbody, and was quickly replaced by a new purpose-built "stud" bar-shaped bridge/tailpiece, phased in around 1953. The new unit was mounted on to the top of the body with twin height-adjustable studs, hence the nickname.

The original gold-top sold well at first in relation to Gibson's other models. Electric guitars were clearly catching on. In 1954 Gibson's historian Julius Bellson charted the progress of the company's electric instruments. Consulting records, Bellson estimated that back in 1938 electric guitars had made up no more than ten per cent of Gibson guitar sales, but that the proportion of electrics to the rest had risen to 15 per cent by 1940, to 50 per cent by 1951, and that by 1953 electric guitars constituted no less than 65 per cent of the company's total guitar sales.

In a move designed to widen the market still further for solidbody electrics, Gibson issued two more Les Paul models in 1954, the Junior and the Custom. The cheaper Junior was designed for and aimed at beginners, although over time it has proved itself well enough suited to straightforward pro use.

Although the outline of the Junior's body was clearly Les Paul-like, the most obvious difference to its partners was the flat-top "slab" mahogany body, finished in traditional Gibson sunburst. It did not pretend to be anything other than a cheaper guitar: it had a single P-90 pickup, simple volume and tone controls, and the unbound rosewood fingerboard bore plain dot-shape position markers. It featured the stud bridge/tailpiece as used on the second incarnation of the gold-top.

By contrast, the high-end two-pickup Custom looked luxurious. It came with an all-black finish, multiple binding, block-shape position markers in an ebony fingerboard, and gold-plated hardware. It was, naturally, more expensive than the gold-top.

The Custom had an all-mahogany body, as favored by Les Paul himself, rather than the maple/mahogany mix of the gold-top model, and this gave the new guitar a rather more mellow tone. The Custom was promoted in Gibson catalogs as "The Fretless Wonder" thanks to its use of very low, flat fretwire, different than the wire used on other Les Pauls at the time. It was the first Les Paul model to feature Gibson's new Tune-o-matic bridge, used with a separate

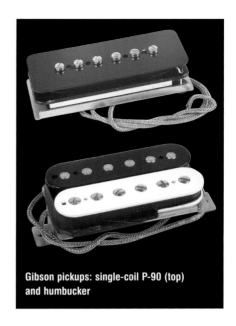

Gibson pickups: single-coil P-90 (top) and humbucker

bar-shaped tailpiece and offering for the first time on Gibsons the opportunity to adjust individually the length of each string, thus improving intonation (tuning accuracy). These new units were gradually added to other models in the Gibson line.

In 1955 Gibson launched the Les Paul TV model, essentially a Junior in what Gibson referred to as "natural" finish – actually more of a murky beige. Also that year the original line-up of Les Paul models was completed with the addition of the Special, effectively a two-pickup version of the Junior finished in the TV's beige color (but not called a TV model).

A number of well-known players from a variety of musical styles were drawn to Gibson Les Paul models during the 1950s. These musicians included rock'n'roller Frannie Beecher, bluesmen such as Guitar Slim, Freddy King and John Lee Hooker, as well as rockabilly rebel Carl Perkins.

Gibson launched three hollowbody electrics during 1955 in a new "thinline" thinner-body style, aiming to provide instruments more comfortable than their existing deep-bodied archtop cutaway electrics which were generally around 3.5" deep. The ES-225T, the ES-350T and the Byrdland had shallower bodies, around 2" deep, and the latter two also boasted a

gold-top's solid body cleverly combined a carved maple top bonded to a mahogany "back," uniting the darker tonality of mahogany with the brighter sound of maple.

Gibson had made a one-off all-gold hollowbody guitar in 1951 for Paul to present to a terminally ill patient whom he had met when making a special hospital appearance. This presentation guitar presumably prompted the all-gold archtop electric ES-295 model of 1952 (effectively a gold-finished ES-175) and was probably the inspiration for the color of the first Les Paul model. Almost all the other design elements of the first Gibson Les Paul have precedents in earlier Gibson models. For example, the instrument's layout of two P-90 single-coil pickups and four controls (which comprised a volume and tone pair for each pickup) was already a feature of Gibson's CES electric archtops that had been launched the previous year.

The general body outline and glued-in mahogany neck also followed established Gibson traditions, and the "crown"-shape inlays on the rosewood fingerboard had first appeared on the 1950 incarnation of the ES-150 model. Several Gibson acoustics had already appeared with the same scale-

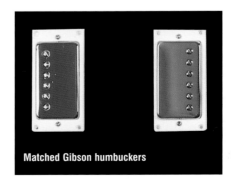

Matched Gibson humbuckers

shorter scale-length and a shorter, narrower neck, all designed for an easier, more playable feel. Top of the new line was the Byrdland, a kind of thinline L-5CES. It was inspired by country guitarist Billy Byrd and sessionman Hank Garland, hence the combined model name.

An important player who grasped the possibilities of these new friendlier electrics from Gibson was Chuck Berry, the most influential rock'n'roll guitarist of the 1950s. Berry chose a brand new natural-finish ES-350T to fuel his startlingly fresh hybrid of boogie, country and blues. In hindsight, it's remarkable that this great player did not appear in any Gibson advertising at the time – but then nor did any other black guitarists of the period.

Jazz players still kept Gibson's name prominent in the archtop electric field. Of the guitarists in the poll for the prestigious US jazz magazine *Down Beat* in 1956, Gibson could count six of the top ten as being loyal to the company: Barney Kessel (most often seen with an ES-350); Tal Farlow (also principally a 350 man); Les Paul (no prizes for guessing his six-string choice); Herb Ellis; Jimmy Raney; and Jim Hall (the last three all favoring Gibson ES-175s).

New humbucking pickups were developed by Seth Lover in the Gibson workshops. The idea was to cut down the hum and electrical interference that plagued standard single-coil pickups, Gibson's ubiquitous P-90 unit included. Lover contemplated the humbucking "choke coil" found in some Gibson amplifiers, installed to eliminate the hum dispensed by their power transformers.

From those beginnings, Lover extrapolated a pickup design that employed two coils wired together electrically "out of phase" and with opposite magnetic polarities. The result was less prone to

---

F A C T   F I L E

The **humbucking pickup** is another significant component first introduced by Gibson, and was developed in the mid 1950s by engineer Seth Lover. The design, as approximated in countless pickup models today, uses two coils side by side that are virtually identical, but are wound in the opposite direction and have opposite magnetic polarities. When the signals from the two coils are combined, the sound of the guitar is retained, while a lot of unwanted noise is rejected. The width of the "magnetic window" of a humbucking pickup usually also produces a fatter, warmer sound than that of the standard single-coil pickup.

Gibson Tune-o-matic bridge and tailpiece, showing mounting lugs

picking up extraneous noise, in the process giving a fatter, thicker tone than single-coil types. Ray Butts came up with a similar principle around the same time while working for Gretsch.

During 1957 Gibson started to fit its electric guitars with the new humbuckers. The Les Paul Custom was promoted to a three-pickup guitar in its new humbucker-equipped guise. Today many guitarists and collectors make a point of seeking out the earliest type of Gibson humbucking pickup, which is now known as a "PAF" because of the small "patent applied for" label that is attached to the underside. The PAF labels appear on pickups on Gibson guitars dated up to 1962 (even though the patent had been granted in 1959). Some who prefer the sound of PAF-label humbuckers say that later humbuckers sound different because of small changes made to coil-winding, magnet grades and wire-sheathing.

Gibson purchased the old Epiphone brand of New York in 1957, relocating the operation to its base at Kalamazoo, Michigan. The following year Gibson released the first of its new Epiphones, effectively creating for itself a second-tier line. Some of these "new" guitars continued existing Epiphone models, but others were new Epiphone equivalents of Gibson models – for example the Casino, very similar to a Gibson ES330 (but with an Epiphone logo, of course).

In fact, 1958 proved to be one of the most significant years in Gibson's entire history. During that heady 12 months the company issued the radical new Explorer

and Flying V solidbodies, changed the finish of its Les Paul model to a gorgeous sunburst, introduced the brand new semi-solid ES-335 and ES-355 guitars, changed the body outlines of the Les Paul Junior and Les Paul Special to a useful double-cutaway shape, and brought out its first double-neck electric guitars. All these various designs would to a greater or lesser extent become classics over the coming years, and today some of them qualify as the most revered electric guitars ever made.

The Gibson Modernistic series of guitars was first seen in public during 1958. Fender's flamboyant designs such as the Stratocaster and the new-that-year Jazzmaster had been leaving Gibson's rather staid electric models behind as rock'n'roll burst forth. Guitar makers became increasingly aware that, beyond the usual considerations of quality and playability, there was an immense and largely untapped value in sheer visual appeal.

So the designers at Gibson temporarily set aside their customary preoccupation with curvaceously elegant forms to come up with the boldly adventurous Flying V and Explorer. Here was a pair of stark, linear creations. The body of the Flying V had an angular, pointed, arrow-head shape, while that of the Explorer was an uncompromising study in offset rectangles.

Most Explorers have a long, drooping headstock with the tuners in a line on one side – a design that would later inspire the superstrat's "pointy" headstock of the 1980s. But a small number of early Explorers (sometimes referred to as Futura models) had an unusual V-shaped head.

Both Flying V and Explorer were made from Korina, which was a timber tradename for an African relative of mahogany, sometimes known as limba. Gibson used a different control layout on the V and Explorer than the one they generally employed on two-humbucker electrics: on the Modernistics, the player was offered a volume knob per pickup but just one overall tone control.

"An asset to the combo musician with a flair for showmanship," insisted Gibson's 1950s publicity for the new Modernistic pair. The company urged its dealers: "Try one of these 'new look' instruments – either is a sure-fire hit with guitarists of today!" But customers ignored the designs as too futuristic, too un-Gibson and too un-guitar. One story has a number of the new oddball Gibsons reduced to hanging as signs outside guitar shops: if you can't sell them, flaunt them.

The small numbers produced would turn the Modernistics into future collectables of the rarest kind. In fact, only 98 of the original Flying V were made, with a further 20 or so assembled in the early 1960s from existing parts. Gibson's factory records for the original Explorer are not so clear, but the best estimates among collectors and other experts put production at just 22 instruments, with a further 16 assembled later. A good number of reissues and redesigns of both the Flying V and Explorer has followed, especially during their bouts of popularity with metal guitarists and others in subsequent decades.

Among players drawn to the Flying V in its various guises were Albert King in the 1950s, Jimi Hendrix in the 1960s, Marc Bolan and Andy Powell in the 1970s, Mick Mars and Michael Schenker in the 1980s, and Jim Martin and Tim Wheeler in more recent times.

Perhaps more importantly (or disgracefully, depending on your viewpoint) this late-flowering popularity of Gibson's Modernistic duo of Flying V and Explorer has been the trigger for any number of outlandishly shaped solidbody guitars, especially during the late 1970s and 1980s.

A third guitar in the original 1958 Modernistic series, the Moderne, was planned but never actually reached general production or distribution, even though a patent for the design was filed in summer 1957 along with similar documents claiming the Flying V and Explorer designs. No prototype or other incarnation of the original Moderne has ever turned up, despite much searching by desperate collectors. Some keen Gibson fans have even described this virtually fictional guitar as the company's "holy grail." If a Moderne should ever surface, it would surely be the ultimate collectable Gibson instrument. It might even prove to be the first million-dollar guitar.

Also in 1958, Gibson made a radical design-change to three of the Les Paul models, as well as a cosmetic alteration to another that would later take on enormous importance. The single-pickup Les Paul Junior and TV models were revamped with a completely new double-cutaway body shape, apparently as a reaction to players' requests for more access to the top frets than the previous single-cutaway design allowed. The new cutaways did the trick. The Junior's fresh look was enhanced with a new cherry red finish. The TV adopted the new double-cutaway design as well, along with a rather more yellow-tinged finish.

When the double-cutaway design was applied to the two-pickup Les Paul Special during the following year, the construction was not an immediate success. Gibson had overlooked the fact that the cavity for the neck pickup in the Special's new body severely weakened the neck-to-body joint. In fact, the neck could potentially snap off at this point. The error was soon corrected when Gibson's designers moved the neck pickup further down the body, resulting in a

stronger joint. The new double-cutaway Special was offered in cherry or the new TV yellow (although the yellow Special was never actually called a TV model).

Sales of Gibson's Les Paul gold-top had gradually declined during the late 1950s, and so in a bid to improve sales in 1958 Gibson changed the look by applying its more traditional cherry sunburst finish. This sunburst Les Paul is generally known as the Les Paul Standard, although Gibson did not refer to it as such in their literature until 1960, and the guitar itself never bore the name.

Gibson must have deduced that the unusual gold finish of the original Les Paul model was considered too unconventional. To some extent they were proved right. Sales of the gold-top had declined from a high of 920 in 1956 to just 434 in 1958, the year of the new Standard. After the sunburst model appeared, sales then climbed to 643 in 1959. But when they dipped again in 1960, Gibson decided that this change of finish had not been enough, and that the only way to attract new customers was to completely redesign the Les Paul.

So the sunburst Standard was dropped, having existed for a little short of three years. Here again was one of Gibson's sleeping giants: almost ignored at the time, this instrument would become an ultra-collectable object in later years. Players and collectors came to realize that the guitar's inherent musicality, as well as its short production run (some 1,700 examples were made between 1958 and 1960), added up to a modern classic. This re-evaluation was prompted originally in the middle and late 1960s when a number of guitarists discovered that the Gibson Les Paul had enormous potential for high-volume blues-based rock. It turned out that the Les Paul's inherent tonality coupled with its humbucking pickups – played through a loud tube amp – made a wonderful noise.

Of course, this newly discovered sonic potential of the Les Paul was something that neither Gibson nor Les Paul could possibly have planned. Leading early members of the Loud Les Appreciation Society were Mike Bloomfield in America and Eric Clapton in England. Demand for the old instruments rocketed. (As we shall see, Gibson would reintroduce original-design Les Pauls in 1968.)

The original sunburst Gibson Les Paul Standard – the "burst" in guitar-speak – has since achieved almost mythological status. The revised model appeared on Gibson's November 1959 pricelist, where it was shown to have a retail cost of $280. That's equivalent to about $3,500 at today's prices, but even this is far short of the five-figure sums that genuine originals now fetch on the active collector's market. Oddly, however, the value of these instruments is not only determined by their sound or playability or

rarity – but often by their individual look.

Gold-top Les Pauls mostly had maple tops made from two or more pieces of wood, safely hidden under the gold paint. Now that this maple top was on show through the transparent sunburst finish of the Standard, Gibson's woodworkers were more careful in selecting wood of good appearance, and would usually bookmatch the timber. This is where a piece of wood is sliced into two, then matched together like an open book, the pieces opened out down a central join to give symmetrically similar patterns.

The most celebrated "bursts" are those that display through the top's finish the most outrageous wood pattern. This is often called "flame," but more correctly "figure." Figure is caused by a kind of genetic anomaly in the growing tree that makes ripples in the cells of the living wood. The visual effect of figure is also determined by the situation of the original tree, and the way in which the timber is cut from it. Quarter-sawing – cutting so that the grain is generally square to the face of the resulting pieces – usually produces the most attractive results. The illusion can exist of roughly parallel rows of three-dimensional "fingers" or "hills and valleys" going across the face of the timber. In extreme cases this can look spectacular.

Another factor that can make sunburst Standard models look quite different from one another is color-fading. The colored paints used to create the sunburst effect, especially the red element, can fade in varying ways over time, depending primarily on how the guitar has been exposed to daylight during its lifetime. Some apparently sharp-eyed collectors claim to be able to tell exactly how long a particular guitar spent in the shop window. In some cases the original shaded sunburst will have almost totally disappeared, leaving a uniform and rather pleasant honey color on such guitars, now affectionately known as "unburst" examples.

A further innovation of 1958, and one that proved to be more successful at the time, was Gibson's new ES-335 guitar. This was a development of the company's thin-body "thinline" design that had begun with the Byrdland and the ES-350T three years earlier. When it came to the new 335, however, Gibson deployed a radical double-cutaway design, as well as the use of a novel solid block within the otherwise hollow body to create a new "semi-solid" structure.

Gibson's idea was effectively to combine a hollowbody guitar with a solidbody, not only in terms of construction but also in sonic effect. A problem for hollowbody electric guitar designers had been the screeching "feedback" that often occurred when the guitar was played with its amplifier set at high volume. The 335's solid maple block inside what Gibson described

1961 Gibson Les Paul/SG

BODY: solid mahogany double-cutaway body with slightly non-concentric pointed horns, beveled edges, no binding; nitrocellulose finish.

NECK: glued-in, one-piece mahogany neck with bound rosewood fingerboard with 12" fingerboard radius, 22 medium nickel-silver frets, and 1 ¹¹⁄₁₆" nut width; 24 ⅝" scale length. Slim, flattish profiles in the early '60s, a little chunkier later in the decade.

HEADSTOCK: symmetrical headstock at 17 degree back angle, with three-a-side tulip-button Kluson tuners; bone nut.

BRIDGE: adjustable tune-o-matic bridge and Maestro vibrola tailpiece.

ELECTRONICS: dual humbucking pickups constructed of single alnico bar magnet beneath, six fixed steel slug pole pieces in one coil and six threaded adjustable pole pieces in the other; DC resistance of 7.5k to 8k; nickel-plated steel cover. Three-way toggle switch to select either pickup alone or both together; four 500k potentiometers for individual Volume and Tone for each pickup.

SOUND: thick, rich and vocal from the neck pickup, punchy and cutting from the bridge, with a slightly airy, woody resonance in all positions; good sustain. Good hum rejection.

guitar facts

as its "wonder-thin" body tamed the feedback and combined pure solidbody sustain with the woody warmth of a hollowbody. This quality would endear the 335-style Gibson to a wide range of players, especially bluesmen such as B.B. King, but also to a number of other guitarists from jazz stylist Larry Carlton to Britpop pioneer Bernard Butler.

The "dot neck" 335 – one with dot-shape fingerboard markers and made between 1958 and 1962 – has become a prime collectable guitar. In 1962 Gibson replaced the dots with block-shape markers. Not that this makes the guitar sound less good, but collectors feel the dot-neck feature marks a "better" period of quality and manufacturing standards, and therefore denotes a more desirable instrument. Players tend to be less selective and will generally tend to choose a 335 from any period, that plays well and feels good, and that is financially within reach.

The earliest 335 models were officially named ES-335T, the "T" at the end standing for "thinline" to emphasize and underline one of its most important features. Soon, however, a "D" was added by Gibson,

meaning double pickups, as well as an extra "N" for natural-finish examples, resulting in the rather overwhelming model description of ES-335TDN. The sunburst 335 was originally made in greater numbers than the natural version, which was dropped in 1960. From that year the 335 was also available in a cherry red finish, known as the ES-335TDC.

A more high-end version of the 335 model also appeared in 1958, a cherry-finish guitar that was named the ES-355. This guitar was distinguished by multiple binding on the neck, body and headstock, the latter also bearing Gibson's luxurious split-diamond inlay. The 355 generally gleamed with gold-plated hardware, as well as boasting an ebony fingerboard and a Bigsby vibrato as standard.

The idea of a stereo guitar had originally been investigated by Jimmie Webster at Gretsch in New York. He had filed a patent for a stereo pickup system in 1956, leading to Gretsch's as-ever wonderfully titled Project-O-Sonic guitars of 1958. Gibson's first take on the stereo idea, the ES-345, appeared in the following year, along with optional stereo wiring for the ES-355. "Stereophonic" and its more common diminutive "stereo" had become buzzwords in the late 1950s, as first stereo pre-recorded tapes and then stereo records hit the market.

Gretsch's pioneering system had worked by effectively splitting each pickup on a two-pickup guitar into two, so that one pickup could feed the output from the instrument's lower three strings to one amplifier, while the other pickup sent the higher three strings out to another amp.

Gibson would certainly have known

1959
Gibson Les Paul
Special

1956
Gibson Les Paul
Junior

1955 Gibson Les Paul Junior & '59 Les Paul Special

BODY: solid mahogany slab body with flat top and single cutaway; double-cutaway on later models (as on Special); no binding.

NECK: one-piece mahogany neck with unbound rosewood fingerboard, joining upper bout at the 16th fret; 22 nickel-silver frets, 1 11/16" nut width and 12" fingerboard radius; 24 5/8" scale length. (Bound fingerboard and 22nd-fret neck joint on '59 Special.)

HEADSTOCK: back-angled symmetrical headstock, with three-a-side Kluson tuners; headstock-end truss-rod adjustment.

Bridge: wrapover bridge/tailpiece.

ELECTRONICS: one single-coil P-90 pickup (two on Special) with dual alnico bar magnets mounted beneath, and six threaded steel pole pieces; single Volume and Tone control on Jr; three-way toggle switch and individual Volume and Tone controls on Special.

SOUND: warm, round and full, with plenty of power and a pronounced midrange honk for rock leads.

about and examined the Gretsch system, and when it came to their own stereo guitars adopted a rather more straightforward system in 1959. Gibson's two-pickup circuitry simply directed the output of each complete pickup to a separate amplifier. In contemporary advertising, Gibson assured the guitarist of the day that it would soon be customary to plug in to a pair of amps and produce "a symphony of warm, full stereophonic sound."

Another new Gibson feature in the search for fresh electric tonalities was the Varitone control, offered on the ES-345 and some ES-355s. This switch selected one of six preset tone options, in combination with the pickup selector expanding to 18 possible tonal shades.

However, Gibson's Varitone and stereo capabilities were never especially popular among guitarists. Often, players would simply disconnect the confusing Varitone and, despite the stereo option, would just get on with playing what was undoubtedly a very good guitar in conventional "mono" mode.

Gibson's doubtless exhausted development team added one more innovation to the line during 1958: the company's first double-neck guitars. Always something of a compromise between convenience and comfort, the double-neck electric guitar was a relatively new idea, the first one having been custom-made by Paul Bigsby in California in 1952. The concept would have been obvious to Bigsby because he also made pedal-steel guitars, on which multiple necks are common.

A double-neck instrument is designed so that it can offer the player two different guitars in one instrument. An instant changeover from one neck to another saves the guitarist having to swap between separate instruments. Clearly, this is especially useful for the stage musician. The most obvious drawback to the double-neck electric is the increased weight of the resulting instrument, as well as the general awkwardness involved in reaching beyond a neck in an ideal playing position to the other that is invariably too high or too low for comfort.

Gibson launched two double-necks in 1958. The EDS-1275 Double 12 had what became the most common combination for electric double-necks, mixing a six-string and a 12-string neck. It looked something like an extended ES-175 with its twin pointed cutaways. The more unusual EMS-1235 Double Mandolin had one standard six-string neck, plus a short-scale neck with six strings tuned an octave higher than a guitar, supposedly to mimic the sound of a mandolin.

These first Gibson double-necks were produced only to special order, their hollow bodies made with carved spruce tops and maple backs and sides. The instruments are rare today. Around 1962 Gibson changed the double-necks to a solidbody style, which made them look more like extended SG models. They remained custom-order-only instruments. The most famous player to opt

for a Gibson double-neck was Jimmy Page who regularly used one on stage.

Gibson's first low-end solidbody – aside from earlier Les Paul Juniors – was the Melody Maker, launched in 1959. At first it had a simple "slab" single-cutaway body, though this was modified to a double-cutaway body two years later. An option was a short scale-length, another feature aimed at the smaller fingers of beginners. The last change to the Melody Maker came in 1965 when it adopted the style of Gibson's SG solidbody. This type of body design would last until the Melody Maker was dropped from the Gibson line during the early 1970s.

Considering all the Les Paul models as a whole, sales declined in 1960 after a peak in 1959. As we've seen, by 1961 Gibson had decided on a complete re-design of the line in an effort to try to reactivate this faltering model. The company had started a $400,000 expansion of the factory in Kalamazoo during 1960 which more than doubled the size of the plant by the time it was completed in 1961. It was the third addition to the original 1917 factory, other buildings having been added in 1945 and 1950. But this new single-story brick-and-steel building was more than twice the size of the previous additions combined, resulting in a plant of more than 120,000 square feet that extended for two city blocks at Parsons Street in Kalamazoo. Clearly, Gibson was expecting its business to

expand rapidly in the coming years.

One of the first series of new models to benefit from the company's newly expanded production facilities was the completely revised line of Les Paul models. Gibson redesigned the Junior, Standard and Custom models, adopting a new, distinctly modern, sculpted double-cutaway design. The "Les Paul" name was still used at first, but during 1963 Gibson began to call these new models the SG Junior, the SG Standard and the SG Custom. (Confusingly, the SG name had been used earlier on old-style Les Pauls: the old-design TV and Special had been renamed as the SG TV and the SG Special in 1959.) The transition models – those produced between 1961 and 1963 – had the

new SG design but the old Les Paul names, and these are now known to collectors and players as SG/Les Paul models.

Les Paul's name was dropped for a number of reasons. Partly it was because the connection with the guitarist was less of a commercial bonus for Gibson than it had been. His popularity as a recording artist had declined: he'd had no more hits after 1955. Crucially, Les Paul and Mary Ford had separated in May 1963 and were officially divorced by the end of 1964, and Paul did not want to sign any fresh contract with Gibson that would bring in new money while the divorce proceedings were underway. So his contract with Gibson was terminated in 1962, and the following year Les Paul models became SG models ("Solid Guitar").

From 1964 until 1967 inclusive there were no guitars in the Gibson line that bore the name of Les Paul, either on the actual guitars themselves or in the company's various catalogs, pricelists, and other advertising material.

Production did increase at the Gibson factory of the new SG-style designs, with the output of Gibson Les Pauls from the Kalamazoo plant settling at just under 6,000 units every year for 1961, 1962 and 1963. SG-style solidbodies have attracted a number of players over the years, including John Cipollina, Eric Clapton, Tony Iommi, Robbie Krieger, Tony McPhee, Pete Townshend, Angus Young and Frank Zappa.

Gibson produced a number of new electric archtop signature models in the 1960s named for jazz guitarists such as Barney Kessel and Tal Farlow, both best known for their fine playing which had come to the fore in the previous decade. The body of the Gibson Barney Kessel (1961) featured an unusual double "sharp" cutaway. More successful as an instrument was the Tal Farlow model (1962), visually distinguished by an ornate swirl of extra binding at the cutaway. Back in the solidbody department, Gibson was determined to take on its chief rival, Fender, and came up with the Firebird guitars (and matching Thunderbird bass). Launched in 1963, the Firebirds clearly recognized the solidbody style of the West Coast firm while retaining the style and workmanship for which Gibson was known. Gibson called upon car designer Ray Dietrich to out-Fender Fender.

Dietrich devised the new Firebird line with sleek, asymmetrical bodies that looked a little as if Gibson's old Explorer design had been modernized with some additional curves. The new elongated body shape featured a "horn-less" upper portion that had the effect of making the lower cutaway appear to protrude further. This unbalanced "lop-sided" effect has since gained the original Firebirds the nickname "reverse body" among collectors and players.

There were four models in the 1963 Firebird line. The Firebird I had a single pickup and was the only model without a vibrato unit. The Firebird III had two pickups and a "stud"-style bridge, while the Firebird V had two pickups and a Tune-o-matic bridge. The glorious top-of-the-line Firebird VII had three pickups.

They were the first Gibson electrics to employ through-neck construction. They were also unusual in that they featured a "flipped Fender" headstock which was fitted with banjo-style tuners. This meant that players had to adjust tuning in an unfamiliar way, reaching around to the back of the headstock. But at least the design of the headstock showed a clean outline to the audience. The Firebirds were all fitted with special smaller-than-normal humbucking pickups, which were without adjustable polepieces. Standard finish for the Firebirds was sunburst. However, Gibson did go further than simply adopting a Fender vibe for the new line.

The company also borrowed Fender's custom color idea, applying to the new line of guitars a range of paints more often employed to brighten up the look of the latest automobiles. One of Gibson's ten new Firebird colors was in fact identical to a Fender color. However, Gibson used the Oldsmobile name for it – Golden Mist – while Fender had opted for the Pontiac term, Shoreline Gold.

Despite the striking appearance of the Firebirds, and their prominent use in the 1960s and later by players such as Brian Jones and Johnny Winter, the ploy didn't work. Gibson's sales of electric guitars during the 1960s had to rely on classic 1950s designs such as the great semi-solid ES-335. Fender understandably complained about similarities to its patented "offset waist" design feature, pointing primarily to the Jazzmaster and Jaguar in its line, and so Gibson tried to fix things by reworking the Firebirds in 1965.

Gibson came up with a new Firebird shape that flipped the old one into a slightly more conventional if still quite Fender-like outline, known now as the "non-reverse" body. Gibson also dropped the through-neck construction in favor of its customary set-neck. The new Firebird I had two single-coil pickups, the Firebird III three single-coil pickups, the Firebird V two mini-humbuckers, and the Firebird VII three mini-humbuckers. Still unsuccessful, the Firebirds were grounded by 1969. Since then, the non-reverse Firebirds have been used even less by well-known players than the marginally more favored reverse versions. However, Oasis's new rhythm guitarist Gem Archer was to be seen on the band's 2000 dates occasionally strapping on a non-reverse Firebird, which must have pleased a

number of vintage guitar dealers.

Back in the 1960s, Gibson enjoyed good sales in Britain amid the mushrooming of pop music talent there. Distribution of Gibson in Britain had been patchy until Selmer, a wholesale company that was based in London, started officially to import Gibson guitars to the UK during 1960. In fact, British musicians had virtually been starved of any American-made guitars between 1951 and 1959, thanks to a government ban on importation during that period.

Selmer was in the right place when the ban was lifted. The company's famed retail store in London's Charing Cross Road was at the heart of an area alive with music publishers, small studios and instrument retailers, a mecca for both the budding and successful musician. Jeff Beck bought his first Les Paul Standard from the Selmer store; Steve Howe purchased his favorite ES-175D there; and Robert Fripp acquired his prized Les Paul Custom at the store in 1968.

As noted earlier, Gibson had since the 1930s used the Kalamazoo brand – named for the location of its factory in Michigan – for cheaper products unworthy of the full Gibson marque. In 1965 the Kalamazoo brand was revived as Gibson decided to feed a strong demand for bargain electric guitars. At first the entry-level Kalamazoo electrics had Fender-style offset cutaways, although later in the 1960s a shape more like Gibson's own SG was adopted. A handful of different models appeared in this KG series, but they were all dropped by the turn of the decade.

There was a newly revised version of the Flying V launched by Gibson during the second half of the 1960s. The reworked model had more conventional hardware than the original late-1950s V, without the through-body stringing. Gibson also redesigned the control layout for these models first issued during 1967, with the three knobs now forming a triangular group rather than the three-in-a-line style of the original. These new-style Vs would stay in the Gibson catalog until the late 1970s.

Guitar sales in general in the United States – including acoustic as well as electric instruments – had climbed throughout the early 1960s, hitting a peak of some 1,500,000 units in 1965, after which sales declined and fell to just over a million in 1967. CMI's sales of Gibson guitars and amplifiers hit a fiscal peak of $19million in 1966, but then began to fall in line with the general industry trend, and were down to $15million-worth by 1968. As well as the general decline in demand for guitars, Gibson's production had been hit by a number of strikes in the 1960s, including a 16-day stoppage in 1966. Gibson president Ted McCarty and his number two, John Huis, left that year after purchasing the Bigsby

FACT FILE

Neck pitch is the angle of a guitar's neck relative to the body face (top). Most Gibson guitars – and many other set-neck and archtop electric guitars – are made with a considerable backward pitch to the necks, whereas most bolt-neck guitars, as typified by Fender, are made with the necks nearly parallel to the top of the body.

musical accessories company of California, which they re-established in Kalamazoo.

In February 1968, after a number of short-stay occupants in the president's chair, Stan Rendell was appointed as the new president of the Gibson operation. Rendell immediately set about his task of improving the company's fortunes.

Meanwhile, as we've seen, the blues-rock boom had made players aware of the potential of old Les Paul guitars. Musicians began to hunt for the instruments, and prices for secondhand examples began gradually to climb. Gibson at last decided to do something about their deteriorating position in the electric guitar market, and specifically about the increasing demand for their old-style Les Paul guitars.

Les Paul's musical activities had been very low-key since the mid 1960s, but in 1967 he began a new association with Gibson that resulted in a reissue program for Les Paul models. By the time Stan Rendell became president of Gibson in early 1968 the decision to re-commence manufacturing Les Paul guitars had been made by the CMI management in Chicago, principally by Maurice Berlin and Marc Carlucci, and a new contract was negotiated with Paul. For some reason, Gibson decided to re-introduce the relatively rare two-humbucker Les Paul Custom, and the gold-top Les Paul with P-90 pickups and Tune-o-matic bridge. They were launched at a June 1968 trade show in Chicago. Gibson's ads publicizing the revived guitars admitted that the company had virtually been forced to re-introduce the guitars: "The demand for them just won't quit. And the pressure to make more has never let up. Okay, you win. We are pleased to announce that more of the original Les Paul Gibsons are available." The new Les Pauls sold well, and Gibson clearly had a success in the making. The only mystery so far as many guitarists were concerned was why they'd waited so long.

An important change to Gibson's ownership occurred in 1969. The new owner, Norlin Industries, was formed that year with the merger of Gibson's parent company, CMI, with ECL, an Ecuadorian brewery. The Norlin name was arrived at by combining the

1964 Gibson ES-335

BODY: semi-acoustic construction with back, sides, and top of laminated maple, with a pressed arch on the top and solid maple center block; top and back binding; double cutaway with 20th fret neck/body joint. Finished in nitrocellulose lacquer.

NECK: glued-in, one-piece mahogany neck with bound rosewood fingerboard with 12" fingerboard radius, 22 medium nickel-silver frets, and 1 $1\frac{1}{16}$" nut width; 24 $\frac{5}{8}$" scale length.

HEADSTOCK: symmetrical headstock at 17 degree back angle (14 degrees from 1966), with six-a-side Kluson tuners (Grover replacements on this example); bone nut.

BRIDGE: adjustable tune-o-matic bridge with six double-notched vinyl saddles and stop tailpiece.

ELECTRONICS: dual humbucking pickups constructed of single alnico bar magnet beneath, six fixed steel slug pole pieces in one coil and six threaded adjustable pole pieces in the other; DC resistance of 7.5k; nickel-plated steel cover. Three-way toggle switch to select either pickup alone or both together; four 500k potentiometers for individual Volume and Tone for each pickup.

SOUND: thick, rich and vocal from the neck pickup, punchy and cutting from the bridge, with a slightly airy, woody resonance in all positions, perhaps a little thick for some full chords; good sustain. Good hum rejection.

guitar facts

1959
Gibson Flying V

1959 Gibson Flying V

BODY: slab-style solid korina body (usually two-piece).

NECK: chunky korina neck with unbound rosewood fingerboard, joins body at the 22nd fret; otherwise similar in materials and proportions to the LP/SG standards.

HEADSTOCK: arrow-shaped three-a-side headstock with Kluson tuners.

ELECTRONICS: dual PAF humbucking pickups; three-way toggle switch for each pickup individually or together; three 500k potentiometers for individual volume and master tone.

SOUND: round, rich and resonant, with good power and excellent sustain.

the 1970s (and, to some extent, to those made into the 1980s). Generally, such alterations were made for one of three reasons. The first and apparently most pressing requirement was to save money. Second, Gibson wished to limit the number of guitars returned for work under warranty. Lastly, there was a distinct desire to speed up production of Gibson guitars at the Kalamazoo factory.

The guitar design department at Gibson gave a change of style and name to the recently re-introduced Les Paul gold-top model in 1969, when the Les Paul Deluxe took its place. The Deluxe was the first

"new" Les Paul model for 14 years, and was prompted by calls for a gold-top with humbucking pickups rather than the single-coil P-90s of the existing reissue model.

Gibson ended up using small Epiphone humbuckers for the Les Paul Deluxe model that were surplus to requirements. At first the Deluxe was only available with a gold top, but gradually sunbursts and other colors were introduced, and it lasted in production until the mid 1980s.

Back in the 1950s and 1960s one of guitarist Les Paul's more out-of-step tastes had been for low-impedance pickups. Today, low-impedance elements are more often used as part of a pickup design, thanks to improvements in associated components, but back then Paul was largely on his own. The vast majority of electric guitars and guitar-related equipment was (and still is) high-impedance.

The chief advantage of low-impedance is a wide and all-encompassing tonal characteristic. This might appear at first to be an advantage, but in fact the tonal range offered isn't necessarily to everyone's taste. Another disadvantage is that low-impedance pickups must have their power boosted at

first syllable of ECL chairman Norton Stevens' name with the last syllable of that of CMI founder Maurice Berlin.

Norlin was in three businesses: musical instruments, brewing, and "technology." The takeover was formalized in 1974 and Maurice Berlin, a man widely respected in the musical instrument industry, was moved sideways in the new structure, away from the general running of the company.

Many people who worked at Gibson during this period feel that there was a move away from managers who understood guitars to managers who understood manufacturing. Some of the instruments made during the period soon after Gibson were taken over have a bad reputation today. The new owners are generally felt now to have been insensitive to the needs of musicians. Clearly this was a sign of the times, as economic analysts were busily advising many of the big corporations that they should diversify into a range of different areas, pour in some money... and sit back to wait for the profits.

There was a shift in emphasis at Gibson toward the rationalization of production, and this meant that changes were made to some of the company's instruments built during

1964 Gibson EDS-1275 Double 12

BODY: solid mahogany dual-cutaway body with concentric pointed horns, beveled edges, no binding; nitrocellulose finish.

NECK: two one-piece mahogany necks with bound rosewood fingerboards; 22 nickel-silver frets, 1 11/16" nut width, 12" fingerboard radius, and 24 5/8" scale length on each.

HEADSTOCK: back-angled symmetrical headstocks; top neck has elongated headstock with six-a-side Grover tuners; bottom neck has standard Gibson SG-style headstock.

BRIDGE: two tune-o-matic bridges, the top unit with double-notched saddles; simple steel string-retainer tailpieces.

ELECTRONICS: four humbucking pickups with single alnico bar magnets mounted beneath, one coil with six steel slug pole pieces and one with six adjustable threaded steel pole pieces; DC resistance approximately 7.5k; two-way toggle switch mounted between tailpieces to select upper or lower neck; three-way toggle switch for either pickup independently (of selected neck) or both together; individual Volume and Tone controls.

SOUND: warm, full and resonant, with some of the SG's characteristic 'sizzle,' but a little more woody ring to it. Excellent sustain and power. This particular instrument also belongs to Steve Howe of Yes.

1964
Gibson EDS-1275

some point before the signal reaches the amplifier (unless the player is plugging the guitar straight into a recording studio mixer, as Les Paul did).

When Paul had gone to Gibson in 1967 to discuss the revival of Les Paul guitars, he'd talked with great passion about his beloved low-impedance pickups, and how Gibson should use them on some of their instruments. So in 1969 along came the first wave of Gibson Les Paul guitars with low-impedance pickups: the Les Paul Professional and the Les Paul Personal. The Personal was, as the name implied, in keeping with one of Paul's own modified Les Paul guitars, even copying his odd feature of a microphone socket on the top edge of the body. The Personal and Professional had a complex array of controls, seemingly aimed at recording engineers rather than guitarists. These included an 11-position Decade control, "to tune high frequencies," a three-position tone selector to create various in- and out-of-circuit mixes, and a pickup phase switch. The Personal also provided a volume control for that handy on-board microphone input. Both guitars required connection with the special cord supplied, which had an integral transformer to boost the output from the low-impedance stacked-coil humbucking pickups to a level suitable for use with normal high-impedance amplifiers.

Predictably, the guitars were not a great success, and did not last long in the Gibson line. Their rather somber brown color, achieved with a natural mahogany finish, could not have helped in an era when most of the competition was busily turning out simple guitars finished in bright colors.

The company did have another go at low-impedance instruments during 1971. First, Gibson decided to scale down the body size of the Professional/Personal style, virtually to that of a normal Les Paul, and to give it a contoured back. Second, the company located the still-necessary transformer into the guitar itself, and provided a switch on the guitar to give either low-impedance output or normal high-impedance output. Third, Gibson re-titled the guitar to the more appropriate Les Paul Recording. It would remain in the line until 1980. Another low-impedance-equipped model came along in 1972, the L-5S. The name of this single-cutaway solidbody alluded to Gibson's great old electric hollowbody model, the L-5CES – but beyond that, any obvious kind of connection was unclear.

There seemed to be even less chance of guitarists being attracted to low-impedance pickups on an instrument that didn't even have the cachet of the Les Paul name. So it was that a few years into its life the new L-5S was changed from low-impedance pickups to regular humbuckers – but that still made no difference to its popularity. Even the use

FACT FILE

Most electric guitars with traditional magnetic pickups and no active (powered) onboard electronics provide a **high-impedance** output. This is a good match for the input of a standard tube guitar amplifier, but a high-impedance signal has more difficulty traveling over long cable lengths without some frequency loss, in the highs in particular. Makers have occasionally offered guitars with low-impedance pickups to counter the pitfalls of signals, and onboard preamps powered with 9-volt batteries – which can convert a standard guitar's output to low-impedance – are also available; but the majority of players have continued to prefer the traditional sound and performance of high-impedance pickups.

of the new L-5S by the fine jazzman Pat Martino had apparently little impact on other musicians. Gibson's final fling with low-impedance pickups was reserved for the company's thinline style, and was launched during 1973 as the two-pickup gold-colored Les Paul Signature.

Some of the new Signature model's controls were similar to those found on previous low-impedance models, but an extra feature on the Signature was the inclusion of two jack sockets. One was on the side of the body, for normal high-impedance output; the other on the face of the body was for connection to low-impedance equipment such as recording mixers. (A similar facility was offered on the final version of the Recording model.) The Signature models never really fired players' imaginations, and by the end of the 1970s they were out of production. By now Gibson employed around 600 people at its Kalamazoo factory, and was producing something like 300 guitars every day. Demand for guitars had increased during the early 1970s, and so management decided to build a second Gibson factory at Nashville, Tennessee, some 500 miles south of Kalamazoo. Recent strikes at Gibson had cost Norlin dear, and the new plant of 100,000 square feet was also constructed with a view to decreasing costs through advantageous labor deals.

Work began in 1974 on the new facility, five miles to the east of Nashville, and the factory eventually opened in June 1975. Gibson's original intention was to keep both Kalamazoo and Nashville running. Nashville was designed to produce very large quantities of a handful of models, while Kalamazoo was more flexible and had the potential to specialize in small runs.

Nashville was thus the obvious choice to produce the models in Gibson's solidbody line required in the greatest volume at the time – the Les Paul Custom and Deluxe models – along with various other solidbody models.

As if to highlight the contrast between the capabilities of the two plants, Gibson introduced two new Les Paul models in 1976. First was the Les Paul Pro Deluxe, effectively a Deluxe with P-90 pickups and an ebony fingerboard. It was produced in large quantities at Nashville.

The other new model was The Les Paul, a spectacular limited-edition model that was notable for Gibson's employment of various fine woods for virtually the entire instrument. Many parts that on a normal electric guitar would be made from plastic were hand-carved from rosewood. These included the pickguard, backplates, control knobs and truss-rod cover.

Raw bodies and necks of attractive maple and an ornate ebony and rosewood fingerboard for the The Les Paul were produced at Gibson's Kalamazoo factory. Further work on the multiple colored binding, abalone inlays and handmade wooden parts was continued at the workshop of freelance luthier Dick Schneider, who was based about a mile from the factory in Kalamazoo.

Very few of The Les Pauls were made, with probably well under 100 produced from 1976 to 1979, primarily in the first year. During this time Schneider moved away from Kalamazoo, and later examples of The Les Paul were therefore produced entirely at the Gibson factory. As the limited stocks of Schneider's handmade wooden parts ran out, so normal plastic items were substituted, along with less ornate binding.

Each example of The Les Paul had a numbered oval plate on the back of the headstock. Number 25 was presented to Les Paul just prior to the 1977 Grammy Awards ceremony where Paul and Chet Atkins received a Grammy award for their *Chester & Lester* album. The $3,000 price tag on The Les Paul made it four times the cost of the next most expensive Les Paul model on the 1976 pricelist. During the previous year, Gibson had in fact introduced a number of other new models and a reissue. These included a revitalized Explorer, plus two new solidbodys: the all-maple single-cutaway L-6S, as endorsed by Carlos Santana, and the Les Paul-shape bolt-on-neck Marauder with humbucker and angled single-coil pickups. The S-1 was a sort of three-pickup Marauder that also sported that model's V-shape headstock, and it joined the line in 1976. None of these lasted long.

The 25/50 Les Paul was intended to celebrate Les Paul's 25th year with Gibson (presumably it had been planned for 1977)

and his 50th year in the music business. The silver and gold themes generally associated with these anniversaries were reflected in the guitar's chrome- and gold-plated hardware, while Chuck Burge in Gibson's R&D (research and development) department designed the special intricate inlay in pearl and abalone on the guitar's headstock.

The guitar bore a three-digit edition number on the back of the headstock as well as a standard serial number. Once again Les Paul himself was presented with a special example: this time he received guitar number one at a party given in his honor by Gibson, who launched the Les Paul 25/50 Anniversary model during 1978. Despite its relatively high price the Kalamazoo-made 25/50 sold well, bringing into sharp focus for Norlin the ready market for more costly Les Paul models

Gibson's new RD models first appeared in 1978, and incorporated a package of complex "active" electronics. This kind of circuit had been popularized by Alembic at the start of the 1970s and was designed to boost the signal and widen the tonal range of a guitar. The circuit was powered by an on-board battery. The body of the RD series was an even curvier version of the previous decade's Firebird "reverse body" design.

This kind of "hi-fi" guitar was prompted by the apparent competition from synthesizers, which had become big business during the late 1970s. Gibson's parent company Norlin figured that a hook-up with Moog, one of the synthesizer field's most famous names of the time, might re-capture some of the ground that guitars seemed to be losing to the new keyboards.

In fact one of the RD models – the Standard – was a regular electric, without the active circuit, which was reserved for the Custom and Artist models. Gibson's RD line did not, however, prove popular and was soon gone from the catalog. Many guitarists disliked what they considered the "unnatural" sounds of active circuitry, and this was a major factor in the downfall of the RD series. Gibson believed that the radical styling was more to blame for the lack of popularity, and moved to combine the RD technology with some of its traditional body designs.

In 1979 Gibson did this, expanding the RD concept into two of its more mainstream electric series, the ES thinlines and the Les Pauls. Gibson had to re-design the large RD circuit board to fit into these more confined body designs. Each of the new Artist models had three knobs, for volume, bass and treble, and three switches for brightness, expansion and compression. However, these models also failed to grab many guitarists, and the Artists did not last for very long: the Les Paul Artist hobbled on to 1981, while the ES Artist managed to last until 1985.

A happier project was the Les Paul Heritage Series, one of the first conscious attempts by Gibson to try to make Les Pauls in a way that many players thought was no longer possible. A reasonably healthy market had been building since the late 1960s in so-called "vintage" guitars (which used to be called merely "secondhand," or "used," or just plain "old guitars").

This trend was fueled by the general feeling that Gibson "didn't make them like they used to," combined with the prominent use of older instruments by many of the most popular guitarists of the day. While to some extent this was flattering in general to the Gibson name (and to others such as Fender and Gretsch whose guitars were also associated with the vintage trend), it did not help a manufacturer whose main priority was to continue to sell new guitars and especially its new models.

Some US dealers such as Strings & Things and Music Trader who specialized in older instruments had already begun to order selected new models with vintage-style appointments from Gibson's Kalamazoo plant, which since the onset of the Nashville factory was beginning to lean more heavily toward shorter, specialized runs of guitars. For the Heritage Series Les Pauls, Gibson's team used a 1954 pattern sample for the carving of the body top, changed the then-regular neck construction to three-piece mahogany, disposed of then-current production oddities such as the "volute" carving below the back of the headstock, and moved a little closer to older pickup specifications. Especially attractive maple was selected for the tops of these new Les Paul models, which were touted as limited editions and were not included on the company's general pricelist.

Launched in 1980, the two Heritage Series models were the Heritage Standard 80 and the Heritage Standard 80 Elite, the latter with an ebony fingerboard and an even more desirable "quilt" figured maple top.

Whether as a result of the influence of the Heritage models or a general awareness of market demands, Gibson began at this time to rectify some of the general production quirks instituted in the 1970s, removing from its standard models the volute, for example, and gradually reverting to one-piece mahogany necks.

An oddity issued in 1980 was the Les Paul-shape Sonex 180 which had what Gibson called a Multi-Phonic body. This was in fact a wooden core with a plastic outer skin, following a relatively shortlived 1980s trend for experimental non-wood guitars. The Sonex lasted less than four years in the Gibson line. The idea for a combination of wood and non-wood materials would find a firmer foundation with Parker in the 1990s. Also during 1980 Gibson issued one of its first signature guitars for a black player, the double-cutaway thinline B.B. King model, in Standard and Custom versions. Both had stereo wiring and were without f-holes, the Custom adding a Varitone six-way tone selector. The King models were based on the Gibson ES-355 that had been the great bluesman's favored instrument since 1959. The Standard was dropped in 1985, but the Custom soon became known as the Lucille – "Lucille" is King's nickname for his cherished 355 – and is still in Gibson's line at the time of writing.

The Victory MV models of 1981 were yet further attempts by Gibson to compete directly with Fender, the exaggerated Strat-like bodies clearly influenced by the California competitor. The Victorys were gone from the line by 1984.

During the early 1980s Gibson continued to attempt to update its image, as it had during the previous decade, but in the process was coming up with some wildly inappropriate new designs – none more so than the ugly Corvus line of 1982. The Corvus was available (though largely unpurchased) with one, two or three pickups, and had a peculiar body shaped like a misguided can-opener. While it would be kind to say that other companies were also trying odd-shaped models at this time, the Corvus models must be some of the most pointless guitars ever created. These too were gone from the Gibson pricelist by 1984.

Despite such aberrations, Gibson was also becoming more and more aware of the value of its old, hallowed "traditional" designs. We've already seen how this had prompted the Heritage Les Paul series in 1980. During the next few years – and with even less publicity – Gibson also put into production a small number of Heritage-series versions of the old Flying V and Explorer, modeled as close as possible on the originals, including the use of korina wood.

More unusually, Gibson also produced a recreation of the third "missing guitar" of the original late-1950s Modernistic series. The peculiar Moderne had never been put on sale back then, but in 1982 it finally appeared as part of the limited-edition korina-body Heritage series, looking as if the lower half of a Flying V body had been lopped off and curved away underneath. The club-shape headstock of the Moderne was unusual too, and the overall impression was that Gibson's initial decision in the 1950s had been correct.

Gibson, aware of the continuing demand at the monied end of the market for "vintage" Les Pauls, realized that the Heritage Series of 1980 had only been a half-hearted approach to recreating the most celebrated old Les Pauls.

So in 1983 a proper reissue program was instituted by Gibson. These reissue guitars have been known over the years by a

1965 Gibson Firebird V

BODY: "reverse" style solid mahogany body with treble horn longer than bass horn; through-neck design with central body core cut from same lengths of timber as neck, slightly raised from side "wings" of guitar.

NECK: mahogany through-neck (see above) with bound rosewood with 12" fingerboard radius, 22 medium nickel-silver frets, and 1 ¹¹⁄₁₆" nut width; 24 ⅝" scale length.

HEADSTOCK: back-angled asymmetrical headstock with beveled edge, six-inline Kluson "banjo style" tuners on treble side.

BRIDGE: tune-o-matic bridge and vibrola tailpiece.

ELECTRONICS: two mini-humbucking pickups with DC resistance of 5.5k to 6k ohms; individual Volume and Tone controls for each pickup and three-way selector switch.

SOUND: bright, sharp, aggressive and even glassy – particularly in the bridge position – with considerable body and snarl.

number of different titles, including Reissue Outfits, Replicas and, at the time of writing, the Historic Collection. Gibson's reissue series stepped backward and forward at the same time, using old specs but made with modern methods. By 1985 the company's pricelist showed a gold-top Reissue and a sunburst Standard Reissue, effectively high-quality versions of the existing sunburst-finish and gold-top Les Paul models, the former with a selected "curly" maple top.

Gradually since then Gibson has tried gradually to improve the authenticity and accuracy of its reissues, driven by the persistent demands of fastidious customers who seek "perfect" duplication of those hallowed 1950s originals. In a way, that will never happen, of course. Trying to recapture the past is an expensive and largely impossible business. But that does not stop some guitar manufacturers making an attempt.

At present the basic reissue sunburst Standard is referred to as the 1959 Les Paul Flametop because of its general proximity to a 1959-style model with "flamed"-maple top. Little "corrections" have been made since the reissue model's introduction in 1983, including moves to a smaller-sized vintage-style headstock; the use of especially attractive figured maple for the top; the adoption of carving that matches the original body contours; re-tooling of the neck for similar reasons of authenticity; a slight reduction in the neck pitch; holly veneer for the headstock face; "correct" routing of the control cavity; early-style Tune-o-matic bridge; and the reinstatement of a longer and wider neck "tongue" at the neck/body joint.

Other reissue Les Pauls in the Historic Collection on Gibson's 2000 pricelist included the 1958 Plaintop and Figured Top, the 1960 Flametop, the 1952, 1954, 1956 and 1957 Goldtops, the 1954 and 1957 Custom Black Beautys (two or three pickups), and single- or double-cutaway Juniors and Specials. At a high price, these bring accurate reproductions of the classic Les Paul originals within the grasp of mere (wealthy) mortals.

During the early 1980s Norlin decided to sell Gibson. Sales fell by 30 per cent in 1982 alone, to a total of $19.5million, against a high in 1979 of $35.5million. Of course, Gibson was not alone in this decline. The guitar market in general had virtually imploded, and most other American makers were suffering in broadly similar ways. Their costs were high, economic circumstances and currency fluctuations were against them, and Japanese competitors increasingly had the edge.

A hostile takeover of Norlin by Rooney Pace occurred in 1984, and chairman Norton Stevens was off the board. Norlin had relocated some of its administration personnel from Chicago to Nashville around

1980
Gibson Explorer
prototype

1958 Gibson Explorer
BODY: slab-style solid korina body (two or three-piece).
NECK: chunky korina neck with unbound rosewood fingerboard, joins body at the 22nd fret; otherwise similar in materials and proportions to the LP/SG standards.
HEADSTOCK: 'split V' shaped three-a-side headstock with Kluson tuners early on; dropped six-a-side headstock later.
ELECTRONICS: dual PAF humbucking pickups; three-way toggle switch for each pickup individually or together; three 500k potentiometers for individual volume and master tone.
SOUND: round, rich and resonant, with good power and excellent sustain.

1980. All the main Gibson production was now handled at the Nashville plant. Kalamazoo had become a specialist factory making custom orders, banjos and mandolins, and as far as Norlin was concerned its closure became inevitable.

The last production at Kalamazoo was in June 1984, and the plant closed three months later, after more than 65 years' worthy service since the original building had been erected by Gibson. It was of course an emotional time for managers and workers, many of whom had worked in the plant for a considerable time. Three of them – Jim Deurloo, Marv Lamb and J.P. Moats – rented part of the Kalamazoo plant and started their new Heritage guitar company in April 1985. Although the emphasis at the Nashville plant had been on large runs of a small number of models, this had to change when it became Gibson's sole factory.

Norlin had put Gibson up for sale around 1980, and by summer 1985 they finally found a buyer. In January 1986 three businessmen – Henry Juskiewicz, David Berryman and Gary Zebrowski, who had met while classmates at Harvard business school – completed their purchase of the Gibson operation for a sum undisclosed at the time, though since confirmed as $5million.

The inevitable "restructuring" of the Gibson business occurred, and as seems so often to be the case in such undertakings many employees lost their jobs. However, today the company appears to be relatively healthy again. As well as tailoring the reissue program to sensible and defined areas, the new owners – with guitar-fan Juskiewicz at the helm – also continued to attempt innovations and to introduce new models. However, such new designs still apparently had little effect on players who thought that Gibson meant classics.

Luck played a part, however: Chet Atkins had severed allegiance with the Gretsch company, and now switched to Gibson. A number of "signature" electric thinline hollowbodies appeared from 1986, not dissimilar in style to some of the well-known Gretsch Chet Atkins models, but with distinct Gibson touches. Models include the Country Gentleman and the Tennessean.

The superstrat-like US-1 model debuted during 1986 and introduced musicians to a new idea from Gibson in the construction of solidbody guitars. For the new US-1, the company decided to employ a core of "chromite" (balsa wood) at the heart of the guitar, primarily for the material's low weight and its resonant qualities.

Chromite had the effect of reducing the weight of the maple-top US-1, and Gibson also applied the new material to the Les Paul Studio Lite model in 1991.

New in 1991 was the solidbody M-III line, a series of radically styled double-cutaway guitars fitted with flexible circuitry. The M-III guitars used the popular humbucker/single-coil/humbucker pickup layout, in the process aiming to provide Stratocaster-like and Les Paul-style tones from a five-way switch.

Unfortunately, Gibson's customers felt the design and the electronics of the new M-III guitars were, again, too "un-Gibson," and they did not rush to buy the instruments. So

it was that in a move reminiscent of the marriage of RD and Artist ten years before, Gibson decided to apply the electronics from the strange M-III to the more familiar environment of the Les Paul design. This resulted in two new models, the Classic/M-III and the Studio Lite/M-III. However, even this made little difference to players' allegiances, and the original M-IIIs as well as these Les Paul versions were gone from the Gibson line by the late 1990s.

Gibson's first official Custom Shop had started in the 1960s at Kalamazoo, building one-offs to customers' requirements, although of course non-standard orders had been undertaken from the company's earliest days. The Custom Shop idea was revived in the 1980s at Nashville, running from 1983 to 1988, and has now been running again since another new start in 1992.

The present Custom Shop at Gibson continues the traditional role of making oddities for wealthy players, but also provides more mainstream inspiration for the current Custom Shop Collection series that includes everything from a Zakk Wylde signature Les Paul to Tony Iommi's SG model.

The most recent new solidbody from Gibson was the single-cutaway humbucker/single-coil/humbucker Nighthawk, launched in 1993 in Standard, Special and Custom guises, but dropped by the end of the decade. Semi-hollow versions, the Blueshawk and B.B. King Little Lucille, followed in 1996 and 1999.

A relatively simple cosmetic alteration provided Gibson with its Gothic series that first appeared in 1999, with matt black finish and matt black hardware. Two of the models chosen for this line of instruments aimed at the solid rocking guitarist were obvious: the Flying V and the Explorer. However, the all-black 335 was a more surprising choice, and did not last in this particular category of Gibson's Designer Collection, which also found room to contain models such as the Explorer 1976 and the EDS1275 double-neck reissues.

Reissue "repros" of more vintage glories were featured in Gibson's 2000 catalog, including Firebirds, Flying Vs, 175s, 295s,

335s, Explorers, CESs and SGs. These are in addition to a long list of Les Paul reissues, some of which were mentioned earlier. One interesting addition to the burgeoning line of Gibson's "new/old" Les Pauls was the Aged 40th Anniversary model, which first appeared in 1999. Essentially, this was yet another move toward a more accurate reproduction of those hallowed 1959-period flame-top Les Paul Standards. The engineers at Gibson responsible for this particular attempt explained that they had virtually started again from scratch (which is what they usually say), finding new sources of materials and components.

But the major difference with the 40th Anniversary recreation was, however, the aged finish. There's no doubt that this was influenced by the success that Fender had found with its Relic series, introduced in the mid 1990s after the company had almost jokingly displayed a couple of aged repros of early models at a trade show – and received an incredibly positive reaction (for which read many orders from dealers visiting the show). So it was that a trained team at Gibson set about giving the 40th Anniversary model a look that suggests it has actually been gigged and used for 40 years. thus, the paint colors were made to appear faded, the nickel parts on the instrument such as the pickup covers were realistically tarnished, the lacquer "skin" was cracked and effectively dulled, and there were all manner of dings and knocks over the guitar. Like Fender and its Relics, Gibson aimed to recreate the almost indefinable allure of a vintage guitar with this model – at a stiff price, of course. Meanwhile, good examples of original sunburst Les Pauls with PAF humbuckers, manufactured nearly 50 years ago, have reached the quarter-million-dollar mark on the collector's market.

More signature models have also appeared from Gibson, including an L-5CES named for Wes Montgomery (1993) that reproduces the great jazzman's custom requirement of a single pickup, and Les Pauls for Jimmy Page (1995), Joe Perry (1996), Slash (1997), Ace Frehley (1997) and Peter Frampton (2000). As these latest models come off the Gibson production line in Nashville it's curious to observe that the company's classic designs, many of which are dozens of years old, seem more than ever before to reflect the needs of contemporary musicians.

At the start of the 21st century, the Gibson group of companies enjoyed annual revenues of around $200million and had 1,200 employees. It must be apparent to them that, among the greatly increased competition of today's guitar market, Gibson is uniquely placed to serve up its own true, traditional flavor – but with all the benefits of the improvements made in modern

manufacturing. Gibson designs look set for many new adventures, in the hands of succeeding generations of inspired musicians, and in the care of its industrious creators.

Godin

This Canadian maker has long been recognized for its original designs and bold innovations, yet the company has arguably failed to attain the appreciation it deserves among the better brands from North American and Japan.

Godin popularized "synth-access" guitars, and is also among those offering "hybrid" instruments that mix electric and acoustic qualities. The company is located in Canada and the US, headed by Robert Godin.

Godin first set up his LaSiDo shop in La Patrie, Quebec, in the early 1980s to build replacement electric-guitar necks and bodies. Soon LaSiDo was building instruments and parts for a number of big-name guitar brands – this continues today – but also developed its own models, of which Godin is the sole electric brand.

Godin is still probably best known as a maker of acoustic and electric-acoustic guitars (making brands such as Seagull, Norman, Simon & Patrick etc). Godin came to prominence with its innovative Acousticaster model of 1987, a Telecaster-size bolt-on-neck electric-acoustic with unusual harp-shape "sound fork" under the bridge, which was designed to improve the guitar's response.

Moves by Godin into the market for solidbody electric guitars proved relatively unsuccessful for the company until the launch of its LG-X model in 1994. This was a "synth-access" guitar – in other words an instrument with special built-in pickup and circuitry that enables it to be linked directly with (and control) a remote synthesizer module, thus giving the guitarist access to synth sounds. Guitar synthesizers had foundered in the 1980s due to poor compatibility between special "controller" guitars and the synthesizers available, but this new MIDI-based system pioneered by Godin offered much better performance. One of the most popular guitar-ready synthesizer modules used by synth-access players is the Roland GR series.

The Les Paul-style LG-X now heads a small series of similar instruments, some also with piezo "acoustic"-sounding bridge pickups. The LG-XT of 1998, for example, incorporated the piezo-loaded L.R. Baggs vibrato X-bridge, and as such offers the adventurous player the potential for a variety of different sounds and applications from one instrument.

Godin's first synth-access guitar had in fact been the Multiac, launched in 1993, which was a thinline nylon-strung electric-acoustic, and it's joined in the Godin line

today by the Multiac Classical and Multiac Steel, plus the budget-price Solidac. Godin clearly believes that many more players will become attracted to the idea of playing synthesizer sounds with a guitar, and later the LGX-SA and LGXT were aimed at players who prefer a solidbody feel.

Despite this innovation and industry, the mass-produced, well-made Godin line lacked "classic" styling. So in the late 1990s attempts were made to introduce some guitars with retro-inspired designs. These included the Radiator, launched in 1999, which illustrated a desire by Godin to go beyond its specialist status and move into the mainstream market. Similarly, the Triumph model, launched in 2006, blended retro looks with contemporary design touches in a solidbody that could be called more "standard" than many Godin offerings. Certainly Godin guitars are unusual in offering hybrid pickups and synth-access, but they are almost an underground force within the guitar industry. In the past brand often struggled to attain big-name endorsement, although that situation seems to have changed, and artists such as John McLaughlin, Al DiMeola and Steve Stevens can now be seen sporting Godin electrics. Godin now also has factories in Berlin, New Hampshire, and Princeville, Quebec, as well as at the original location in La Patrie.

Gretsch

The look – and arguably the sound – of the Gretsch electric screams "rock'n'roll" more than any other guitar. With their flashy and colorful looks, and cutting, aggressive tones, Gretsch models of the mid 1950s captured the interest of a surprising number of formative players of this radical new music, and were for a time possibly even better recognized by non-playing music fans than the Fender and Gibson guitars that would eventually outsell them.

In addition to making a distinct mark with some visually arresting guitars, Gretsch has also attracted key players in its long history, including Chet Atkins, Duane Eddy and George Harrison. The company's founder, Friedrich Gretsch, emigrated to the United States from Germany in 1872 at the age of 16. After working for a manufacturer of drums and banjos in New York City, Gretsch set up his own Fred Gretsch Manufacturing Company there in 1883 to make drums, banjos, tambourines and toy instruments.

Friedrich's son Fred, the eldest of seven children, took over at age 15 on his father's premature death in 1895. By 1900 Fred Sr, as he became known, had added mandolins to the company's drum- and banjo-making activities. In 1916 construction was completed of a large ten-story building at 60 Broadway, Brooklyn, just by the Williamsburg Bridge in New York. This imposing building continued to house the factory and offices of the Gretsch company for many years.

In the early 1930s the guitar began to replace the banjo in general popularity, and about 1933 the first Gretsch-brand guitars appeared, a line of archtop and flat-top acoustics. They were offered alongside Gretsch's burgeoning wholesale list of other makers' instruments, including guitars from the "big two" Chicago companies, Kay and Harmony.

The first Gretsch-brand archtop electric was introduced around 1939, the shortlived Electromatic Spanish model, which was made for Gretsch by Kay. At this time Fred Sr was still nominally president of Gretsch, but in fact had effectively retired from active management in the early 1930s to devote himself to banking. He officially retired from Gretsch in 1942, and died ten years later. He was replaced as company president in 1942 by his third son, William Walter Gretsch (generally known as Bill), who headed Gretsch until his premature death at the age of 44 in 1948. Bill's brother Fred Gretsch Jr, already the company's treasurer, then took over as president. It was Fred Jr who would steer the company through its glory years during the 1950s and 1960s.

After the war, Gretsch placed a new emphasis on guitars for professionals. The first new Gretsch electric guitar of the post-war era revived the Electromatic Spanish name, this archtop debuting in 1949 alongside a number of Synchromatic acoustics. The single-coil pickup of the Electromatic Spanish was the first of many made for Gretsch by Rowe Industries of Toledo, Ohio, a company run by Harry DeArmond. A few years later that DeArmond pickup would receive its official Gretsch name, the Dynasonic.

Cutaway-body electrics followed in 1951, the Electromatic and Electro II, in effect proving that Gretsch now took seriously the new electric guitar business. Helping to launch the new models was a new Gretsch man, Jimmie Webster, a qualified piano-tuner and inspired guitarist. Webster used an unusual "touch" playing system, similar to that popularized much later by Eddie Van Halen. Webster became an important ambassador for Gretsch, probably doing more than anyone else in the coming years to spread the word about Gretsch guitars, as well as doing much in the process to promote electric guitars and guitar-playing in general.

Gretsch certainly noticed Fender's new solidbody guitar of 1950, mainly because the upstart California company called it the Broadcaster. This was a name that Gretsch still used, spelled Broadkaster, for a number of its drum products. (Gretsch had made drums since its earliest days, pioneering new manufacturing techniques along the way as well as instigating the important switch to smaller-size drums in the kit during the 1940s.) At Gretsch's request, Fender dropped the Broadcaster name, changing it to Telecaster. When Fred Jr saw that Fender and Gibson were actually beginning to sell these new-style solidbody guitars, he acted swiftly: in 1953 Gretsch launched its first "solidbody", the single-cutaway Duo Jet.

In fact, the guitar was a semi-solid with some air space between the arched portion of the laminated maple top and the mahogany body (which also had channels and routings for the electronics), but the visual effect was certainly of a solidbody instrument, and it was clearly intended as competition for the Telecaster, and for Gibson's Les Paul in particular.

In its early years the new Duo Jet had, unusually, a body front covered in a black plastic material, as used on some Gretsch drums. It also had Gretsch's unique two-piece strap buttons (an early take on the idea of locking strap buttons) and the Melita Synchro-Sonic bridge. The Melita was the first bridge to offer independent intonation adjustment for each string, beating Gibson's Tune-o-matic version by at least a year.

FACT FILE

The term **semi-solid** is used to describe electric guitars that are proportionally more solid than hollow, and are often made by routing out solid wood sections rather than by constructing a thinline acoustic body and adding a solid center block, as with a semi-acoustic. The Gretsch Duo Jet, Rickenbacker 360, and Fender Telecaster Thinline are classic examples of the format.

Three more solidbodies in the style of the Duo Jet were added to the Gretsch line in 1954 and 1955: the country-flavored Round Up, the red Jet Fire Bird, and the Silver Jet. The latter came with a silver sparkle finish on the body front, another product of Gretsch's drum department.

That same year in the hollowbody lines the non-cutaway Electromatic Spanish became the Corvette, the cutaway Electro II became the Country Club, and the Electromatic became the Streamliner. The Country Club would go on to be the most enduring model name in Gretsch's history.

Another significant addition to the Gretsch line in 1954 was the option of colored finishes for some models, beyond the normal sunburst or natural varieties. We've already noted the company's use of drum coverings on the Silver Jet and the

1955 Gretsch Chet Atkins Hollow Body

BODY: 16" wide, 2 ⅞" deep fully hollow single-cutaway body with pressed arched maple ply top, and maple ply back and sides; multi-ply top and back binding; transparent nitrocellulose finish.

NECK: glued in maple neck with bound rosewood fingerboard with 12" radius; 14th fret neck/body joint, 21 narrow nickel-silver frets, and 1 ¹¹⁄₁₆" nut width; large mother of pearl block position markers etched with western themes; 24 ¾" scale length.

HEADSTOCK: symmetrical back-angled headstock with three-a-side tuners; aluminum nut.

BRIDGE: fixed-arm Bigsby vibrato tailpiece with cast aluminum one-piece compensated rocker bridge, mounted on floating rosewood base; adjustable for height only (or approximate intonation by moving the base).

ELECTRONICS: two single-coil DeArmond 200 (Dynasonic) pickups, made with six adjustable alnico slug pole pieces, DC resistance approximately 8.5k. Three-way toggle switch for either pickup independently or both together; four controls for individual Volume for each pickup, master Tone, plus master Volume (on treble bout).

SOUND: thick, cutting, twangy and a little bit raunchy, with a whisper of air and openness to round out the package.

1955 Gretsch
White Falcon

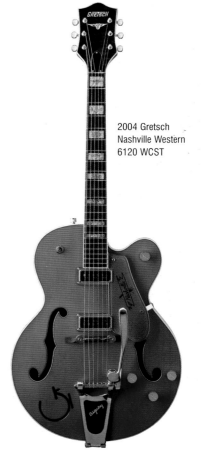

2004 Gretsch
Nashville Western
6120 WCST

black Duo Jet, but equally flamboyant paint finishes were on the way. Automobile marketing was having a growing influence on guitar manufacturers in the early 1950s, and the theme was especially evident in Gretsch's colorful campaign of 1954, with a Cadillac Green option for the Country Club and a Jaguar Tan (a sort of dark gold) for the Streamliner. The paints came from DuPont, which also supplied most of the car companies (and later Fender too). Gretsch drew yet again on its experience in finishing and lacquering drums in different colors, artfully applying know-how that already existed within the company to help its guitars stand out in the marketplace.

There were isolated precedents for colored guitars – Gibson's gold ES-295 and Les Paul of 1952, Fender's infrequent and as-yet unofficial custom colors – but for a few years Gretsch made the use of color into a marketing bonus almost entirely its own. Through the middle 1950s Gretsch added a number of pleasant two-tone options – yellows, coppers, ivories – contrasting a darker body back and sides against a lighter-colored body front, for example on archtop electrics such as the Streamliner (launched 1954), Convertible (1955) and Clipper (1956). This two-tone style was yet further evidence of inspiration from long-standing techniques used in the drum department.

The success of Gibson's new Les Paul guitar – well over 2,000 were sold in 1953 alone – alerted other manufacturers, including Gretsch, to the value of a "signature" model endorsed by a famous player. Today the practice is very familiar, but back in the 1950s it was a new, exciting and potentially profitable area of musical instrument marketing. Around 1954 Jimmie Webster succeeded in securing talented Nashville-based country guitarist Chet Atkins for this role, a move that in time would completely turn around Gretsch's fortunes.

After various discussions and meetings between the company and the guitarist, the Gretsch Chet Atkins Hollow Body 6120 model appeared in 1955. Atkins wasn't keen on the Western paraphernalia that Gretsch insisted on applying to the guitar – including cactus and cattle inlays, and a branded "G" on the body – but relented because he was so keen to get a signature guitar on to the market.

In fact, the decorations on the Hollow Body model were gradually removed over the following years. Gretsch had also given ground by adding a Bigsby vibrato to the production model, in line with Atkins's request. There was a Chet Atkins Solid Body, too, essentially a Round Up with a Bigsby vibrato – although, despite the name, the Solid Body still had Gretsch's customary semi-solid construction. Atkins had little to do with the Solid Body model, and it was dropped after a few years.

The Hollow Body, however, became Atkins's exclusive instrument for his increasingly popular work. It remained one

of the most popular Gretsch models for many years, and Gretsch did good business from the new endorsement deal. Its 1955 catalog trumpeted: "Every Chet Atkins appearance, whether in person or on TV...

guitar facts

and every new album he cuts for RCA Victor, wins new admirers to swell the vast army of Chet Atkins fans." The new Chet Atkins model effectively put Gretsch on the map.

Not content with the coup of attracting Chet Atkins to the company, Jimmie Webster also devised Gretsch's brand new top-of-the-line sensation, the White Falcon. First marketed by Gretsch in 1955, it was an overwhelmingly impressive instrument. The guitar's single-cutaway hollow body was finished in a gleaming white paint finish, as was the new "winged" design headstock, and both bore gold sparkle decorations that again were borrowed from the Gretsch drum department.

All of the White Falcon's metalwork was gold-plated, including the deluxe Grover Imperial "stepped" tuners and the stylish new tailpiece, since nicknamed the "Cadillac" because of a V shape similar to the auto company's logo. The fingerboard markers of the White Falcon had suitably ornithoid engravings, and the gold plastic pickguard featured a flying falcon about to land on the nearby Gretsch logo. It was, simply, a stunner.

"Cost was never considered in the planning of this guitar," boasted the Gretsch publicity. "We were planning an instrument for the artist-player whose caliber justifies and demands the utmost in striking beauty, luxurious styling, and peak tonal performance and who is willing to pay the price." To be precise, $600. The next highest in the line at the time was a $400 Country Club. Gibson's most expensive archtop electric in 1955 was the $690 Super 400CESN – but by comparison that was a sedate, natural-finish product of the more conventional Kalamazoo-based company. Meanwhile, over in New York, Gretsch proclaimed the idiosyncratic White Falcon as "the finest guitar we know how to make – and what a beauty!"

Some of Gretsch's more ostentatious banjos used gold trim, fancy fingerboard markers and rhinestone inlays, so it's fair to deduce that features of the White Falcon such as the distinctive jeweled knobs and feathery fingerboard inlays may well have been inspired by the company's banjos. There's no reason to suppose that borrowings would be limited to the drum department. Jimmie Webster was probably fond of wandering around the entire factory and warehouse in his search for new ideas.

An early White Falcon prototype had been displayed at one of Gretsch's own local promotional events in March 1954, but the guitar's first big showing was at the major NAMM instrument trade show in Chicago four months later. Gretsch enticed dealers by billing the still experimental Falcon as one of their "Guitars Of The Future" along with the green Country Club

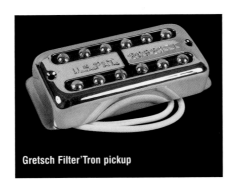

Gretsch Filter'Tron pickup

and tan Streamliner. Gretsch also produced a partner to the White Falcon in the company's standard-shape semi-solid style. This was the White Penguin, complete with all the Falcon features and released in 1956. It even had a little penguin waddling across the pickguard.

Very few Penguins were sold, and the model has since become regarded as one of the most collectable of all Gretsch guitars.

Gretsch benefited from some big success stories among two early rock'n'roll guitarists, both of whom used Chet Atkins Hollow Body guitars to power their sound. Eddie Cochran was an accomplished guitarist who landed a cameo spot in the 1956 movie *The Girl Can't Help It* and then made some blasting rock'n'roll with his Hollow Body at the center of a churning mix of rockabilly, country and blues. Duane Eddy turned out a string of hit records from the late 1950s, based on his deceptively simple instrumental style that will forever be known by the word attached to so many of his albums: Twang. That twangy tone came when Eddy concentrated on playing melodies on the bass strings of his Hollow Body. He made full use of the pitch-bending potential of the guitar's Bigsby vibrato, his amplifier's tremolo, and the studio's echo facilities.

Ray Butts, a music store owner and electronics wizard from Cairo, Illinois, met Chet Atkins in 1954 and showed the guitarist his new combination amplifier that offered echo from a built-in tape loop, an unusual facility at the time. Atkins and players such as Carl Perkins and Scotty Moore became customers for Butts's amp. Then Atkins, who didn't like Gretsch's DeArmond pickups, asked Butts to come up with an improved type of pickup. Butts devised a humbucking model, around the same time that Seth Lover at Gibson formulated his humbucker. Gretsch was fitting the new Filter'Tron pickups to most electrics by 1958.

Two new models in the Chet Atkins series were the dark brown Country Gentleman and the red Tennessean. The Country Gent, new in 1957, was the first Gretsch hollowbody to be made with a thinline body – about two inches deep, unlike most of the company's existing hollowbodies which were around three

inches deep. The thinline concept had been popularized by the Gibson company in the preceding years.

The Country Gent was also the first Gretsch Chet Atkins model to be offered with a slightly wider 17″ body, like the company's White Falcon, Country Club and Convertible. The Hollow Body (and indeed the new Tennessean) was closer to 16″ wide. The Gent had what are generally referred to by players and collectors as "fake" f-holes. These have a visual representation of f-holes on the body, to help the general look of the guitar, but are without actual apertures. The Gretsch f-holes would not revert to true holes until the early 1970s.

The new Space Control bridge appeared around this time, another Jimmie Webster design. It was simpler than the Melita, and lacked intonation adjustment. Also new were "Neo-Classic" half-moon-shape markers at the edge of the fingerboard, which appeared around 1957.

In 1958 Gretsch marked the 75th anniversary of the company's founding with special Anniversary model guitars in one- and two-pickup versions, remarkably lasting in the line until 1977. Meanwhile, the tireless Jimmie Webster collaborated with Ray Butts to come up with the first stereo guitar system, "Project-O-Sonic." At first they achieved this by splitting the output of the pickups, sending the sound of the top three strings to one amplifier and the bottom three to another.

This stereo circuitry was first launched as an option on the Country Club and White Falcon models during 1958. Various modifications appeared over subsequent years, but stereo seemed too complex to capture many players' imaginations. Another questionable piece of Webster weirdness was "T-Zone Tempered Treble," which translates to the more simple description "slanted frets." Webster claimed that they improved intonation. The White Falcon and the new high-end Viking model bore the skewed frets from 1964, the fingerboard helpfully marked with offset dot markers in the slanted zone to warn innocent players.

The Country Gent, Hollow Body and White Falcon changed to a double-cutaway style during 1961 and 1962. Gibson was as ever the primary inspiration for this decision: since 1958 the Kalamazoo guitar-maker had increasingly employed double cutaways to successful effect. With such a body design, players could more easily reach the higher frets of the fingerboard and make fuller use of this upper register when soloing. George Harrison, who'd previously used a Duo Jet, was a very visible player of the double-cutaway Country Gentleman in the 1960s. Gretsch's solidbody line also moved to double-cutaways, from 1961.

During the early 1960s Gretsch toyed

with a number of peculiar solidbody designs, and the Bikini was among the oddest. It consisted of a hinged, folding body-back which could accept slide-in, interchangeable guitar and bass necks. The body-backs were in both single- and double-neck styles. Few Bikinis were made.

The colorful Princess model of 1962 was, according to the boys at Gretsch, "engineered to meet the needs and standards of young women all over the world." Gretsch had, in fact, simply finished one of its existing models in special pastel color combinations designed to appeal to the delicate female sensibility. Another opportunist solidbody was the Twist of 1962, exploiting the contemporary dance craze. It sported a pickguard with a twisting red and white "peppermint" design. The Astro-Jet of 1963 was a very strange looking guitar, almost as if it had been left out too long on a hot Brooklyn summer day and melted into several disfigured lumps. It also had an apparently randomly styled headstock, with four tuners on one side, two the other.

During the guitar boom of the middle 1960s Gretsch decided to move its drum department out of the Brooklyn factory to another location a few blocks away, while a good deal of the company's wholesaling operations were either ceased or moved to the Chicago office. All this was to allow the whole of the seventh floor in Brooklyn to be turned over to guitar making, not least because of the popularity afforded Gretsch by George Harrison's prominent use of a Country Gentleman.

No Harrison signature model ever appeared, but Gretsch did produce a shortlived Monkees model to cash in on the TV pop group of the 1960s. Through a marketing deal the group featured Gretsch instruments including drums and the company's 12-string thinline electric introduced in 1966. The six-string Monkees model that Gretsch issued that same year had the group's distinctive guitar-shape logo on the pickguard and truss-rod cover.

By the mid 1960s models such as the high-end White Falcon came fitted with a gamut of guitar gadgets created by the ever-fertile mind of Jimmie Webster. They included the weird slanted frets in the upper register that we've already seen. Additionally there was a "standby" on/off switch, which on a stereo-equipped model meant a total of two control knobs and six switches, as well as a couple of levers behind the back pickup to operate padded string-dampers. Also, the vibrato tailpiece would sport a telescopic adjustable arm, while a Floating Sound frame-like device sat on a "fork" passing through the body and contacting the back. It was positioned in front of the bridge with the strings passing through it and was supposed to enhance tone and increase sustain. Webster's inspiration came from the tuning forks he used regularly as a piano tuner. Thus the top-of-the-line Gretsch models of the day were probably the most gadget-laden instruments on the market, assaulting players' imaginations with a plethora of possibilities. But some musicians were simply scared off.

Shockwaves had been sent through the guitar manufacturing industry in 1965 when the Fender companies were sold to the Columbia Broadcasting System corporation for $13million. D.H. Baldwin, an Ohio-based musical instrument company specializing in the manufacture of pianos and organs, was like many actively seeking to purchase a guitar-making operation at this time. In 1965 the firm had bid unsuccessfully for Fender. So Baldwin bought the Burns guitar company of England and then in 1967 purchased Gretsch.

Baldwin began to diversify away from its original core of music and into financial services, including banking and insurance. The company's Annual Report for 1969 noted a 12 per cent drop in Gretsch sales, conveniently attributing over half the fall to a three-month strike that began in October 1969.

By 1970 plans were underway by Baldwin to move the Gretsch factory out of its 54-year-old home in Brooklyn to a site in Booneville, Arkansas, well over 1,000 miles away. Baldwin already operated a number of factories there, enjoying cheaper and more amenable labor. Of course, the move did not please an already disgruntled workforce at Gretsch, and very few personnel made the move south-west in September 1970. The Brooklyn building continued to house Gretsch sales until that too was moved, first to the Illinois office and then in 1972 to Baldwin's HQ in Cincinnati, Ohio. Thus by the summer of 1972 the very last Gretsch connection had been severed with 60 Broadway, Brooklyn, New York City.

The first new Gretsch model of the Baldwin era was the undistinguished twin-cutaway thinline Rally, although it did have an unusual built-in active treble-boost circuit. More interesting, though hardly devastating, was a new line of Chet Atkins models. In 1972 the Deluxe Chet and the Super Chet were launched. The big, deep-body, single-cutaway archtop style was the result of a collaboration between Chet Atkins and Gretsch men Dean Porter and Clyde Edwards. The highly-decorated Super Chet sported an unusual row of control "wheels" built into the pickguard's edge, while the plainer Deluxe Chet had conventional controls. The Deluxe did not last long, but the Super stayed in the line for some seven years.

Two new low-end guitars came along in 1975, the Broadkaster solidbody and semi-hollow electrics. As usual Gretsch were to some extent following Gibson's lead – and on this occasion the path was an unpopular one. Gibson had launched the Marauder, its first solidbody guitar with a Fender-style bolt-on neck, in 1974; likewise, the Broadkaster solidbody was the first Gretsch with a bolt-on neck, while also displaying strong Strat-style influences. Neither of these new Gretsch guitars drew much praise.

More new Chet Atkins signature models appeared in 1977, the effects-laden Super Axe and the gadget-less Atkins Axe. The distinctive look of these big new solidbody guitars with their sweeping, pointed cutaway was the subject of a patent issued to Gretsch designer Clyde Edwards for "ornamental design." Both were gone from the line by 1980.

The last new Gretsch guitars to appear under Baldwin ownership were the unappealing Beast solidbodys, launched in 1979. While nobody realized it at the time, they marked the end of an era with a depressingly low note. If Baldwin's performance in handling its fresh acquisition was measured by the aptitude and success of the new Gretsch models it launched in the 1970s, then the score would be low. Baldwin fared little better in the business affairs surrounding Gretsch. Although sales picked up a little in the early 1970s, Baldwin was not seeing a profit from the business, despite various cost-cutting exercises.

1962 Gretsch Corvette Princess

BODY: solid mahogany body with beveled edges and dual equal-depth cutaways with pointed, non-concentric horns; finished in ivory nitrocellulose lacquer.

NECK: one-piece mahogany neck with rosewood fingerboard; 21 nickel-silver frets; and 1 23/32" nut width; 24 ½" scale length.

HEADSTOCK: back-angled symmetrical headstock, with three-a-side tuners; headstock-end truss-rod adjustment.

BRIDGE: slotted bar bridge adjustable for height only; trapeze tailpiece; optional clip-on vibrato unit.

ELECTRONICS: single HiLo'Tron single-coil pickup with DC resistance averaging around 3.5k. Two 250k potentiometers for individual Volume and Tone.

SOUND: bright, tight and well-defined, with a little roundness and warmth from the all-mahogany construction.

Gretsch/Bigsby vibrato with bridge

gretsch

1955 Gretsch Duo Jet

BODY: single-cutaway mahogany body with routed chambers, pressed arched maple ply top with black plastic covering; top binding.

NECK: glued-in, one-piece mahogany neck with bound ebony fingerboard with 12" radius, 22 narrow gauge nickel-silver frets, and 1 ¹¹⁄₁₆" nut width; 24 ⅝" scale length.

HEADSTOCK: symmetrical back-angled headstock with three-a-side Grover tuners.

BRIDGE: Simple rocker-bar bridge on floating rosewood base, with Bigsby vibrato tailpiece.

ELECTRONICS: two single-coil DeArmond 200 pickups (also known as Gretsch Dynasonics), with individually adjustable alnico slug pole pieces; DC resistance of approximately 8.5k. Three-way toggle switch to select either pickup alone or both together; controls for individual pickup Volumes, master Tone, and master Volume.

SOUND: snappy, bright, round and gritty, with plenty of bite and edge.

guitar facts

1963 Gretsch
Country Gent

In early 1979, Baldwin bought the Kustom amplifier company, and by the end of the year had merged Gretsch with Kustom, moving the sales and administration office for the new combined operation to Chanute, Kansas. Probably during 1980 Baldwin finally decided that they would stop production of Gretsch guitars. Very few guitars were manufactured beyond the start of 1981 (two years short of Gretsch's 100th anniversary). A man called Charlie Roy was running the Gretsch/Kustom operation, which he bought from Baldwin in 1982, moving the offices to Gallatin,

Tennessee, just outside Nashville. By now Chet Atkins's endorsement deal had come to a natural end, and he soon transferred allegiance to Gibson. (Gibson began making a number of Chet Atkins signature models from 1986.)

Baldwin once again took control of Gretsch around 1984, when the deal with Roy ceased. Around this time there was a last-ditch plan to revive Gretsch guitar production at a Baldwin piano-action factory in Ciudad Juarez, Mexico, but only a small trial batch was assembled, after which the idea was dropped. Baldwin then sold Gretsch to yet another Fred Gretsch, the grandson of Fred Sr, whom we shall call Fred III.

Fred III had originally worked for his grandfather at Gretsch from 1965 until 1971, when he began his own musical instrument importing and wholesaling business. He acquired the Synsonics brand in 1980 from Mattel, which led to some success with acoustic and electronic percussion as well as electric guitars. He bought Gretsch from Baldwin at the very beginning of 1985. Gretsch drum production – which had never ceased – continued in Arkansas for a year, then moved to Fred's own premises in South Carolina. It was then that Gretsch guitar manufacturing was started again.

Fred III, with the help of old Gretsch hand Duke Kramer, decided to introduce updated versions of the classic Gretsch models of the past, no doubt having noticed the increasing prices that certain Gretsch instruments had been fetching for some time on the "vintage" guitar market. Kramer drew up specifications for the proposed new models, and visited many American makers with a view to US production. But negotiations were unsuccessful, so Gretsch

went "offshore," in guitar-biz-speak, meaning they contracted a manufacturer a good distance beyond the shores of the US. After some searching, Gretsch selected Terada in Japan as its new factory.

However, in 1989 Gretsch offered an unusual forerunner to its forthcoming guitars with a series of Korean-made electrics intended to capitalize on the popularity of the fictional-family supergroup, The Traveling Wilburys. The cheap and somewhat primitive guitars were loosely based on the group's old Danelectro instruments, and various models were issued, all boldly finished in what Gretsch called "original graphics" with an appropriate travel theme.

Gretsch delivered its first proper models later in 1989. Clearly it could no longer use Chet Atkins's name, now a Gibson property, so while some of the model names were familiar, others were necessarily modified. Nine new Gretsch models were launched. There were five hollowbodys: the Tennessee Rose, recalling a Tennessean; the Nashville; Nashville Western with G-brand and Western appointments; Country Classic, recalling a Country Club; and Country Classic double-cutaway. There were four solidbodys: the Duo Jet; Silver Jet; Jet Firebird; and Round

1995 Gretsch
Blue Pearl sparkle Jet

Padded back on rear of White Falcon

guitar facts

Up. This initial selection was soon joined by a pair of White Falcon models in single- or double-cutaway styles.

Since then the revitalized Gretsch operation has, like so many of its contemporaries, placed increasing emphasis on revisiting the past. This has resulted in the reissue of various oldies that bear re-activated pickup and hardware designs, including the reincarnation of Filter'Tron humbucker and DeArmond (Gretsch Dynasonic) single-coil pickups. The company also launched signature models honoring well-known Gretsch players such as Brian Setzer (1993), Malcolm Young (1997), Keith Scott (1999), Duane Eddy (1999), Stephen Stills (2000), Elliot Easton (2000), and Reverend Horton Heat (2005).

During recent years Gretsch has added more models to its line, including a Black Falcon, an Anniversary reissue and a variety of fresh color options, as well as a low-end Korean-made series that revives the old Electromatic name. At first this was offered for sale only in Japan, but by 2000 was available elsewhere.

The Fender Musical Instrument Corp. took over the manufacturing and distribution of Gretsch guitars in 2002, and has continued to expand the range of standard and signature models, mostly still made in the Terada factory in Japan. While Gretsch's own Dynasonic pickups are highly regarded reproductions of the DeArmond 200 models, the company has used American pickup manufacturer TV Jones's reproductions of classic Filter'Tron humbuckers on some recent models, including the Country Classic, the Nashville Golden Anniversary, and the Power Jet. In recent years, US-made lines of selected "Custom USA" classics and "Custom Limited Edition" models have also appeared, and with this return to American manufacturing sources – albeit in limited numbers – the Gretsch electric guitar has come full circle.

F A C T   F I L E

Both alnico and ceramic magnets are used to make guitar pickups. The former, a more expensive material by weight, is often associated with vintage designs or reproductions thereof, and is considered to have a relatively sweet, smooth tone. More powerful ceramic magnets are often a maker's choice for high-gain designs, or for those where cost is a major consideration. Pickup and guitar manufacturers such as Bill Lawrence and G&L have also, however, made very successful general-use pickups from ceramic magnets.

Guild

Occasionally forgotten amid the other two "big G" makers – and of course the "big F" – Guild is nevertheless a much-respected American manufacturer, and deservedly holds a place among the six classic A-list American electric guitar manufacturers, putting them alongside Fender, Gibson, Gretsch, Rickenbacker, and Epiphone.

For players who've discovered them, Guild guitars since their inception in the early 1950s have always offered a high-quality alternative to the market leaders. Founded in New York City by jazz guitarist Alfred Dronge, Guild was born just as the Epiphone company was embroiled in a labor dispute and was relocating to Philadelphia. Many former Epiphone employees joined the new company and brought their skills to Guild, especially in making carved archtops.

So it's no surprise that Guild's first guitars, introduced around 1953, were non-cutaway and single-cutaway archtops – either electric, or acoustics with an optional pickup. Guild's archtops would always command respect, although the company quickly began to make its reputation with high-quality acoustic flat-tops. The full-bodied, rounded "F"-series and dreadnoughts that debuted in 1954 were played through the years by stars such as Eric Clapton, Ralph Towner and Charlie Byrd (who chose the classical Mark series).

Among Guild's 1953 non-cutaway electric archtops were the one-pickup X-100 and two-pickup X-200, replaced the following year by the one-pickup Granada (and renamed the Cordoba X-50 in 1961) which was offered until 1970. Single-cutaway models included the shortlived one-pickup X-300, two-pickup X-400 and three-pickup X-600, plus the luxuriously appointed Stuart X-500 which remained Guild's flagship archtop until 1994. Other long-running single-cutaway electric archtops introduced the following year were the one-pickup Savoy X-150, two pickup Manhattan X-175, and 13 1/2"-wide two-pickup hollowbody Aristocrat M-75, a model that lasted until 1963 and then reappeared a few years later as the semi-hollow BluesBird, transforming into the solidbody M-75 BluesBird in 1970.

In 1956 Guild moved its factory to Hoboken, New Jersey, and picked up its first pro endorsement by pop-jazz great Johnny Smith, beginning a string of artist models. The single-cutaway, single-DeArmond-equipped Johnny Smith Award was introduced that year – renamed the Artist Award in 1961 – and became another high-end mainstay of the Guild line. In 1962 jazz ace George Barnes entered the fold with his single-cutaway, twin-humbucker George Barnes AcoustiLectric model, followed by

the "George Barnes Guitar In F" model in 1963, both offered until the early 1970s.

Twangy instrumentalist Duane Eddy also came on board in 1962 with his single-cutaway, twin-DeArmond Duane Eddy Deluxe (lasting to 1987) followed by the Standard in 1963 (until 1974). From 1963-65 the single-cutaway Bert Weedon Model, with two DeArmonds and a Bigsby vibrato, was available, endorsed by the British sessionman and *Play In A Day* author.

Guild entered the thinline market in 1960 with its Starfire series, initially single-cutaways (Starfire I with one single-coil pickup, II with two single-coil pickups, III with added Bigsby), all but the Starfire I lasting into the mid 1970s. These were joined in 1963 by the double-cutaway Starfire IV (two humbuckers) and V (Bigsby), followed in 1964 by the VI (gold hardware, pearl/abalone block inlays) and the XII 12-string. All but the IV (still produced) ceased during the 1970s.

In 1963 Guild began making solidbody electrics, producing many excellent instruments – even some classics – yet never really finding great success. Guild's first solidbody was one of the most unusual American guitars of the 1960s, the lumpy "Gumby"-shaped S-200 Thunderbird, available from 1963-68. Not only was the shape unusual, but the guitar featured a very early example of phase-switching (for a different pickup sound) and more importantly was one of only two guitars ever to incorporate a metal stand built into the back.

Despite these oddities, the Thunderbird had enough appeal to win over an eclectic

bunch of players, including Muddy Waters, Zal Yanofsky, Jorma Kaukonen and Banana. The Thunderbird was joined by two other similarly shaped solids, the plainer S-100 Polara (also with built-in stand) and the single-pickup S-50 Jet-Star, both gone by the late 1960s. The S-200 and S-100 featured Swedish Hagstrom vibratos.

In 1966 Guild was purchased by Avnet Inc, an electronics firm that also purchased the Hershman company and its Goya guitar brandname that year. Alfred Dronge was retained to manage Guild, and production began to shift over to a new factory in Westerly, Rhode Island. Guild production continues there today. When Hoboken production ended in 1971 corporate headquarters were moved to Elizabeth, New Jersey.

In 1970 Guild revisited the solidbody market and introduced a new S-100 Polara, more conventionally styled with a slightly offset double cutaway, and twin humbuckers. It's often referred to as "Guild's SG" because of its similarity to the Gibson model, though it was more closely modeled on Hagstrom's mid-1960s solidbody design. Two low-end companions were also introduced at this time, the S-90 and S-50. An S-100 Deluxe joined the line in 1973 with optional stereo output, followed by the S-100C in 1974, a version with an oak leaf carved into the front. The previously mentioned M-75 solidbody was offered from 1970-80, along with a Deluxe version and, beginning in 1975, the M-85CS.

In 1972 Dronge was killed in an aircraft crash and was succeeded by Leon Tell. Guild briefly participated in the "copy era" in 1973-74 by offering Japanese-made Madeira-brand copies of its own S-100 as well as of Fender and Gibson designs. The "SG" S-series was retired in 1976, supplanted by a new design with offset double-cutaways and a "bell"-shaped lower bout. With different appointments (some sporting DiMarzio pickups) these included the S-60, S-65, S-70, S-300, and S-400, all offered through 1982.

From 1980-83 the M-80 was available, a double-cutaway version of the M-75. In 1981 Guild introduced its first Strat-style solids, the S-250 and S-25 (both with set-necks) and its first "pointy" guitars, the X-82 Nova and X-79 Skylark. The X-82 Nova was essentially a hybrid Explorer/Flying V similar to Dean's ML model, while the X-79 Skylark was more radically pointed and had a dramatically extended upper horn and sloped lower bout, and a matching headstock shape. Both lasted into the mid 1980s. In 1983-84 the X-80 Skyhawk joined the line, essentially a variant on the X-79. The Madeira brand was revived briefly on a series of original and copy designs in the early 1980s.

In 1983, Guild began offering a number of fairly popular Strat-style models, often with

a bewildering variety of model names for the same or similar guitars, and all distinguished by set-necks and Guild's first six-tuners-in-line headstocks. The S series differed primarily in details such as pickup types and layouts and included Flyer, Thunderbolt and Aviator models among others.

In 1984-85 Guild offered perhaps its most exotic solidbodies with the X-88 Crue Flying Star (a very pointy variant on the X-82, named for Motley Crue's Mick Mars), the X-100 Bladerunner (almost "X"-shaped, with large holes cut out of the body, designed by luthier David Andrews) and the X-90 Citron Breakaway (shaped something like a Jackson Randy Rhoads V but with detachable wings to make it a travel guitar, designed by luthier Harvey Citron).

In 1985 the single-cutaway solid Bluesbird and semi-hollow Nightbird electrics debuted. It was also during this mid-1980s period that Guild introduced one of its more collectable models, the Brian May MHM1, promoted as a "copy" of the Queen guitarist's homemade axe, even though it wasn't an exact replica.

A period of turmoil began for Guild. In 1986 Avnet sold Guild to an investment group headed by banker Jere Haskew from Chattanooga, Tennessee. Around this time Guild introduced Telecaster-style guitars in two versions, the fancy T-250 and the T-200 Roy Buchanan, endorsed by the great Tele ace. These were Guild's first bolt-on-neck guitars. In 1987-88 Guild returned to imports with a line of high-quality Japanese-made solidbodies carrying the Burnside brandname, including both Strat- and Tele-style guitars and original "pointy" designs (often with flashy paint jobs). Some had set-necks, others were bolt-ons.

In 1987 Guild experienced financial difficulties, yet managed to introduce some fine electrics including the high-end semi-hollow Nightbird I and II, the solidbody Liberator series and the well-made but otherwise conventional Detonator superstrat. The Liberator Elite was a spectacular set-neck guitar with a carved flamed-maple body cap and fancy rising-sun inlays.

In 1988 Guild went into bankruptcy and ceased solidbody guitar production, though it continued to make the semi-hollow and hollowbody electrics (which often appear to be solids) for a couple more years. In 1989 the company was sold to the Fass Corporation of New Berlin, Wisconsin (subsequently US Music Corporation). While domestic electric production was in hiatus, the Madeira brand was again revived in 1990-91 for a brief run of Strat- and Les Paul-style guitars.

After a period when Guild concentrated on its traditional strengths – mainly flat-top guitars – the company ventured back to solidbodies in 1993-94 by reviving the Brian

---

1958 Guild Stuart X-550

BODY: 17" wide fully hollow single-cutaway body with arched spruce ply top, maple back and sides; multi-ply top and back binding.

NECK: glued in five-piece maple neck with bound ebony fingerboard with 12" radius; 14th fret neck/body joint, 20 medium nickel-silver frets, and 1 $^{11}\!/_{16}$" nut width; 25 $^{9}\!/_{16}$" scale length.

HEADSTOCK: symmetrical back-angled headstock with three-a-side pearl button Grover tuners; bone nut.

BRIDGE: floating two-piece ebony bridge with thumb wheels for height adjustment; lyre-shaped trapeze tailpiece.

ELECTRONICS: two wide single-coil pickups, made with alnico bar magnets beneath and six adjustable threaded steel pole pieces; three-way toggle switch for either pickup or both together, controls for independent Volume and Tone controls for each pickup.

SOUND: full, airy and resonant, with good balance and clarity, and just a little bite for cutting power (later Stuart's with Guild humbuckers sound a little fuller and warmer, though with a shade less snap and cut).

May guitar with the limited-edition Signature, this time a little closer to the original. It was followed in 1994-95 by three more May models: the Pro, Special and Standard, differing in appointments. In 1994 Guild reissued its venerable SG-style solidbody, the S-100 of the 1970s, after its high-profile use by Kim Thayil.

In late 1995, Guild was sold to Fender. The new owner decided to bring Guild designs to a wider market with an additional line of less expensive equivalents marketed with the DeArmond name, after Harry DeArmond whose Rowe company made many of Guild's early pickups.

At the other end of the price scale the Guild electric line was rationalized. The Brian May models were dropped, and the accent was now on traditional design. Late-1990s guitar included revivals of the 1960s single-cut Starfire semi-hollow models alongside the continuing Bluesbird and S-100 solidbodies.

Famed archtop builder Bob Benedetto was brought in during 2000 to redefine Guild's Artist Award and Stuart archtops and to launch a new custom-shop Guild Benedetto line, including the small sealed-body Benny model.

Benedetto's association with Fender/Guild ended in mid 2006, by which time Fender had also temporarily suspended production of Guild electrics other than the high-end Stuart and Johnny Smith Award models. Fender's stated purpose was that it would refocus on a new line of Guild flat-top acoustic guitars to be issued during the latter part of 2006 and early 2007.

2000
Gulid Starfire IV
reissue

Hagstrom

From their ultra-thin necks to their unique switching configurations, Hagstrom guitars made an occasional splash in western markets, and have even landed in the hands of a few notable professional players, notably grunge and punk artists such as Mark Arm of Mudhoney and Pat Smear of The Germs, Nirvana and Foo Fighters.

Hagstrom of Älvdalen, Sweden, was a major global operator during the guitar boom of the 1960s. It was founded as an accordion importer in 1921 by Albin Hagstrom. Guitar-making began in 1958 with the sparkle-plastic-covered hollowbody De Luxe and Standard models.

These single-cutaway guitars could be played "acoustically," or electrically with modular plug-in assemblies featuring one, two or four single-coil pickups. Their popularity was later boosted when bands like Roxy Music and ABC displayed them in publicity material. (The guitars were imported into the US 1959-61 by Hershman, with the Goya brand.)

In 1962 Hagstrom introduced the Kent-brand line of Strat-influenced solidbodies

1963 Hagstrom Kent PG24G

Body: alder with screwed-on plastic facing; offset double cutaway design.

Neck: bolt-on, maple neck with rosewood fingerboard and distinctively narrow/thin profile; 22 nickel-silver frets; 25 ½" scale length.

Headstock: asymmetrical headstock with six-in-line no-name tuners; black plastic nut and full-width retaining bar.

Bridge: one-piece rosewood bridge with plastic saddle; Hagstrom vibrato system.

Electronics: two single-coil Hagstrom pickups with medium-low output; potentiometer for Volume control; slide switches for individual pickup on/off, preset Tone selections, and Mute.

Sound: bright and light, with a certain graininess when pushed.

featuring vinyl-covered backs and Lucite (plastic) covered fronts. These were sold in the US by Merson as Hagstroms (the Kent name was already in use by Buegeleisen & Jacobson) and in the UK by Selmer as Futurama guitars. The patented Hagstrom vibrato was licensed to Guild and Harmony and appeared on some of their 1960s solidbodies. The asymmetrically shaped two-pickup Impala and three-pickup Corvette (later Condor) with pushbutton controls appeared from 1963-67.

Kents later lost the Lucite, became distinctly more Strat-like, and gained the Hagstrom brand. By 1965, body-horns had become more pointed, hinting more at Gibson's SG, a classic Hagstrom style. The line included 12-string models (Frank Zappa used one) and Viking thinlines. Hagstrom's most popular model, the Les-Paul-like Swede, was offered from 1973-82. Equipped with a synthesizer pickup it was also offered as the Patch 2000 from 1976-79 (see Ampeg). A fancier Super Swede was made from 1978-83.

In 1968 Hagstrom hired New York luthier James D'Aquisto to design an archtop model, the Jimmy, with f-holes or oval soundhole. A number were produced in 1969; supply problems delayed main production until 1976-79. Hagstrom considered Japanese sourcing in the early 1980s, but ceased production in 1983 to concentrate on retailing.

Hamer

Although never as big a company as PRS, Hamer preceded that maker in establishing itself as a quality American electric guitar brand rooted mainly in designs that updated the Gibson set-neck template to the needs of contemporary players. As Such, Hamer became one of the first enduring American manufacturers to successfully establish itself after the

1963
Hagstrom Kent
PB24G

2000 Guild Starfire IV

BODY: semi-acoustic construction with back, sides, and top of laminated maple, with a pressed arch on the top and solid maple center block; top and back binding; double cutaway with 19th fret neck/body joint. Sunburst finish in nitrocellulose lacquer.

NECK: glued-in mahogany neck with bound rosewood fingerboard with 12" fingerboard radius, 22 medium nickel-silver frets, and 1 ¹¹⁄₁₆" nut width; 24 ¾" scale length. (Many earlier models had three-piece maple/rosewood/ maple neck with rosewood finberboard).

HEADSTOCK: symmetrical back-angled headstock, with three-a-side Grover tuners; bone nut.

BRIDGE: adjustable tune-o-matic style bridge and stop-bar tailpiece.

ELECTRONICS: dual Guild humbucking pickups constructed of single alnico bar magnet beneath, six fixed steel slug pole pieces in one coil and six threaded adjustable pole pieces in the other; DC resistance of approximately 6k to 7k; chromed steel cover. Three-way toggle switch to select either pickup alone or both together; four 500k potentiometers for individual Volume and Tone for each pickup. Master volume control on some models.

SOUND: fat, woody, resonant, with decent cutting brightness for humbuckers and a slightly raw edge.

guitar facts

classic makers of the instrument's heyday in the 1950s and '60s.

One of the new-generation American makers of the 1970s, Hamer has survived with an enviable reputation. Established around 1975, Hamer grew out of Northern Prairie Music, a respected repair workshop in Wilmette, Illinois, that included co-founders Paul Hamer and Jol Dantzig.

Hamer and chief ideas-man Dantzig preferred Gibson designs and construction. Their early instruments reflected this with liberal use of mahogany, Gibson scale-length, 22-fret glued-in neck and twin humbuckers. First up was the Standard, strongly Explorer-based but no clone: high-end features included a bound, bookmatched maple top, and pickups from new maker DiMarzio.

The Sunburst of 1977 had the outline of Gibson's late-1950s double-cutaway Les Paul Junior. It became a classic Hamer, sharing the features and deluxe appointments of the Standard and adding Fender-like through-body stringing and a fixed bridge. By 1980 it was joined by the more basic Special model, and in that same year Hamer relocated to larger premises in Arlington Heights, located on the north-west side of Chicago.

The 1981 Prototype was the first with original styling, though far from radical. The odd triple-coil pickup did attract Andy Summers of The Police, however. Multi-string basses became a Hamer specialty, including eight- and 12-string versions. Although Cheap Trick's Rick Nielsen was Hamer's highest-profile fan, his unusual taste in guitars precluded a signature production model, so Hamer's first signature guitar was

1979 Hamer Sunburst

BODY: dual-cutaway body made from solid mahogany back and bookmatched arched maple top; single-ply top binding.

NECK: glued-in mahogany neck with unbound rosewood finberboard; 22 medium nickel-silver frets, 1 $^{11}/_{16}$" nut width and 12" fingerboard radius; 24 ¾" scale length.

HEADSTOCK: back-angled symmetrical headstock, with three-a-side Schaller tuners; headstock-end truss-rod adjustment.

BRIDGE: through-body stringing into fixed bridge base plate with six individual saddles adjustable for both height and intonation; string ball-ends set in individual ferules in back of guitar.

ELECTRONICS: two custom-wound DiMarzio humbucking pickups (of the 'Gibson PAF' format), each with one coil with six steel slug pole pieces and one with six adjustable threaded steel pole pieces; three-way toggle switch for either pickup independently or both together; individual Volume controls and master Tone.

SOUND: warm and rich, but with good cut and definition, as well as excellent sustain.

the Steve Stevens model, launched in 1984.

In 1988 Hamer was acquired by Ovation's manufacturer, Kaman. Paul Hamer had left a year earlier, and it was around this time that significant changes were made to the line. Most Gibson-influenced models disappeared, largely replaced by superstrat designs catering for the new breed of fast-gun guitarists. More unusual were the 36-fret Virtuoso and seven-string Maestro, while the Sustainiac infinite-sustain system was a novel option on the Chaparral.

A stylistic balance returned with the reissued Sunburst in 1989, amid a fashionable revival of guitars with two humbuckers and a fixed bridge. Since then this original Hamer has been reborn several times, including high-end Archtops and cheaper Specials.

The line became further diversified during the 1990s, with Fender derivatives as well as the Korean-made Slammer series, launched in 1993, bringing the US designs to more affordable levels. The Duo Tone was Hamer's hybrid guitar, launched in 1994. In 1998 Hamer revived the 1980s Phantom name but using the shape of the Prototype model. A year later the company issued a suitably deluxe 25th Anniversary model. Also in 1999, the double cutaway Newport became Hamer's first semi-solid model, followed by the single-cutaway Monaco III semi. Artists such as Lyle Workman, Keb' Mo' and David Grissom count themselves among the names on the Hamer roster for the new millennium.

Harmony

While Fender, Gibson, and Gretsch grabbed all the glory, Harmony managed to put guitars in the hands of countless future stars during an era before Asian imports were considered even playable.

Before the guitar boom of the 1960s one of the largest mass-manufacturers of "beginner" and middle-market guitars was the Harmony company of Chicago, founded by German immigrant Wilhelm J.F. Schultz in 1892. By about 1905 the company had

become a large supplier of instruments to the Sears, Roebuck mail-order catalog, with a variety of "parlor" guitars. In 1914 Sears introduced Supertone-brand guitars, virtually all Harmony-made, and purchased Harmony in 1916.

Schultz died in 1925 and was succeeded by Jay Kraus. In 1928 Harmony introduced a line of acoustics endorsed by Roy Smeck. During the Depression of the 1930s, fancier trim was replaced by stenciled designs, typical of cheaper Harmonies through the 1950s. Archtops appeared around 1934, and in 1940 Sears sold Harmony to a group of investors headed by Kraus. Sears changed its brandname to Silvertone, no longer exclusively Harmony-made.

Harmony came relatively late to electric guitars, with an amplified Spanish archtop and Hawaiian lap-steel appearing in 1939. From around 1948 Harmony increasingly applied pickups to full-sized archtops, which they continued through the 1960s. Harmony's first solidbody debuted in 1953, the small copper-finished, Les-Paul-shaped Stratotone with neck and body made from one piece of wood.

The Stratotone line expanded in 1955 with the black Doublet and the yellow or

c1964
Harmony Rocket H59

green Newport, with aluminum and vinyl strips on the sides. In 1955 electric Roy Smeck guitars appeared, a Spanish archtop and a lap-steel. In 1956 Harmony introduced the one-pickup H65, the company's first cutaway archtop.

Harmony thinlines began with the single-cutaway Meteor hollowbodies in 1958. By this time electrics featured DeArmond single-coil pickups and bolt-on necks. Harmony's solid Stratotones were replaced by slightly larger hollow versions: the one-pickup Mercury, two-pickup Jupiter, and one- or two-pickup Mars, differing in finish and trim. Both lines lasted till 1965.

Harmony's famous thin hollowbody single-cutaway Rocket line debuted in 1959, offered through 1967 after which the model became a double-cutaway, lasting to 1973. Other thinline electrics introduced in the early 1960s included the high-end three-pickup double-cutaway H75 (1960) and three models with a Tele-style curve on the upper shoulder: H74 Neo-Cutaway, H66 Vibra Jet with onboard transistorized tremolo (both 1961), and another Roy Smeck, the H73 (1963).

Solidbodies returned in 1963 with Harmony's Silhouette line, shaped roughly like Fender Jaguars and sporting six-tuners-in-line headstocks, one or two pickups and several vibrato options, including a Hagstrom-made unit. These models lasted until 1973.

In 1966 Harmony put a six-tuners-in-line headstock on its H72 double-cutaway thinline and introduced the H79 thinline electric 12-string. In 1968 most of its previous thinlines were supplanted by the Rebel models that featured pointy double-cutaways, six-tuners-in-line heads and sliding volume and tone controls.

Jay Kraus died in 1968 and management passed to a trust. Hit hard by imported competition, Harmony electrics were gone by 1975, the year Harmony purchased Ampeg to handle its distribution. In 1976 Harmony was auctioned off, the name going to the Global company. In the 1980s some imported low-end double-cutaway solidbodies appeared. The brand entered the 1990s with inexpensive beginner guitars, including near-copies of Strats, but many of its formative electrics of the late 1950s and '60s have continued to make stirring music at the hands of creative musicians who have discovered that these budget-minded designs can often produce bold, vibrant and very original tones.

Heritage
Seen by players in the know as the heirs to the Gibson tradition, Heritage remains a respected but undersung American maker.
Established in 1985, Heritage occupies the former Gibson factory in Kalamazoo, Michigan, and the staff includes many ex-employees of that company. Some early guitars displayed Fender tendencies, but predictably enough the most popular Heritage models echo various facets of Gibson design, often using deliberately similar model designations.

The H-535 and H-555 are equal-double-cutaway thinline semi-solids in ES-335- and ES-355-style, while the H-575 is a Gibson ES-175-style single-cutaway archtop electric. Naturally, Les Paul-like solidbodies abound, including the H-150CM, a fancy-fronted limited edition. Other models such as the Prospect Standard semi and the latest Millennium series continue to emphasize this "Gibson alternative."

Hofner
Early Beatles associations never gave Hofner guitars the same boost that they did to models from Rickenbacker and Gretsch, but these solidly built German electrics gave a start to many aspiring British and European rock'n'rollers.
In the late 1950s and early 1960s German-made Hofner guitars served a growing army of young three-chord hopefuls in the UK, although this popularity seems often to have been the result of simple availability rather than inherent quality.

Hofner saw the potential of the fast-growing market for electric guitars before many of its competitors. The company had been founded in the 1880s by Karl Höfner in Schoenbach, Germany, initially producing violins, cellos and double basses. Guitars were first introduced in 1925, by which time sons Josef and Walter had joined their father, and the business had developed into one of the largest in the Schoenbach area. After World War II the Höfner family moved to the Erlangen district, home to many instrument makers in what became West Germany. Hofner production began again in 1949, and two years later the company and its factory was relocated to Bubenreuth.

Archtop acoustic guitars were added to the German line in the early 1950s, and were soon partnered by versions with floating pickups attached. Hofner electric guitars with built-in pickups followed on to the German market in 1954; these thinline, small-bodied, single-cutaway instruments reflected the growing influence of Gibson's Les Paul model. Although without f-holes, the Hofners were actually hollow, and consequently relatively lightweight.

The first Hofner "solids" were launched in Germany in 1956, but in fact these too were more semi-acoustic than solidbody. Also at this time came Hofner's first bass guitar, the 500/1, another small hollowbody. It is better known today by its descriptive nickname, the "Violin" bass, and even more as the "Beatle" bass for its most famous player, Paul McCartney, who played one on-stage throughout his mop-top career.

In 1953 Hofner acoustic archtop guitars were introduced into the UK by the busy importer and distributor Selmer. This London-based company began to offer a selection from Hofner's comprehensive lines, and most models were specifically made or modified to Selmer's requirements. Selmer soon realized the value of the instruments coming from their new German supplier, and chose to ignore the numbered model designations of the instruments they'd commissioned for the British market, instead giving them distinct model names that were more likely to attract British players. Thus Selmer would launch the Golden Hofner, Committee, President, Senator, Club, Verithin, Colorama and Galaxie.

As already noted, Hofner had introduced its first electric guitars with built-in pickups on to the German market in 1954, and these appeared in the UK the following year as the Club 40 and Club 50. These small, single-cutaway six-strings were hollowbodies without f-holes, in a loosely Les Paul style, offered with one pickup (40) or two pickups (50). They were joined in 1958 by the Club 60 which had a bound ebony fingerboard and fancy position markers. The affordable Club line (£28-£50, about $45-$80) quickly became essential to many aspiring beat-groups, including an embryonic Fab Four wherein John Lennon thrashed a battered Club 40.

Selmer's timing with the introduction of Hofners to Britain was perfect. As the 1950s progressed, Britain was beginning to embrace rock'n'roll – but there was a very limited choice of electric guitars available,

---

1958 Hofner Club 50

BODY: single-cutaway semi-solid construction with back and sides of maple, and carved top of solid spruce; three-ply top binding and back binding; 14th fret neck join.

NECK: glued-in five-ply maple and rosewood neck with no truss-rod; unbound rosewood fingerboard with approximately a 10" fingerboard radius, 22 narrow nickel-silver frets; 24 7/16" scale length.

HEADSTOCK: symmetrical back-angled headstock, with three-a-side tuners; zero fret.

Bridge: two-piece rosewood floating bridge adjustable for height, inset with fret wire for string saddles.

ELECTRONICS: two low-gain single-coil Fuma pickups; individual toggle switches for pickup on/off, individual Volume and Tone controls for each pickup.

SOUND: resonant, round and woody, with a fairly bright, crisp edge.

mostly due to a ban on US imports that was in effect from 1951 to 1959. British players welcomed the variety, quality and value offered by the Hofner line, and the brand soon became a leading name in the UK, seen in the hands of famous artists such as Bert Weedon and Tommy Steele.

The electric archtop Committee, which appeared in 1957, was designed in conjunction with an advisory group of six leading UK players: Frank Deniz, Ike Isaacs, Jack Llewellyn, Freddie Phillips, Roy Plummer and Bert Weedon. With an ornate, high-end image, the Committee featured two pickups, a flowery headstock inlay, a harp-style tailpiece, multiple binding all around, and figured maple veneer on the body's sides and back (which also sported a fancy inlaid fleur-de-lis). As with most Hofner hollowbody guitars, finish options were sunburst and natural – or, as Selmer preferred to call them, brunette and blonde.

Slotting into the electric archtop line below the Committee were the more austere two-pickup President and single-pickup Senator, although the general image of the President was improved by triple-dot position markers and the company's six-"finger" Compensator tailpiece.

The Golden Hofner was launched in 1959 and was by far the most luxurious Hofner, going to extremes in size, opulence and price. This top-of-the-line hollowbody electric boasted a hand-carved body, ebony fingerboard, fancy inlay and binding, and gold-plated hardware – including an engraved, shield-shaped tailpiece. The ornate Golden Hofner also bore the Committee-style inlaid fleur-de-lis on the back of the body, and was described with some justification in Hofner advertising as "a masterpiece of guitar perfection."

By the time the Golden Hofner model was launched in 1959 the Hofner catalog had increased considerably, with a wide variety of large-bodied archtops, thinline versions, smaller semis and an assortment of solids. In Britain at the time Selmer offered eight UK-only electric models in addition to the Golden Hofner: the Committee, President, Senator, Club 40, Club 50, Club 60, and Colorama. The single-cutaway Colorama solids had first appeared in the UK in 1958, in one- or two-pickup models. Later versions of the Colorama modified the body shape to twin cutaways (1960) and Fender-like offset cutaways (1963).

Gibson's successful thinline electrics of the period had prompted Hofner to offer slim versions of the existing archtop electric best-sellers. The Verithin model, first introduced in 1960, offered an even thinner cross-section to the body, as well as some notably Gibson-like touches such as a equal-double-cutaway design and a bright cherry-red finish. The stylish approach and keen pricing

---

---

proved very popular, and the Verithin became something of a classic among cost-conscious British beat groups.

As 1950s rock'n'roll gave way to the beat group music of the early 1960s, Hofner maintained a healthy share of the market. Most Hofners targeted beginners and second-time buyers, and while not matching Fender or Gibson for quality, Hofner guitars invariably offered character, impressive visuals and fair performance, and attracted many soon-to-be-famous guitarists in their formative years, including Ritchie Blackmore, Joe Brown, David Gilmour and Roy Wood.

Hofner's second UK solidbody model appeared in 1963, the Strat-inspired Galaxie. It was bedecked with slider switches and roller controls, in keeping with trends at the time. Hofner sales peaked in the UK during the 1960s, but the transition into rock music by the end of the decade saw Hofner's British popularity diminishing as competition increased at all price levels. Hofner seemed reluctant to move with the times, with the ever-stronger Japanese challenge and the 1970s "copy era" increasing the pressure. Ironically, Hofner instruments from the late 1970s to mid 1980s period are of better quality than the earlier guitars, but have attracted far less attention.

Hofner has battled on through the 1980s and 1990s into the 21st century, with sales mainly limited to "Beatle" basses. Undeterred, it introduced new models, some reflecting changing market trends while others recreated former glories. But today, for guitar collectors of a certain age in Britain, it's the UK-only electric archtops that

---

Hofner produced from 1957 to 1965 that are the most desirable, mainly for their image and artist-association – but also, of course, for pure nostalgia.

Ibanez

The Ibanez company has achieved a perspective-shift in the eyes of players like that of few other brands, from "cheapo imports" to quality copies to professional-grade instruments favored by jazz and metal stars alike.

No Japanese guitar manufacturer has had more global impact than Hoshino Gakki Ten, a company best known for its primary brandname, Ibanez. Its guitars are in the hands of some of the world's top players, and for half a century Hoshino has contributed classic designs, efficient instruments for working musicians, and countless players' first guitars.

Hoshino was founded in 1909 in Nagoya, Japan, by Matsujiro Hoshino as a supplier of books and stationery, also retailing musical instruments. The company began importing instruments in 1921. Later in the 1920s, Yoshitaro Hoshino succeeded his father and in 1932 the first acoustic instruments appeared carrying the Ibanez brand. However, the company's buildings were destroyed during World War II, and Hoshino did not resume business until 1950.

Yoshitaro's son Junpei became president in 1960 and opened a new factory called Tama Seisakusho (Tama Industries). By 1964 Hoshino was making and exporting guitars with brandnames such as Ibanez, Star, King's Stone, Jamboree and Goldentone. While it's an oversimplification that ignores the many original creations, one can characterize Ibanez guitars historically in terms of stylistic influences. The 1960s reflected the design influence of Jim Burns of England; the 1970s were heavily dominated by Gibson-style guitars; and the remainder of the century was given primarily to offset-double-cutaway guitars derived from Fender's Stratocaster design.

In the early 1960s Hoshino first reached the US when they sold acoustic guitars to Harry Rosenblum, founder of Elger Guitars and owner of Medley Music in Ardmore, Pennsylvania. Interested in obtaining an American distribution arm, Hoshino purchased a half interest in Elger around 1962. By that time Hoshino still only made acoustic guitars, but was offering a line of solidbody electrics sourced from other Japanese factories such as Fujigen Gakki, Kasuga, Chu Sin Gakki and others. These early Ibanezes were small-body short-scale beginner guitars that came in two basic shapes, similar to a pointy-horned Burns Bison or a Fender Jazzmaster, and fitted with up to four small single-coil pickups.

ibanez

1998 Ibanez JS 10th Anniversary:

BODY: chrome-covered synthetic 'luthite' with slightly scalloped back; double cutaway (standard JS Series models usually have bodies of solid basswood, sometimes covered in a thin aluminum skin that is chromed).

NECK: bolt-on maple neck with rosewood fingerboard; with 9 ½" fingerboard radius, 22 nickel-silver frets, thin 'JS' profile and 1 ¹¹⁄₁₆" nut width; 25 ½" scale length.

HEADSTOCK: asymmetrical headstock with six-inline Schaller tuners; steel locking nut and full string retainer.

BRIDGE: locking Edge Pro vibrato system.

ELECTRONICS: dual DiMarzio custom model humbucking pickups; two 500k potentiometers for master Volume and Tone controls; standard three-way switching.

SOUND: hot and lithe, with a firm emphasis on performance through high-gain amplification. Prone to good sustain and easy harmonic feedback.

guitar facts

c1963
Ibanez Model 882

distributor Summerfield Brothers, and Jason-brand guitars in Australia. Technical advice from Maurice Summerfield in the UK and Jeff Hasselberger in the US made Ibanez copies even better, with necks lowered into the body and squared-off fingerboard ends.

By 1974, the Ibanez line had exploded with both bolt-on-neck and set-neck variations on Gibson designs, including instruments in the style of the SG (including double-necks), Flying V (called the Rocket Roll), Firebird, Les Paul, Explorer (the Destroyer), Moderne, ES-345 and ES-175, plus a full complement of Fender copies. A number of these were marketed in the UK with the Antoria brand.

No sooner had these full-blown copies arrived than Hoshino began to innovate. In 1974 Ibanez introduced maple fingerboards on Les Paul and thinline copies, plus a rosewood-capped "Les Paul" with elaborate fingerboard inlays – before Gibson adopted such features. Ibanez had introduced original designs by 1974 (which, combined later, would yield its most popular and respected 1970s model, the Artist).

The 1974 models included four "Artist" electrics, two double-cutaway thinlines and two solidbodies, with fatter horns than the later Artist, but with bolt-on necks with the "castle" headstock shape associated with the later-style Artist. Another solidbody debuted at this time, bearing two small sharply-pointed cutaways, but with an early version of the later Artist's glued-in heel-less neck joint.

Company literature dates the appearance of the carved-top, equal-double-cutaway Ibanez Artist to 1975,

though it was not advertised until the following year. The new Artist's fast, heel-less, glued-in neck and twin humbuckers competed with Yamaha's similar SG-2000. The Artist models would proliferate, to include versions with active onboard EQ and various switching and appointment options through 1982. The two players most associated with the Artist were John Scofield and Steve Miller. The Artist solidbody line was revived in 1997, but not before the model name had seen more use.

In 1975 a number of Ibanez guitars appeared which are now considered some of the most collectable. They included the Custom Agent (a Les Paul-alike with a Gibson F-5 mandolin-style head and pearl belly inlays), the Artwood Nouveau (Strat-style with a dragon-carved body) and the Artwood Twin (a copy of the Rex Bogue double-neck played by John McLaughlin).

These special guitars led to a variety of Les-Paul-style single-cutaway and Artist-style double-cutaway carved ash models that had various features, including "tree-of-life" inlays. Most were produced in limited runs and called Artist and/or Professional models, although common names had little to do

Around 1964 Hoshino revised the Burns-style with a closer interpretation, including three-part pickguards, and replaced the little Jazzmaster-shaped body with one slightly more Strat-like. But throughout most of the 1960s Hoshino's principal focus was on acoustic guitars.

Hoshino's serious interest in electric guitars strengthened after Shiro Arai of Aria encountered the newly-reissued Gibson Les Paul Custom – effectively Gibson's own "copy" of the original – at a US trade show in 1968. Arai took back to Japan the notion of making Les Paul copies, launching what would become the "copy era."

By 1969, bolt-neck Ibanez "Les Pauls" had joined those of other Japanese manufacturers, followed around 1971 by an Ibanez version of the Ampeg Dan Armstrong "see-through" Lucite guitar.

Around this time other Japanese manufacturers began to produce full lines of Fender, Gibson and Martin copies, increasingly closer to the originals, as did Hoshino by 1973. It was during the early 1970s that Hoshino began selling Ibanez- and CSL-brand guitars in the UK through

1981
Ibanez Artist 2618

1981 Ibanez Artist 2618

BODY: solid mahogany body with carved maple top; dual-cutaway body with concentric horns; top binding; polyurethane finish.

NECK: three-ply maple neck (birch on some models) with bound rosewood fingerboard; 22 nickel-silver frets, 1 11/16" nut width and 12" fingerboard radius; 24 ¾" scale length.

HEADSTOCK: back-angled symmetrical headstock, with three-a-side Velve-Tune Ibanez tuners; headstock-end truss-rod adjustment.

BRIDGE: Ibanez Gibralter bridge (adjustable tune-o-matic derivative); Quick Change tailpiece with plate.

ELECTRONICS: two humbucking Super 70 pickups with no covers, alnico magnets (possibly alnico VIII) and adjustable pole pieces; three-way toggle switch for either pickup independently or both together; individual Volume and Tone controls.

SOUND: this Artist model, which is similar to the later AR100 series, is obviously very LP-ish – fat, full and ringing, but with decent cut and excellent sustain.

with consistency of features and design. Musicians playing these guitars included Randy Scruggs, Carl Perkins and Bob Weir.

An original Ibanez model, the Iceman, debuted In 1976. It was popularized when a custom-made model faced with broken mirror parts was played by Paul Stanley. The Iceman featured a medallion-like body shape with a point on the end and a large, Mosrite-style extended lower-cutaway horn. It was offered in both set-neck and bolt-on-neck versions.

It was at this time that original US distributor Harry Rosenblum sold his interest in Elger to Hoshino, although Hoshino's American subsidiary did not change its name to Hoshino USA until 1981. The strategy of copying US classics was very successful for everyone marketing Japanese guitars in the 1970s, especially Hoshino, and the American companies being copied became increasingly alarmed at the erosion of their market share. In 1977 Norlin, the parent company of Gibson, filed a federal lawsuit against Elger. It claimed trademark infringement based on the copying of Gibson's headstock design – even though Ibanez had changed to a more Guild-like shape the previous year. It's from this action that copy guitars are sometimes nicknamed "lawsuit" instruments. The suit was settled out of court and, in the US at least, this particular "copy era" ended.

Ibanez's move away from copies was dramatic. First to appear in 1978 was the Performer series, basically set-neck or bolt-on-neck Les-Paul-style guitars with an extra Tele-style curve on the upper shoulder, plus that Guild-style headstock. These were followed by the Concert series, which combined more of a Strat-style offset-double-cutaway body with the carved top of a Les Paul.

Ibanez quickly settled on the Studio and Musician series, both with rounded slightly-offset double-cutaways with short, pointed horns clearly taking their cue from the designs of Alembic. The Musicians were through-neck guitars with figured ash or walnut wings and, on the top models, onboard active pre-amps and equalization, again Alembic-like.

In 1978 Ibanez began what became a long tradition of artist-endorsed models, introducing the Artist Autograph line including versions of the ash-bodied Professional, now renamed the Bob Weir, a limited edition Iceman called the Paul Stanley, and two new fancy twin-humbucker single-cutaway archtops named for jazz sensation George Benson, the full-sized GB-20 and the narrower GB-10. The Weir and Iceman models did not make it into the 1980s, but the Benson models, including several variations, would remain Ibanez's flagship archtops.

A sign of Ibanez's shift from Gibson-like designs to Fender styles was the introduction in 1979 of the Roadster. This Strat-style guitar had a bolt-on-neck, non-vibrato bridge and three single-coils. It came with either ash or mahogany bodies, and flamed-maple tops peering through semi-opaque finishes. A year later Ibanez helped start the Dyna factory in Japan to produce Fender-style guitars and introduced the new Strat-style oil-finished Blazer, soon altered to feature slightly "hooked" body-horns. The Blazer caught on and set the pattern for the upcoming Roadstar II series.

Ibanez reintroduced in 1981 a version of their Explorer-style guitar, the Destroyer II, with a rather more stylized, pointy body shape. Some models sported fancy tops. Two more endorsement guitars appeared, the LR10 Lee Ritenour Model, an equal-double-cutaway thinline semi-hollowbody in ES-335-style, and a full-size single-cutaway archtop hollowbody, the JP20 Joe Pass Model. In 1982 Ibanez revived its Flying V-style model as the Rocket Roll II, along with the Iceman II, some with flamed-maple tops.

In 1982 the Blazers were replaced by what would become the enormously successful Roadstar II series, hitting the market as both Strat-style guitars and heavy metal pyrotechnics enjoyed a popular revival. By 1983 Roadstar IIs ranged from the ash-bodied RS-100, a three-single-coil descendent of the Roadster, to the RS-1000 with carved birdseye-maple top, and two through-neck models with twin humbuckers or three single-coils. Locking vibrato systems appeared in 1984, as did the company's first model with a humbucker/single-coil/single-coil pickup layout, the RS-440.

Steve Lukather endorsed a Roadstar, 1985's basswood-and-maple RS-1010SL, which had two special humbuckers and a Pro Rocker locking vibrato system. Jazz-fusion legend Allan Holdsworth helped design his own Roadstar: the twin-humbucker AH10 and AH20 appeared in 1985-86. The Roadstar II shape continued through 1986, although at the end the prefix changed to RG – confusing because subsequent RGs had different styling. The birdseye models were gone, but the hardtail RG-600 still sported a bound flamed-maple

top as well as low-impedance active pickups.

The V-shaped Rocket Roll was rolled into a new X series of heavy-metal-style guitars in 1983. These included a new Destroyer, combining the V and Explorer shapes into a model similar to a Dean ML, and the dramatic stretched-x-shape X-500.

Ibanez launched a brief foray into synth-access guitars in 1985-86 with the IMG-2010 guitar ("controller") that had a space-age minimalist shape. It featured a clever electronic vibrato system that reproduced the analog effect without tracking problems.

The move away from the Roadstar II era began in 1985 as Ibanez introduced the Pro-Line, with Roadstar styling but superstrat features. The guitars had the now ubiquitous superstrat features – humbucker/single-coil/single-coil pickup layouts and locking vibrato systems – plus a row of small pushbuttons for presetting pickup settings.

Also debuting in 1985 was the RG series, distinct from the renamed Roadstar-style RGs by virtue of a more modern superstrat design with deep, pointed double cutaways. These guitars came in a wide array of pickup and trim configurations, in vibrato or stop-tail versions, with or without pickguards, and some with flamed-maple tops. They had a remarkable run and anchored the Ibanez solidbody line right through the 1990s. The RG7620 (vibrato) and RG7621 (fixed bridge) seven-strings catered to the late-1990s rage for the extra low-tuned string, with the cheaper 7420 and 7421 models following in 2000.

Four new guitars appeared in 1987 – three basic bolt-on-neck Pro-Line models and the shortlived, more radical looking Maxxas line. The Pro-Lines included the Pro-540R Radius, a pointy-horned offset-double-cutaway with a wedge-shape cross-section, quickly adopted by solo virtuoso Joe Satriani, and the Pro-540S Saber of similar shape but with a wafer-thin contoured body. Both would achieve considerable success in the 1990s.

Ibanez's involvement with endorsers had accelerated and expanded during the 1980s. By the end of the decade the redesigned Pro-Line Power model was endorsed by fusion ace Frank Gambale, and the JEM77 appeared in 1988, designed in conjunction with former Frank Zappa guitarist Steve Vai. It had deeply offset, sharp double-cutaways, vine inlays, humbucker/single-coil/humbucker pickups, locking vibrato system, floral pattern finish and a "monkey grip" cut-out body handle. A number of colorful versions, some with aluminum pickguards, subsequently appeared. A 10th Anniversary JEM with engraved metal pickguard and fancy trim would appear in 1998.

Ibanez faced a dilemma common to other Japanese makers in the late 1980s.

Successful marketing had made Ibanez one of the largest guitar producers in the world, but inherent costs and currency exchange rates made it increasingly hard to market guitars manufactured in Japan at the lower price points customers had come to expect. In order to continue offering high-end options, in 1988 Ibanez opened a US custom shop operation in Los Angeles, California. At first the shop dealt with custom graphics, but by 1989 introduced the American Master Series, high-end neck-through-body versions of regular models, including the basswood MA2HSH and maple-topped-mahogany MA3HH, which lasted to 1991.

In 1990 the US shop began making the Exotic Wood series with fancy, unusual timbers. Two years later the USA Custom Graphic series appeared with colorful imaginary painted landscapes. Custom models can feature highly figured woods and extremely elaborate PRS-style multicolor inlays. By 1994 Ibanez had moved its American production to the PBS factory in Pennsylvania operated by innovative luthier Dave Bunker. This lasted until about 1997, when PBS folded. Ibanez began producing the low-cost bolt-on-neck EX series in Korea from 1989-94. These deep, sharp double-cutaway superstrats reflected the RG series, the better models with bound fingerboards and triangular inlays.

At the start of the 1990s Ibanez introduced a new Artist series of set-neck double-cutaway electrics, twin-humbucker guitars only vaguely reminiscent of the old Artists. They included the semi-hollow f-hole AM200, the all-mahogany solidbody AR200, and maple-capped AR300, all lasting until mid-decade.

In 1990 Ibanez began to shuffle its Japanese solidbody lines. The wedge-cross-section Radius was endorsed by Satriani and transformed into the JS Joe Satriani Signature series, a variety of twin-humbucker models in finishes ranging from oiled mahogany to custom graphics. In 1998 came the JS 10th Anniversary Chrome Limited Edition, made of synthetic "luthite" material and finished in chrome. Ibanez's relationship with Steve Vai yielded the seven-string Universe series in 1990, essentially a JEM without the "monkey grip" handle. By 1992 the UV77 was available with pyramid inlays and swirled, multi-colored "bowling ball" finishes.

Yet more changes occurred in 1991. The thin-bodied Saber guitars were renamed the S-series, adding a seven-string model and proliferating as the decade progressed. By 1997 variants included the S Classic SC620 with a bound, flamed-maple top, and the S Prestige S2540 NT made of figured sapelle mahogany. Frank Gambale got his own Signature FGM series in 1991, a version of

the thin Saber with humbucker/single-coil/humbucker pickups, locking vibrato system and "sharktooth" inlays. In 1994 the Gambale line split into vibrato and stop-tail models, and three years later these were replaced by the FGM400, an high-end version with a quilted maple top and block inlays that lasted until 1998.

Reb Beach helped design the Voyager, offered from 1991 to 1996. Behind the vibrato was a wide, wedge-shaped cutout designed to make extreme double-action vibrato work easier. The RBM1 had a maple neck; the RBM2 had a koa top and Bolivian rosewood neck. These were replaced in 1994 by the mahogany-bodied RBM10 and oil-finish RBM400, available through 1996.

Ibanez's respected Benson electric archtops were joined by the Artstar series, beginning with the AF2000 in 1991. These were conceptually related to the late-1980s Artist line, with full-size hollow bodies and a single rounded cutaway, twin humbuckers, a headstock shaped somewhat like the old Artist "castle," and a trapeze tailpiece. A new Artstar AS200 semi-hollowbody thinline also debuted in 1991, with a larger body than the contemporary Artist AM200. These too would continue to be available in various versions through the following decade.

While the Radius guitars had earlier been transformed into the Satriani Signatures, their success inspired the less expensive R series in 1992. These lasted only a year, except for the R540 LTD which, with its humbucker/single-coil/humbucker pickups and sharktooth inlays, lasted to 1996.

By the early 1990s guitar manufacturers with any longevity had begun to realize that they were not only competing with other makers, but with their own "vintage" models which were increasingly prized by players and collectors alike. This resulted in two trends: the introduction of "retro" guitars with pseudo-1960s styling; and the reissuing of the company's own vintage classics. For Ibanez this was reflected in 1994 with the retro Talman series and the reissue of its radical Iceman guitars.

The Talman had an offset cutaway shape, like a lumpy Jazzmaster. The initial line was made in Japan and featured synthetic Resoncast (MDF) bodies. Some had Sky "lipstick" single-coil pickups and photogravure pseudo-figured-maple on bodies and necks.

In 1995 Ibanez expanded the Talman line to include models with pearloid pickguards, metallic finishes and retro-looking fulcrum vibratos. In 1996 Talman production was shifted to Korea where the line changed to wood-body construction. They were gone by 1999.

The 1994 Iceman series included two bolt-on-neck reissues, the IC300 with a bound body and fingerboard, the IC500 with

fancier pearloid binding. The Iceman was quickly adopted by guitarist J of White Zombie. In 1995 Ibanez added the limited-edition Paul Stanley PS10LTD, with a carved maple top and set-neck, and the general-production PS10II. In 1996 the Paul Stanley PS10CL replaced the IC500, and a year later the glued-neck ICJ100 WZ with abalone binding supplanted the Paul-Stanley-endorsed models.

The Ghostrider was new in 1994. An equal-double-cutaway solidbody with a bound top, two humbuckers and three-tuners-a-side headstock, it provided an early-to-mid-1980s feel with a late-1950s name, and lasted two years. While pointy-double-cutaway superstrats were still the principal fare for Ibanez, the retro vibe brought back traditional Strat-shaped guitars in 1994 with the RX series. These ranged from the RX750 with a padauk/mahogany/padauk sandwich body and the RX650 with a figured-maple top, to models with Strat-style pickguards – all in various pickup configurations. The RX series continued through 1998 when it was renamed the GRX series and downsized. In

Ibanez Lo-Pro vibrato

1999 the series was augmented with a beginner-level equal-double-cutaway, the twin-humbucker GAX70.

Ibanez added yet another pro endorsement in 1994 with the Paul Gilbert series. The first guitar was the PGM500, basically a deep-cutaway RG with a reverse headstock, humbucker/single-coil/humbucker pickup layout and fixed bridge assembly. The most distinctive decorative feature was white finish with painted-on black f-holes. This was available for two years.

The first Gilbert model was joined by the PGM30 in 1995, the same guitar except for the addition of a double-locking vibrato system. This guitar would become the principal Gilbert model. In 1998 the Gilbert line was briefly enhanced for about a year by Ibanez with the transparent red PGM900 PMTC, essentially a Talman with twin humbuckers, stop tailpiece and the distinctive fake f-holes.

Another celebrity series was introduced in 1996, endorsed by jazz guitarist Pat

Metheny, a long-time Ibanez player. The first model was the fancy PM100, a uniquely shaped offset-double-cutaway f-hole hollowbody archtop with a small pointed cutaway on the bass side and a deeper, pointed cutaway on the treble side. It was joined in 1997 by the PM20, a more traditional single-rounded-cutaway archtop with a rosewood fingerboard and ivoroid trim, still with one neck humbucker.

In 1997 Ibanez brought back the Blazer, its Fender-influenced double-cutaway of 1980. The new Blazers revived the "hooked-horn" body, "blade" headstock, pearloid pickguard and a humbucker/single-coil/humbucker pickup arrangement. The BL1025 featured a Wilkinson vibrato; the BL850 had a Gotoh unit. These late-era Blazers were available until 1999.

The last new endorsement of the 1990s came from another long-time Ibanez player, John Petrucci. The JPM100 of 1998 was another pointy deep-double-cutaway guitar with the RG profile, but finished in a camouflage pattern.

At the start of the 21st century the Ibanez line looked much as it had for more than a decade. Solidbodies were represented by the pointy RG guitars and their many six- and seven-string variations, the Satriani versions of the old wedge-section Radius, the thin S series Sabers, and the Strat-style GRX series, plus the reissued Iceman and Artist models. Semi-hollowbody thinlines included the Artstar series, and hollowbody "jazz" electrics included the venerable George Benson and more recent Pat Metheny.

Signaling future directions, a new feature for 2000 was the Double Edge Bridge, a locking vibrato with built-in L.R. Baggs piezo pickups for a switchable "acoustic" sound. A Millennium series of high-price limited editions included a clear plastic Satriani, a swirly-painted Vai Jem and a George Benson Masquerade. Meanwhile, new signature models such as the Mike Mushok MMM1 Baritone, Andy Timmons AT300, and Noodles NDM1 indicate that Ibanez continues to value its endorsee program.

Jackson

This California maker helped to set the trend for high-performance instruments designed specifically to suit the changing needs of heavy rock players, who previously often had to modify existing models to get the sound and performance they needed from a guitar.

Grover Jackson's brand came to symbolize the "superstrat" rock guitar of the 1980s. His update of Fender's classic Stratocaster design offered more frets, deeper cutaways, a drooped "pointy" headstock, altered pickup layouts and a high-performance

vibrato system. He attracted many of the emerging fast-gun players such as Randy Rhoads, George Lynch and Vivian Campbell, as well as more mainstream guitarists like Jeff Beck, Gary Moore and Frank Stepanek.

Guitarist Jackson liked to tinker with guitars, and joined Wayne Charvel's guitar-parts supply operation in San Dimas, California, in September 1977. The company had financial problems, and in November 1978 Jackson bought the outfit for $40,000. Initially it was business as usual for the small workshop and its three-strong staff, producing necks, bodies and other components as well as repairing and modifying instruments. Charvel-brand bolt-on-neck instruments debuted in 1979 (see Charvel).

In late 1980 Jackson met 24-year-old up-and-coming guitarist Randy Rhoads. Together they designed a custom guitar based on a Gibson Flying V. In 1981 they collaborated again on a more radical variant of the original design with an offset body style. For these clear departures from the Charvels, Jackson began to use his own name as a brand. The operation's two brands remained distinct until early 1986: Charvels mostly Fender-style, with bolt-on-neck; Jacksons more original, with through-neck construction. Both made a feature of flashy graphics and custom paint-jobs.

With the tragic death of Rhoads in 1982 and the subsequent interest in his unusual Jacksons, the value of player-association was underlined. So, early in 1983 the first Jackson-brand production model appeared, the Randy Rhoads.

More exaggerated-shape custom designs were built for players such as Australian band Heaven's guitarist Kelly (a curved Explorer-style design) and Dave Linsk of Overkill (a Flying V-like "Double Rhoads"). At first, Jackson reserved his own brandname for these custom instruments built to various designs for individual musicians. Gradually favorites emerged, and all Jackson's significant body styles, later given model names, were developed at San Dimas between 1983 and 1986: Randy Rhoads (offset V, from 1983); Kelly ("curved" Explorer-style, from 1984); Soloist (superstrat, from 1984); Double Rhoads and later King V (Flying V-style, from 1985). More or less from the start, these were offered with two levels of trim – Student (rosewood fingerboard, dot markers, unbound neck/headstock) and Custom (ebony fingerboard, "sharkfin" markers, bound neck/headstock) – though variations existed.

Jackson gradually developed and modified the original Strat-style guitars he'd made with the Charvel brandname, at first as the blatantly-named Strat Body, but more importantly as the Jackson Soloist. From about 1984 the Soloist came to define what

we now know as the superstrat, the most influential electric guitar design of the 1980s. With input from players regularly shaping the changing design, Jackson built on the classic Strat-style guitar, squaring the body's sides while making the contouring bolder and overall shape slimmer, and "stretching" the horns.

While his early superstrat-inclined guitars continued with 22 frets, Jackson began to capitalize on the extra upper-fret access provided by his through-neck and deeper cutaways by increasing the number of frets to 24, giving players a wider range. The revamped body carried powerful combinations of single-coil and humbucker pickups, evolving to the "standard" superstrat combination of two single-coils plus bridge humbucker, partnered by a locking heavy-duty vibrato system. Jackson also instigated the drooped "pointy" headstock. So was the superstrat born: a new tool for high-speed, high-gain guitarists, able to meet, match and foster their athletic excesses.

The Charvel logo was transferred to a Japan-built line in 1986, with the Jackson brand retained for the high-end US-made line. By 1987 production of the US Jacksons switched to a large new facility at Ontario, California. By late 1987 the King V was a production model. Two years on, the Strat Body's name was changed to the less

1984
Jackson Double Rhoads
Custom

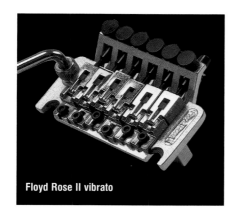

Floyd Rose II vibrato

contentious Vintage Style, while the line expanded to include the Dinky, a Soloist-style bolt-on-neck variation of the Strat Body. Also new was the strange Phil Collen six-string, its radically carved and contoured body far removed from the established idea of a rock guitar. A more affordable Collen model, the PC3, appeared in 2000.

In 1985 Jackson himself had started a joint venture with Texas-based instrument distributor IMC, and left the company in 1989. He later designed instruments for Washburn and others. Subsequently three different Jackson lines emerged: Custom Shop; US series; and Jackson Professional.

The Custom Shop editions were US-made special pieces at prices too rarefied for most mortals to even consider. The limited-production US series models each came with the option of ten different hand-painted airbrush graphic finishes. The Japanese-made Jackson Professional line was intended to bring Jackson to a wider market with high-quality versions of the American originals. These included the unusual Phil Collen model, along with the new Fusion Pro and ultra-pointy Warrior Pro. Prices were relatively elevated for Japanese factory-built instruments.

Despite such price variety, the choice of models remained limited, although the company wasn't slow to pick up and exploit changing trends. As part of the 1992 Professional series, the PRS-style Infinity model insisted on retaining pointy headstock and heavy-duty vibrato. The retro-influenced JIX appeared in 1993, as did the Kelly Standard version of a Custom Shop line. High-end limited editions and variations on continuing themes appeared through the 1990s. In 2000 a seven-string Rhoads, the Pro RR7R, was offered.

Jackson has concentrated on established strengths, while continuing to expand into lower-price markets. The Concept series launched in 1993 featured relatively affordable Japanese-built versions of the best-known Jackson designs, while the Performer line of 1994 was manufactured in Korea to attain even cheaper prices. By 2000 the X Series was made in India.

The acquistion of Jackson by the Japanese electronic musical instrument company Akai in 1997 saw the demise of sister-brand Charvel. But the Charvel Surfcaster survived as a Jackson production model, introduced the following year (it had begun earlier as a Jackson custom-shop guitar). Jackson continues to refine its body shapes, for example in 2000 melding the Kelly and Rhoads styles for the Kelly Star KS2.

Kay

It might be difficult for younger players today to appreciate the significance of Kay in the 1950s, 1960s, and early '70s. But for players starting out on the instrument at that time, Kay was an omnipresent brand, provider of both entry level guitars and some models aimed at the needs of the professional .

Of the huge Chicago-based guitar powerhouses, only Kay approached the size and influence of Harmony on the lower to middle ranges of the mass market. Kay was founded in 1890 as the Groehsl Company, a mandolin manufacturer, adding guitars and banjos around 1918.

In 1921 the company name was changed to Stromberg-Voisinet and two years later Henry Kay "Hank" Kuhrmeyer joined the company. The guitars were called Strombergs, and the company was known as Voisinet (distinguishing it from the Boston company making Stromberg-brand archtop acoustics). By the mid 1920s Voisinet was supplying some of mail-order company Montgomery Ward's fancier instruments, often using pearloid, a popular Kay material. Voisinet (Kay) also supplied many guitars for the Spiegel catalog and other distributors, including Continental, Chicago Musical Instruments (CMI) and Oahu.

In 1928 Voisinet introduced some very early production "electric" guitars, the Stromberg Electros. These were in effect acoustic instruments with a transducer that picked up vibrations of the body's top (not the strings). They came with a primitive amplifier. The Electro models were greeted with some enthusiasm, especially among Chicago's hillbilly radio performers, but very few were in fact made – and they soon disappeared with the Depression.

Stromberg-brand instruments, often with a decal decoration, continued to be sold until around 1932. In 1931 Kuhrmeyer became president and the KayKraft brand debuted on both regular Spanish and distinctive two-point Venetian guitars. Through the 1930s the line was anchored by KayKrafts, cheaper Arch Krafts, and small-bodied guitars often of plywood. By 1934 the company was known as the Kay Musical Instrument Company. The Kay brand began to appear around 1936.

Kay resumed making electrics in 1936 with a pickup-equipped flat-top for Ward's. Unique violin-shaped guitars were made in 1938, and in 1939 the high-end Television archtop appeared. Kay also made a few guitar models for National and Gretsch during the 1930s. In 1940 Sears' new Silvertone brandname was first applied to a Kay-made archtop.

More serious involvement with electric guitars began in 1947 when Kay began putting pickups on its archtops, which continued through the 1960s. In 1952 Kay introduced its first cutaway archtop, the K-1. That year also saw the Thin Twin, a flat-topped single-cutaway semi-hollowbody with two pickups, known popularly as the Jimmy Reed for his use of the model. Kay's first solidbody, the K-125, a small Les-Paul-shaped guitar, also debuted that year. The similar one-pickup K-136 and two-pickup K-142 replaced the K-125 from 1955-57, while a more exaggerated version called the Sizzler was offered between 1956-58. The bizarre and shortlived "map of Ohio" Solo King appeared in 1960.

c1958
Kay Barney Kessel
semi-solid Pro

In 1955 Kuhrmeyer retired and was succeeded by Sidney M. Katz. In 1956 Kay picked up its first professional endorsement when jazz guitarist Barney Kessel put his name on three better-grade electric archtops, the Jazz Special, Artist and Pro, part of the Gold K line with plastic-covered "Kleenex box" pickups and elaborate extruded-plastic headstock facings (known among collectors as "Kelvinators" because of their resemblance to the Sears appliance logo). Kessel's name was dropped in 1960, but the guitars continued with abridged headstock designs. Other popular electrics of the time included the mid-size Upbeat and thinline single-cutaway Swing Master.

In 1960 the hollowbody Les-Paul-shaped thinline Value Leader, Style Leader and Pro arrived in various finishes and pickup configurations, with metal "Art Deco" pickguards. Versions without the metal were offered by St. Louis Music with the Custom Kraft brandname. From this point Kay increasingly employed bolt-on necks on most electrics.

The Vanguard line of solidbodies followed in 1961. These had slab bodies shaped something like a Fender Jazzmaster. A more attractive solidbody was introduced the following year, the Strat-style K-300. Three new electric thinline hollowbodies also joined the Kay line in 1961: the pointy single-cutaway Speed Demon and Galaxie, and double-cutaway Jazz II. In 1965 the Vanguards were redesigned with a "German carve." Kay's six-tuners-in-line "bushwhacker" headstock also debuted in 1965.

In 1964 Kay relocated to a huge ultra-efficient factory in suburban Elk Grove Village, Illinois. Three more solidbodies were introduced in 1965 – the Artiste, Apollo and Titan I – with the new bushwhacker head, short cutaways, heavy contouring, and a shape that seemed like a cross between a Strat and a Jazzmaster.

In 1966 Kay was purchased by Louis J. Nicastro's Seeburg Corporation, best known for its juke boxes. Katz remained in control of the new musical instrument division. Most

of the guitars from the early 1960s were eliminated, but the frumpy early Vanguards became the budget Value Leader line. The mid-1960s models expanded. The somewhat high-end K400 Series Professional solidbodies were introduced, with equal cutaways similar to a Gibson SG and a tapered lower bout like a Strat. The Speed Demon name was also applied to a couple more similarly-shaped solidbodies at this time.

Seeburg's tenure as a guitar-maker was brief. In 1967 Kay changed hands again, purchased by long-time competitor Valco (formerly National and National-Dobro), headed by Robert Engelhardt who was keen to obtain the new manufacturing capacity. The Kay line remained unaffected, though a number of hybrid Supro-brand guitars including the solidbody Lexington began sporting Kay components and Japanese-made parts. The Valco-Kay marriage was also shortlived. In 1968 the market for electric guitars collapsed. Valco-Kay declared bankruptcy and closed its doors.

During 1969 Valco-Kay's assets were auctioned off and rights to the Kay name passed to Sol Weindling and Barry Hornstein of WMI, importer to the US of Teisco Del Rey guitars from Japan. In the early 1970s both the Teisco Del Ray and Kay brands appeared on Teisco-made instruments, but by about 1973 WMI was using only the Kay brand. The bolt-neck K-20T Gibson SG "copy" appeared that year, and most 1970s Kay guitars were low-end copies of popular American models.

In 1980 the Kay name was sold to Tony Blair of AR Musical Enterprises of Indianapolis, Indiana. From that point on the Kay name was used on guitars for the beginner market, with production continually migrating to developing countries in order to maintain the low price point.

Kramer

From modernistic aluminum-necked creations to high-powered superstrats, Kramer followed original and occasionally radical lines that helped it become, for a time, a major force in the guitar market.

Kramer began in the late 1970s as part of the movement to improve guitar technology with aluminum necks, but before its demise at the end of the 1980s it had become one of the largest guitar-making companies in the United States.

Kramer guitars were made by the BKL Corporation founded in 1976 in Neptune City, New Jersey, by former Travis Bean associate Gary Kramer, music retailer Dennis Berardi and ex-Norlin executive Peter LaPlaca. Financial backing came from real-estate developer Henry Vaccaro. Kramer himself left the company shortly after it began.

The first Kramers (450G, 350G) were designed in conjunction with luthier Phil Petillo and featured fancy hardwood bodies with slightly offset double-cutaways and bolt-on "T-bar" aluminum necks with wood inserts in the back, synthetic ebonol fingerboards and "tuning fork"-shape headstocks. Kramer switched from its own to DiMarzio pickups with the DMZ series beginning in 1978. In 1980 Kramer briefly launched a series of exotic shapes, including the B.C.-Rich-inspired XL series, the V-shaped XKG models, and the legendary battle-axe-shaped Gene Simmons Axe.

In 1979 Kramer ran into financial problems and until 1982 management was assumed by Guitar Center of Los Angeles. They recommended a switch to more economical wooden necks, and these were introduced as an option in 1981. This was another big year for Kramer, seeing the introduction of the popular minimalist aluminum-necked headless Duke (similar to a Steinberger), the pointy Voyager series (similar to Dean's ML) and the first series of Strat-style Pacers and high-end Stagemasters. German Rockinger vibratos also began to be offered that year. Aluminum necks began to lose popularity in the early 1980s and the last few were produced in 1985.

In 1982 Kramer began a long-time association with locking-vibrato innovator Floyd Rose, becoming the exclusive distributor while introducing the asymmetrical pointy Floyd Rose Signature model. The link with Rose brought Edward Van Halen into the Kramer camp, the brand's most important endorser who further boosted Kramer's success. In 1983 the Pacer series was slimmed down, with the Deluxe model becoming one of the first guitars to feature the "superstrat" pickup configuration of humbucker/single-coil/single-coil which along with Strat-based shapes and drooped "pointy" headstocks would dominate the rest of the 1980s.

In 1984 the popular single-slanted-humbucker Baretta with "banana" headstock debuted. That year Kramer also introduced the Ripley Stereo, with electronics by luthier Steve Ripley that had individual volume and stereo fader controls for each string. In 1985 a revised Voyager, the Vanguard (reminiscent of the Jackson Randy Rhoads) and the Explorer-like Condor appeared. A sign of Kramer's growing muscle were 1985 endorsers Ed Ojeda, Brad Gillis, Neal Schon, Jeff Golub and John McCarry. Also that year Kramer purchased Spector Guitars & Basses, designed by Stuart Spector and Alan Charney and available in American- and Japanese-made versions.

Along with other major US guitar companies, Kramer began importing its own budget versions of its main guitars, starting

with the Japanese-made Focus line in 1984, followed by the Korean-made Striker series in 1985 and Korean Aero-Stars in 1986. Kramer's strangest models, the spaceship-shaped Enterprize and Triaxe, appeared in 1986 only. That year also saw the limited-edition through-neck Paul Dean Signature. By the end of 1986 Kramer was the largest American guitar company.

By 1987 Kramer's golden age of superstrats had begun, with revamped Pacers, Baretta and luxurious carved-top, through-neck Stagemasters, plus a host of other models. Elliot Easton joined the ranks with the EE Pro guitars, Vivian Campbell began endorsing the NightSwan models, and in 1988 Richie Sambora got his own model. The Kramer Sustainer with the Floyd Rose distortion-generating pickup also appeared in 1988.

By this time Dennis Berardi had started a management company that handled Russian band Gorky Park, and Kramer introduced a Korean-made balalaika-shaped Gorky Park model in 1989.

Following the introduction in 1989 of the Metalist and Showster lines that used some metal parts to improve sustain, the Kramer empire suddenly collapsed in bankruptcy. New management under James Liati took over but by late 1990 Kramer was gone. In 1995 Henry Vaccaro intended a revival, but in 1997 the rights to the Kramer name and most model designations were sold to Gibson.

Magnatone

Magnatone offered well-made electric guitars in the 1950s that were intended to rival the best solidbodies from Fender and Gibson, but the brand never gained a foothold and descended to offering beginner models before vanishing entirely.
Best known for amplifiers that propelled Buddy Holly's glassy rhythms and Lonnie Mack's pulsing sound in the 1950s, Magnatone also made a series of unusual electric guitars. The amps descended from a line introduced around 1937 by Dickerson Brothers of Los Angeles. Dickerson evolved into Magna Electronics and the Magnatone brand, run by Art Duhamell in Inglewood, California, from about 1947.

Innovative steel guitars of the early 1950s with stamped metal and chrome-and-colored-Lucite bodies led to Magnatone's first single-cutaway Spanish Mark III solidbody in 1956, followed by the hollowed-out, set-neck, double-cutaway Mark IV and Mark V, professional-grade guitars designed by Paul Bigsby in 1957. Following a merger with Estey organs in 1959, the Mark models were succeeded by the bolt-on-neck double-cutaway Artist Series, similar to Rickenbacker's 600 and probably designed

by former National/Rickenbacker executive Paul Barth.

In 1961 Barth certainly contributed Magnatone's "golden-voiced Magna-Touch" line, Telecaster-like in shape with hollow-core construction similar to Danelectros. These lasted until 1965 when the best-known Starstream Series appeared, consisting of Zephyr, Tornado, and Typhoon, small offset-double-cutaway beginner-level solidbodies (some with metalflake finishes) inspired by Fender's Stratocaster.

In 1966 the Starstreams were redesigned with a hooked three-tuners-each-side headstock, endorsed by country legend Jimmy Bryant, and joined by the pointy-horned double-cutaway Semi-Acoustic Thinbody guitars. That same year Magna relocated to Harmony, Pennsylvania, making huge solid-state amps. A few Italian-made Magnatone hollowbodies appeared following the move, but guitars faded away. The end came in 1971 when Magna was purchased by a toy company.

Micro-Frets

Despite its innovative and forward-looking designs, Micro-Frets was perhaps just too quirky a maker to ever gain widespread acceptance.
During the late 1960s increasing attention began to be paid to the improvement of electric guitar technology. Among the more curious results were Micro-Frets guitars, the brainchild of self-educated genius Ralph J. Jones. After working on various prototypes he put Micro-Frets instruments into production in Frederick, Maryland, in 1967.

FACT FILE

A **piezo pickup** (or piezo-electric pickup/element) is a transducer with piezo-electric crystals that generate electricity under mechanical strain. In a guitar, it senses string and body movement, and provides a reasonably accurate means of reproducing an acoustic-like sound in an electric or acoustic-electric instrument.

Micro-Frets guitars featured three curious patented innovations. First, the front and back were made of two hollowed-out pieces of wood joined at the side, a technique dubbed "Tonesponder." Second, the (very thin) bolt-on necks sported the Micro-Nut, a metal device that allowed for the adjustment of the length of each individual string at the nut as well as the tail, theoretically providing more accurate intonation. Third, after 1968 or so Micro-Fret guitars could be outfitted with a Calibrato vibrato, specially designed to keep all strings harmonically in tune during use,

taking into account string gauges, and with less chance of going out of tune after use.

Most Micro-Frets guitars were frumpy-shaped variations on two basic designs: equal-double-cutaway (such as Spacetone and Signature models) or offset-double-cutaway (Wanderer, Golden Melody). The earliest Micro-Frets guitars had a side gasket where the body halves joined, DeArmond-like pickups, an early-Bigsby-style vibrato design, and a bi-level pickguard with thumbwheel controls built into a scalloped edge on the top portion.

Other early guitar models included the Huntington (with a scrolled upper horn), Covington, Golden Comet, Orbiter (extended upper horn and pointed lower bout) and Plainsman. In 1968 Micro-Frets announced one of the earliest wireless systems, using an FM transmitter. Jones apparently got the idea from newly-invented garage door openers. Wireless became a shortlived option on most models, with an antenna protruding from the upper horn.

By around 1970 the side gasket had disappeared and a variety of Jones-designed pickups were used. The bi-level pickguards now had regular knobs mounted on the lower portion. Models from this era include the Calibra I, Signature and Stage II. By 1971 Micro-Frets also offered its first true solidbody, the Swinger, plus the Signature Baritone and Stage II Baritone. While most Micro-Frets finishes were fairly conventional, a wild green-to-yellow "Martian sunburst" was offered. Oddly, some models came with plastic decals of cats or pumpkins affixed. Jones died around 1973, and by 1974 the brand was gone. A very few Diamond S guitars were subsequently assembled in Virginia using leftover Micro-Frets parts.

Mosrite

Players of anything from surf to punk have found themselves some surprisingly well-suited guitars among the throaty snarl and twang of the Mosrite instruments.
One of the most colorful American guitar-makers, Semie Moseley enjoyed an erratic career producing distinctive, boldly-designed instruments. Moseley was born in Durant, Oklahoma, in 1935, and later moved to Bakersfield, California.

At age 13 Moseley was playing guitar with an evangelical music group. He joined Rickenbacker in the late 1950s, and soon formed his own guitar-making business, encouraged and assisted by the Reverend Ray Boatright. Their combined surnames provided the name for their new Los Angeles-based Mosrite company.

From the outset Mosrites had unusual features, including a distinctive "M"-topped headstock. Moseley soon produced what was to be the definitive Mosrite design,

guitar facts

essentially a reversed Stratocaster-like body with stylistic and dimensional changes that gave a new outline. It was streamlined and full of visual "movement" but still comfortable and well-balanced.

This radical design was noticed by Nokie Edwards, guitarist with The Ventures, America's leading instrumental band. Production of Mosrite Ventures models commenced in 1963 at a new factory in Bakersfield, funded by the band in return for exclusive distribution.

The new Mk I guitars each carried a Ventures logo on the headstock. Output soon increased from 35 to 300 instruments per month. None of the subsequent models achieved the popularity of the Ventures guitars. Mosrite closed in 1969.

The next 20 years saw false starts and financial setbacks for Moseley. In 1976 his unsuccessful Brass Rail had a brass fingerboard for extra sustain. Demand increased in Japan for original Ventures models, and a dealer there commissioned recreations, but it wasn't until 1984 that Moseley was able to establish a production facility in Jonas Ridge, North Carolina, making reissues and other models.

Moseley's last production was the 40th Anniversary model of 1992. He died that year; his widow Loretta continued the business. By 1995 all Mosrites were Japanese-made, including Johnny Ramone and Nokie Edwards models.

Music Man

For brief a time the repository of many of Leo Fender's post-Fender design notions, Music Man evolved into being a major US-made alternative to the "big two" brands, and captured an impressive list of virtuoso endorsees along the way.

Two ex-Fender employees, Forrest White and Tom Walker, together with Leo Fender, set up a new company in Fullerton, California, in 1972, naming it Music Man two years later. At first production concentrated on a line of amplifiers based on designs by Walker, but a move into instruments followed in 1976. The distinctive Music Man logo had two guitarists whose legs formed a large "M".

When CBS purchased the Fender companies they had given Leo a contract with a ten-year non-competition clause that expired in 1975. In April of that year Leo was announced as president of Music Man Inc. The first guitar to appear was the StingRay, introduced in mid 1976, along with a fine bass guitar of the same name. They reflected typical Fender styling, but displayed significant and subtle refinements of construction and components.

A three-bolt neck/body joint was successfully employed, contradicting its poor reputation gained when the Fender company used it amid poor manufacturing standards in the 1970s.

1988
Music Man
Silhouette

The StingRay followed trends of the time, favoring twin humbuckers and a fixed bridge, while active circuitry was optional. The instrument was not necessarily what was expected of Leo Fender, and the notorious resistance of guitarists to anything new meant it prompted a low-key reaction. But Leo, typically, saw little point in reworking his past achievements, and aimed to offer genuine improvements in quality, consistency and performance.

The Sabre guitar was added two years later with a body outline slightly different to that of the StingRay. It shared the large, six-tuners-on-one-side headstock and one-piece maple neck construction, and likewise came in two versions – I or II – the former with a 12″-radius fingerboard and jumbo frets, the latter employing a more "vintage" 7.5″ radius and standard-size frets. Once more, neither single-coil pickups nor a vibrato unit were present, while active electrics came as standard, together with more comprehensive circuitry and refinements to hardware. Regardless of such changes and the more streamlined image, the Sabre fared no better with players.

Behind the scenes, all was not well. Part of the business arrangements of the operation meant that Music Man instruments were manufactured by Leo's CLF Research company, but after Music Man tried unsuccessfully to buy CLF in 1978 he decided to break away and set up his own guitar-making business, G&L, in 1979. The first instruments bearing his new brandname appeared in 1980. Music Man continued to manufacture instruments in Fullerton for a time after this upheaval, but later other production sources were used, including Jackson. Despite such turmoil, a limited model selection continued until 1980 when the StingRay guitar went from the catalog, the remainder lasting into the early 1980s.

In March 1984 Music Man was acquired by the Ernie Ball company, production being transferred north, near to Ball's string and accessory works in San Luis Obispo, California, and the second chapter in the Music Man story began. Music Man's basses had been more popular than the guitars thus far, so it was the four-string models that first went into production with the new owner.

The prototype of an all-new guitar, the Silhouette, was previewed in 1986, and production commenced the following year. Designed by ex-Valley Arts man Dudley Gimpel in 1985 with the help of country-rock guitarist Albert Lee, this solidbody was Fender-inspired, but with features that included a compact, stylishly-contoured body and a headstock echoing the Music Man bass design, the tuners arranged in a four-and-two formation.

Options included the 24-fret maple neck with rosewood or maple fingerboard, a fixed bridge or locking vibrato system, and various pickup formats. The most recent variant is the Silhouette Special, launched in 1995, its 22-fret neck and Wilkinson vibrato unit being the most obvious of a number of changes made to the (continuing) standard model. Among the high-profile players of the Silhouette have been Ron Wood and Keith Richards, a rare example of these two favoring contemporary new-design guitars.

Back in the 1980s, the Silhouette was joined by the Steve Morse signature model in 1987 which employed a novel four-pickup configuration favored by this players' player. A very popular Music Man six-string model was the EVH, offered for a couple of years from 1991 and designed in close collaboration with the influential high-speed guitarist Edward Van Halen. Features included his own-design body, custom-profile neck and special DiMarzio-made humbuckers. The original Floyd Rose-equipped model was joined by a fixed-bridge option, reflecting Van Halen's changing requirements. However, in the mid 1990s the guitarist changed allegiance to Peavey for a new signature model, and so Music Man subsequently altered the name of its EVH model to the Axis. Since then the original Music Man EVHs have become quite collectable, especially examples with pretty woods.

Causing some confusion in retrospect, Music Man had used the Axis model name earlier for a number of prototypes of what would become the Albert Lee model. One of these angular prototypes was made for Paul McCartney, enjoying the distinction of being

the first left-hander solid six-string made by the new Music Man operation. The remarkable Nigel Tufnel had a typically more refined version, too, featuring four humbuckers, rev counter, tailpipes, Woody Woodpecker logo and note names on the fingerboard to increase Tufnel's already frightening speed.

Other 1990s additions to the Music Man guitar line included two more signature editions added in 1993, the Luke and the Albert Lee. The former was designed to the specifications of Steve Lukather, while the latter has an odd-looking angular body shape. New in 1997 was a cheaper Axis variant, the Axis Sport, which has P-90-like MM90 pickups, the first to be made by Music Man in-house. In 1999 Music Man followed the hybrid trend by offering a piezo-pickup option for the Axis.

While the choice is far from vast, the Music Man line offers a high-quality, top-performance selection that represents some of the best of the new generation of American-made instruments.

National

The classic name in resonator guitars has also offered a number of interesting and unusual electric instruments, as well as models that blended properties of the acoustic resonator with electric pickups and thinline styling.

The National brand appeared on some early electric guitars of the 1930s, but the company is especially remembered for its unusual "map shape" electrics of the 1960s.

John Dopyera and his brothers Rudy and Ed emigrated from what was then Czechoslovakia and set up the National String Instrument Corporation in Los

1964 National Newport 84

Angeles, California, in the mid 1920s, at first to produce a metal-body tenor banjo that John had invented. In 1927 National launched its now-famous acoustic "tricone" resonator guitar. Suspended inside its metal body were three resonating aluminum cones that acted a little like loudspeakers. The result was a loud, distinctive instrument. A few rare examples were fitted with pickups.

A complicated set of business maneuvers followed, during which the Dopyera brothers split from National after an argument and formed the Dobro Corporation in 1929 ("Dobro" derives from the first syllables of "Dopyera brothers").

Dobro then started to make single-cone resonator guitars. Dobro and National were merged again in 1935, and it was at this time that National-Dobro marketed a National electric guitar, the Electric Spanish f-hole archtop model (along with a similar Dobro-brand version, plus cheaper Supro-brand electrics). The magnetic pickups on these early electrics were designed by Victor Smith. In 1936 the company relocated to

Chicago. It continued to make a number of National archtop electrics, including some that unusually were without f-holes, as well as one of the earliest guitars with two pickups, the Sonora model introduced in 1939.

In 1942 Victor Smith, Al Frost and Louis Dopyera (another of the Dopyera brothers) bought the National-Dobro company and changed the name to the Valco Manufacturing Company. After World War II, more Valco electrics appeared bearing the National brand, as well as low-end Supro-brand models and catalog-company contracted brands such as Airline. Post-war National archtop electric models included the Aristocrat – at first with an unusual arrangement of control knobs and jack either side of the large bridge/pickup unit, and later with bodies supplied by Gibson – as well as the single-cutaway Club Combo introduced in 1952.

Valco was not the first brand to offer guitars built from synthetic materials. Earlier innovations had, for example, included Rickenbacker's Bakelite models of the 1930s. But the brightly colored and unusually shaped fiberglass Valco-made guitars of the 1960s were without doubt among the most eye-catchingly different instruments of the era.

Valco was never short of impressive sounding names for its guitar innovations, and came up with "Res-O-Glas" and "Hollow-Glas" for the material used in its new line of non-wood instruments, introduced in 1962. This was in fact one of the first composite materials used for guitar manufacturing, a technique that would in later decades become more prevalent with the advent of "carbon-graphite." The material used for the National (and Supro) guitars of the 1960s was described at the time as "polyester resins with threads of pure glass," or fiberglass. Valco intended that this medium, which it trumpeted as "more adaptable and workable than conventional wood," would provide a longer lasting instrument. Two molded body halves were joined together with a strip of white vinyl binding around the edge.

Valco also produced wood-body National models alongside the Res-O-Glas guitars. The various plastic Newport and Glenwood models and wood-body Westwood guitars have become known as "map shape" Nationals among collectors, because the body suggests a stylized outline of part of the map of the United States. By 1964 National had nine map-shape guitars on its catalog, ranging from the wood-body Westwood 72 to the most expensive model in that line, the plastic-body Glenwood 99.

Like some contemporary Supro models, a number of National guitars, including map-shapes, had in addition to the conventional

magnetic pickup(s) an innovative "contact" pickup built into the bridge. The facility was also included on non-map-shape Nationals, including the various Val-Trol models introduced in the late 1950s.

The bridge-pickup scheme was another National idea before its time; similar piezo bridge pickups would take off in the "hybrid" guitars of more recent years.

However, these brave plastic and pickup experiments ended with Valco itself in the late 1960s. Control in Valco had passed to one Robert Engelhardt, who went on to buy its competitor, the Kay guitar company, in 1967. When Kay went out of business during the following year, Valco – and its National and Supro brands – went down with it.

The National brand has resurfaced since the 1960s, including in the 1970s on a line of unremarkable imported electrics. In 1988 National Reso-phonic Guitars was founded in San Luis Obispo, California, and soon began producing resonator guitars. The ResoLectric model followed in the 1990s and has been popular since that time. It is

made from a thinline mahogany body with figured maple-veneer top, with a P-90 pickup in the neck position and a Highlander IP-1X system mounted in the biscuit bridge to amplify the sound of the resonator cone. Meanwhile, National's "map shape" design was revived in 1996 for wood-body guitars with the Metropolitan brandname, made by Robin in Houston, Texas, and marketed by Alamo Music Products.

Ovation
Despite their often novel designs, versatile electronics, and high overall level of build quality, Ovation electric guitars have never been more than a pale shadow to the company's widely accepted acoustics.
Known for revolutionizing electric-acoustic guitars with "Lyracord" fiberglass bowl-back instruments in 1966, Ovation tried for years to market innovative solidbody electric guitar designs with little success. Ovation was founded by aeronautical engineer and

helicopter manufacturer Charles H. Kaman in Bloomfield, Connecticut (relocating to New Hartford in 1967).

The guitar company used aeronautical materials to solve what they considered as problems with the instability of natural wood. Ovation acoustics got an early push when played by Josh White and Charlie Byrd, but it was Glen Campbell's TV show *Goodtime Hour* in 1969 that made the brand. It was on that show that Ovation's first under-bridge-saddle transducer was introduced.

The device paved the way for a revolution in "amplified acoustic" or "electro-acoustic" guitars, as well as the later trend toward "hybrid" instruments that mixed bridge transducers and conventional magnetic pickups.

While waiting for the bowl-backs to catch on, Ovation had in 1968 introduced its first semi-hollow thinline electrics, the Electric Storm series: Thunderhead, Tornado and Hurricane 12-string. They had German Framus-made bodies, Schaller hardware and pickups, and Ovation necks. In 1971 a budget black Eclipse model was added. These were all discontinued by 1973.

Ovation entered the solidbody market with its battle-axe-shape Breadwinner in 1972, followed by the more high-end Deacon with high gloss finish, neck binding and fancier inlays. Featuring onboard FET pre-amps, these were among the earliest American production guitars with active electronics. A 12-string model was available by 1976. While the Breadwinner lasted until 1979 and the Deacon to 1980, they never took off. Toward the end of its life the Deacon had extra contouring added to its body, but this didn't help sales.

Ovation acoustics continued to mature and evolve, most notably with the introduction of the graphite-topped Adamas, with multiple soundholes on the shoulders, in 1976. Ovation's successful Collector Series debuted in 1982, and its domestic and imported electro-acoustic lines continued to proliferate and thrive.

In 1975 Ovation introduced more solidbodies, this time the more conventional-looking double-cutaway Preacher, Preacher Deluxe and single-cutaway Viper models. The Preacher had passive electrics, while the Preacher Deluxe featured active circuitry and fancier appointments. A 12-string version of the Deluxe was also offered. The Viper came with two or three pickups.

In 1979 the curious Ultra Kaman, or UK II, made its debut. This single-cutaway guitar featured an aluminum-framed body that was filled out with lightweight urethane foam. It boasted precise tone and volume control. The aluminum/foam concept was derived from the necks of Ovation's budget Applause acoustics. Alas, none of these efforts caught on with the market and in

1983 Ovation's American-made solidbodies ceased production. The only "stars" to play Ovation solidbodies briefly were Jim Messina, Roy Clark and Glen Campbell.

Around 1984 Ovation attempted solidbodies one more time with the introduction of its Hard Body series, consisting of Korean-made necks and bodies assembled and finished in the US using Schaller hardware and DiMarzio pickups. The GP was a flame-top, offset-double-cutaway with a glued neck that was otherwise in the general mold of a Les Paul Standard; the GS a bolt-on-neck Strat-style guitar, with one or two humbuckers or humbucker/single-coil/single-coil pickup layout. These lasted only a year or so, but have had an enormous revival of popularity thanks to Queens Of The Stone Age guitarist Josh Homme's use of an Ovation Ultra GP. The scarcity of original examples – fewer than 400 Ultras were made – has prompted the Eastwood brand to offer a "tribute" to the model, dubbed the Eastwood GP.

A few hundred more solidbody guitars were briefly imported from Japan, and a shortlived, entry-level, Korean-made Celebrity By Ovation line of superstrats was offered around 1987. None was successful. A few experimental guitars with Steve Ripley's "stereo" electronics were tried (as on Kramer's Ripley Stereo) but the project went nowhere.

Giving up on its own efforts, Kaman purchased Hamer Guitars of Chicago in 1988. Ovation-brand solidbodies were always well considered and carefully designed, but so often seemed out of step with the times.

Parker
Like too many revolutionary makers, Parker has occasionally struggled with acceptance in the wider market, but has been recognized for its quality and innovation by the guitar industry and by an apparently growing number of professional players.
In the mid 1990s, Parker popularized the "hybrid" guitar – an instrument fitted with piezo as well as regular "electric" magnetic pickups – and revolutionized the way electric guitars can be built.

Parker is a partnership between guitar-maker Ken Parker and electronics expert Larry Fishman. The project required considerable finance, provided primarily by Korg USA, better known for electronic musical instruments. A purpose-built factory was established near Boston, Massachusetts, to manufacture the unusually-shaped Parker Fly. The facility was designed to make Parkers in an entirely different way to any other electric guitars. Every part of the Fly, with the exception of its Sperzel locking tuners, is unique to Parker,

including the tangless stainless-steel frets which are glued into the fingerboard, and the unusual "flat-spring" vibrato with built-in piezo-electric pickups.

Parker said that all this was intended to make their new Fly a more versatile guitar – not merely something different. The theory was that the only reason for a guitar's solid wooden body is strength, that the wood's effect on the sound of the instrument is secondary. But Parker knew that acoustic guitars depend much more for their sound on the timbers used, especially that employed for the body's top. So the company intended that its Fly models would have thin, lightweight but highly resonant wooden bodies strengthened by a composite material (glass and carbon fibers in an epoxy matrix) that forms a very thin "external skeleton" all around the wood. The necks are similarly constructed.

1997 Parker Fly Artist
BODY: thin, full-width core of solid carved spruce with non-concentric double cutaways; glass and carbon-fiber epoxy outer shell; polyurethane finish.

NECK: set-neck construction, poplar core with shell and fingerboard formed from glass and carbon-fiber; 24 medium glued-on hardened stainless-steel frets, and 1 11/16" nut width; compound (conical) fingerboard radius that broadens from 10" at the nut to 13" toward the upper frets.

HEADSTOCK: recessed narrow-profile headstock with six-in-line Sperzel locking tuners.

BRIDGE: Parker flat-spring vibrato system with action-tension adjustment wheel.

ELECTRONICS: two DiMarzio magnetic humbucking pickups, six-element Fishman piezo system in bridge saddles; three-way selector plus master volume and master tone for magnetic pickups; master volume and master tone for electro-acoustic (piezo) pickups, plus three-way switch for magnetic/piezo/both operation.

SOUND: full-throated traditional humbucking sounds with broad, open, resonant voice, or bright, snappy electro-acoustic tones, as well as a blend of the two.

Most Fly guitars have two kinds of pickup fitted: a traditional magnetic type for normal electric sounds, plus a piezo in the bridge for "acoustic"-like tones. While these two types of pickup had been offered on individual guitars before, no previous instrument allowed the player to combine magnetic and piezo pickups in a way that allowed the use of either type independently or both mixed together.

The Parker's Fishman-designed pickup-mix facility effectively provides musicians with two guitars in one, effectively merging electric and electric-acoustic sounds. Many other makers have subsequently emulated

this "hybrid" style, and some guitar-industry people are arguing that it provides one possible future direction for the electric guitar.

The first Parker introduced was the poplar-body Fly Vibrato Deluxe, in 1993, followed by the mahogany Fly Classic (1996), the spruce Fly Artist (1997), the rare figured-maple Supreme (1998) and a nylon-string version, the Spanish Fly (1999). The Concert model (1997) is a piezo-only guitar without vibrato. The MIDI Fly (1999) uses a sophisticated synth-access system, while the lower-price NiteFly (1996) has many of the regular Fly's attributes but with a bolt-on reinforced-wood neck and a more conventional soft maple body (ash and mahogany from '99). New non-vibrato versions appeared in 2000: the basswood-body black-hardware Hardtail, which includes a Sperzel D-Tuner on the D-string and is aimed at the modern rock market; and the gold-hardware mahogany-body Jazz.

Parker players – a diverse bunch that includes Pops Staples, Reeves Gabrels and Dave Navarro – seem drawn as much by the guitar's comfort and playability as its light weight and hybrid sounds.

While gaining applause from many forward-looking players, Parker's individual mindset ultimately made it difficult for the company to remain independent in the corporate sense. In 2004 Parker Guitars was acquired by US Music Corp, parent company of Washburn Guitars and Randall Amplifiers, and relocated to the company's headquarters outside Chicago in Mundelein, Illinois. The new owners have continued to offer a wide range of Parker models.

Peavey
From the introduction of its workmanlike debutante model T-60 in the late 1970s, Peavey has grown to be a major player in the electric guitar field, and has won the support of broad basket of big-name artists.
Beginning as an amplifier manufacturer founded by Hartley Peavey in Meridian, Mississippi, in 1965, Peavey Electronics pioneered new guitar construction techniques in the late 1970s and has offered a large, varied and mostly mid-priced guitar line ever since. Peavey guitars originated with Hartley's idea that he could create a relatively inexpensive alternative to Gibson and Fender guitars. Working with Chip Todd, Peavey devised the T-60 guitar ("T" for Todd). It combined a Gibson-like rounded shape and twin humbuckers with a Fender-style maple fingerboard and slightly offset double cutaways.

The T-60 debuted in 1978, lasted a decade and was notable for three innovations: a tone control that doubled as a coil-tap, devised by LA steel guitarist Orville "Red" Rhodes; a patented "bi-laminated"

Mid-1980s Paul Reed Smith Custom

BODY: double-cutaway body with offset horns, made from carved flamed maple '10-Plus Top' with mahogany back, thin nitrocellulose finish.

NECK: set-neck construction, wide/fat mahogany neck with unbound Brazilian rosewood fingerboard with bird inlays; 24 medium nickel-silver frets, 10" fingerboard radius; 25" scale length.

HEADSTOCK: back-angled headstock, with three-a-side PRS locking tuners; friction-reducing nut.

BRIDGE: PRS 'Stay In Tune' vibrato system with back-loading strings in modified steel inertia and six individually adjustable saddles.

ELECTRONICS: uncovered PRS humbuckers; controls for master volume, d five-way rotary pickup selector for full and split-pickup sounds, "sweet switch" tone switch for normal/treble-bleed tone selections.

SOUND: broad and full, cutting and aggressive in the bridge position, smoother and rounder in the neck, with brighter, snappier single-coil-like sounds available.

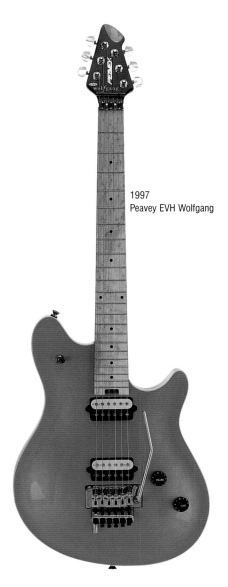

1997
Peavey EVH Wolfgang

began using Kahler locking vibratos on other models in 1985. The popular Strat-style Predator series was introduced in 1985 (the line revived in 1990, with a seven-string added in 2000). An Explorer-inspired "pointy" Vortex appeared in 1985, and the Strat-style Impact series debuted the following year. All these had disappeared by the late 1990s, although the Impact was briefly revived as the figured-top Impact Milano and Torino in 1994.

Peavey guitars always offered high quality at their respective price points, but in the late 1980s the company began markedly improving the quality. In 1987 the popular Nitro series of superstrats and the active and passive Falcon series of near-Strats appeared (both with versions lasting until 1990), as well as Peavey's first ventures into through-neck construction, the Impact Unity. In 1988 Peavey began using Alnico pickups and unveiled the superstrat Tracer series, some models of which survived to 1994.

In 1988 Peavey began working with another celebrity, introducing the violin-waisted Vandenberg Signature designed with Dutch guitar-slinger Adrian Vandenberg. The following year the company introduced the high-end Destiny superstrat and Generation Tele-style model, both with carved figured maple caps, offered until 1994.

In 1990 Peavey introduced its first Les-Paul-inspired model, the single-cutaway Odyssey, available until 1994 and including a quilt-top version. The 1990s saw the continuation of the offset-double-cutaway style – Axecellerator, Defender, Detonator, Firenza (formerly Impact), G-90 and Raptor – and the Tele-style designs – Cropper Classic, for Memphis great Steve Cropper, and Reactor. A PRS-style guitar, the Ltd, appeared in 2000.

Peavey guitars can be said to have finally arrived with the landing of the Eddie Van Halen EVH Wolfgang series in 1996, Eddie having transferred allegiance to Peavey from Music Man. Van Halen had already worked with Peavey on the 5150 amp series (a name Van Halen then used for his own recording studio). The various offset-double-cutaway Peavey Van Halens, with their chunky upper horn, remain high-end, desirable guitars thanks to their endorsement pedigree. Peavey and Van Halen parted ways in 2005; the maker has announced plans to revamp the Wolfgang model as the Corina (not yet release), while the guitarist has begun working with Charvel, creating hand-made reissues of his original striped Charvel parts guitar.

PRS
Whenever it comes time to update the history books – to get past the undisputed classics such as Fender, Gibson, Gretsch and the like and give credit to worthy latter-day makers – the first name set down in ink is usually that of Paul Reed Smith. By listening closely to the needs of contemporary players and updating some proven designs for modern functionality and sound, Smith has become one of the most respected makers in the world.

Back in the mid 1970s, few would have imaged that a lanky, big-haired kid repairing guitars in an impossibly small workshop in Annapolis, Maryland, would one day be running the number three guitar company behind Fender and Gibson. Yet that is the fantastic story of Paul Reed Smith, "the Stradivari of the electric guitar" as one satisfied customer would later call him.

The details of this ascent are more fabulous still. Coming from a musical family, Smith started both his musical and guitar-making career during high school. Initially playing bass before moving on to guitar, Smith built his first instrument toward the end of senior high school by fixing the neck of a Japanese "Beatle bass" copy to a strangely-shaped, solid body. He then managed to get a job repairing guitars at the

1980
Paul Reed Smith

maple neck with opposing grain directions for stability; and the first guitar construction using computer-controlled carving machines, an idea borrowed from gun-stock-making and that is now standard practice among mass-production guitar-makers.

The 1980s were exceptionally fertile for Peavey guitars. The T Series had a facelift in 1982, including a new T-25 Special with a phenolic fingerboard. The profile was slightly reshaped and Super Ferrite blade-style pickups were added; these lasted only about a year. Peavey's first traditional-style vibratos debuted in 1983, and the company flirted with "pointy" body shapes in the mid 1980s with the electric-shaver-shaped Razer, B.C. Rich-style Mystic and V-shaped Mantis. Peavey also began making more conventionally shaped offset-double-cutaway models from 1983-86, including the Horizon, Milestone and Patriot series (the latter with a solid-state amp-in-a-molded-plastic-case, a tribute to Danelectro).

The Hydra double-neck debuted in 1984, and a Kahler-equipped Jeff Cook model appeared the following year. Peavey

guitar facts

Washington Music Center before deciding to go to St. Mary's College in Maryland to study mathematics. The opportunity in the second half of his first year to undertake an independent study project proved a turning point. Smith made his first proper guitar, a single-cutaway solidbody in the style of Gibson's Les Paul Junior, which earned him credits and respect from his teachers.

In that summer of 1975 he turned the top floor of his parents' house into a workshop and, with the help of his brother, set about making more guitars. The bug had bitten, and Smith's return to college proved to be shortlived. By the start of 1976 he had left and moved into his first workshop in West Street, Annapolis.

Smith made his first electric guitar at his new shop, a solidbody Gibson Byrdland-style instrument for Ted Nugent. This was quickly followed by a guitar for British rocker Peter Frampton. The all-mahogany guitar for Frampton was an interesting instrument which, although built in early 1976, laid the foundation for Smith's future.

Its double-cutaway outline apes Gibson's post-1958 Les Paul Special, but features the arched, carved top of a Les Paul Standard. For the first time on a Smith guitar there were mother-of-pearl birds inlaid by hand down the fingerboard, a distinctive feature that would later help to shift a lot of PRS guitars. But why birds? Smith's mother was a keen bird-watcher, and he says that he simply grabbed one of her bird-watching guides and stole the pictures out of it, drawing with friends Billy Armiger and Tim Campbell a couple of others. Along with the motif of an eagle landing that was inlaid into the headstock – a feature that would return to PRS guitars some years later – Frampton's guitar also featured the 24-fret-

neck, twin-humbucking-pickups configuration that would be the basis of Smith's instruments until the beginning of the 1990s.

Smith's dream, however, was to make a guitar for Carlos Santana, one of his guitar-playing idols. Getting to meet players like Santana proved one of Smith's hidden talents. He achieved this by hanging out backstage at the local arenas, begging roadies to let their employer see his instruments. The deal was simple: if you don't fall in love with the instrument you get your money back. It worked.

Apart from Nugent and Frampton, Smith got orders from Al DiMeola (a 12-string with a built-in phase shifter), as well as Frampton's and Bruce Springsteen's bass players, not to mention many local musicians. It also became apparent to Smith from a very early point that big-name guitar players sell guitars to others.

DiMeola said after owning a PRS that he felt Smith had the ability to custom-make the guitar of anyone's dreams. Slowly, the word was beginning to spread.

In 1980, after selling his first maple-topped hand-made guitar to Heart guitarist Howard Leese, Smith got to make an instrument for Carlos Santana. This would be the first of four hand-made Smith guitars that Santana used in the coming years. The association with Santana, and the maple-topped instruments themselves, proved to be massive turning points – although that's not how they appeared at the time. The figured "curly" maple that Smith used for these early maple-top guitars originally came from the drawer-fronts of a friend's dresser. This crucial timber helped to summon up visions of those late-1950s Les Pauls that have influenced so many players and makers.

By the time Carlos Santana owned a Smith guitar he was already on his first comeback. Nearly 20 years later, still playing a PRS guitar, he would be topping the *Billboard* charts again with *Supernatural*, another comeback album. Smith said in 1999 that he couldn't have been successful without Santana's support, because the guitarist gave his instruments instant credibility. Musicians such as Santana, Howard Leese and Al DiMeola all disregarded the overwhelming opinion of the time about which guitars pro players should be using. Their mark of approval was crucial to Smith's early operation. Smith knew that by successfully building a guitar that Santana liked, he had a shot at starting a professional guitar-making operation.

However, building Santana's guitar nearly didn't happen at all. But when, eventually, Santana received his first instrument the guitar player remarked that its special quality was "an accident of God" and that Smith would never be able to do it

again. Santana then said the second guitar Smith made for him was, too, an accident of God. There was a third one, and then a double-neck. When he finally got that, Santana said that maybe this wasn't an accident of God. Finally he thought that Smith might actually be a guitar-maker.

But by 1984 Smith was struggling to survive. He still held some ambition to become a professional guitar player, but with the counsel of his close friends and loyal assistant John Ingram, Smith realized that it was his guitar-building that was making headway, not his playing. He'd set about designing what we know today as the PRS Custom, and after trying unsuccessfully to persuade various big-name manufacturers to make his design under license, he realized he'd have to do it himself.

Armed with a couple of prototypes, Smith headed out on the road and raised orders worth nearly $300,000. Making the guitars to fulfill these orders was another matter. But by the fall of 1985 Smith and his wife Barbara, guided by the business know-how of Warren Esanu, had set up a limited partnership to raise the capital necessary to start a factory in Virginia Avenue, Annapolis. At last, just about a decade after making his first electric guitar, Smith had his production company, PRS Guitars, up and running and in business.

Apart from a few lucky musicians and their fans, nobody knew Paul Reed Smith when the company first displayed its wares at the important American NAMM trade-shows held during 1985. It was a time of high-tech musical fashion. The major trends were in aggressive, futuristic-looking, modern rock guitar designs. In those surroundings, the PRS Custom must have seemed very out of place.

With the Custom, here was an instrument clearly inspired by classic 1950s Gibson and Fender guitars. Often called evolutionary rather than revolutionary, the PRS guitar was substantially more expensive than the high-line Gibson or Fender instruments, but it began to gain interest from players and press. The fabulously-colored carved-maple tops harked back to the classic late-1950s Gibson Les Paul, while the guitar's outline melded the double-cutaway shape of Smith's earlier instruments with elements of a Fender Stratocaster shape, creating a unique hybrid design that was both classic-looking yet original enough to be noticed. This mix of Gibson and Fender – the two major cornerstones of the electric guitar – was crucial to the concept.

PRS's scale-length of 25" (635mm) sat half-way between Gibson's shorter 24.56" (626mm) scale and Fender's longer 25.5" (648mm). The 10" (254mm) fingerboard radius also sat between Gibson's flatter 12" (305mm) camber and the smaller 7.25"

guitar facts

(184mm) radius of vintage Fenders. That wasn't all. With an unusual rotary pickup selector switch, the twin PRS humbuckers created five distinct sounds: a combination of thick humbucking Gibson-like tones and thinner single-coil mixes that approximated some of the Stratocaster's key voices. Augmenting the pickup switch was a master volume control and, instead of a conventional tone control, a "sweet switch" which rounded off the guitar's upper frequencies. (By 1991 the sweet switch had been replaced on all models in favor of a standard tone control.)

The early 1980s had seen the double-locking Floyd Rose vibrato become one of the most popular design features used on contemporary electric guitars. However, as a working musician Smith didn't like the fact that you needed a set of Allen wrenches to change strings. So, with the help of local guitar-playing engineer John Mann, Smith designed his own vibrato system that updated the classic Fender vibrato and employed unique cam-locking tuners, yet still offered fashionable "wide-travel" pitch-bending with near perfect tuning stability.

The Custom used classic "tonewoods," including top-quality curly maple for the distinctly carved top, mahogany for the back and set-neck, and Brazilian rosewood for the fingerboard. The instrument also brought innovations. Instead of employing conventional plastic binding, the edge of the maple top was left natural-colored, contrasting the colored finish of the guitar's top. Along with all this detail, the guitar's double-octave, 24-fret fingerboard was made to feel "as comfortable as an old T-shirt," like a guitar that had been played in.

It was a design that embodied all of Smith's experience to date, made by a guitar player for other guitar players. Although there have been numerous design changes over the years, the PRS Custom is one of the few electric guitars designed outside the 1950s that can genuinely lay claim to the term "design classic."

Launched at the same time as the Custom was the Standard. Originally just called the PRS, it featured an all-mahogany body and as such was the workingman's PRS, though otherwise it had the same specification. The Metal, a Standard with a graphic paint job, bowed to current fashion but was quickly dropped in favor of the more classic-looking instruments. Further models followed that only subtly changed the specification of the main pair. The Special, which appeared in 1987, pandered more to contemporary heavy-rock playing trends, while the Studio, which appeared in 1988, offered a pickup layout that featured a humbucker and two single-coils, and came with or without a maple top.

These early years were fraught with the

problems of production. Smith had a decade of experience in custom one-off building and repairing, but the production of a number of instruments to the high quality of his pre-factory hand-made guitars provided a steep learning curve. Yet apart from the guitars themselves, Paul Reed Smith became a natural figurehead. His own playing experience enabled easy communication with top-line players – he would sometimes guest with name bands – and early on his in-store clinics became a successful if time-consuming part of his job. For many years PRS was quite happy to let people believe that it was Paul Reed Smith himself who made every guitar.

To support these high-end instruments a sequence of simple and classy advertisements became another hallmark of the brand. It didn't go unnoticed: designer Dennis Voss and photographer Michael Ward won an Award of Merit for Graphic Excellence in 1985.

Smith seemed on every level to surround himself with mentors and teachers. Early on, Eric Pritchard had given him valuable advice on numerous engineering and technical matters. Pritchard not only helped to design the locking PRS tuners but also many of the production tools that were used to fabricate PRS guitars for years. Many friends remarked how Smith possessed an uncanny ability to absorb information, like a sponge.

In 1987 Smith introduced a theme that has since become an important part of PRS Guitars: the limited-edition "ultimate quality" guitar. A friend had remarked to Smith that he didn't charge enough for his work. The result was the Signature, basically a Custom but with absolutely top quality woods and maple tops. In all, some 1,000 Signature models were made. Each was hand-signed on the headstock by Smith himself, before the Artist Series took over the top-of-the-line position in 1991. Smith would at this time go on long sales tours, away from the factory, and obviously wasn't available then to sign the Signature models. An interim solution was to have Smith sign decals which could go under the finish, and Smith says the production team even threatened to sign the guitars themselves. So the Signature came to an end.

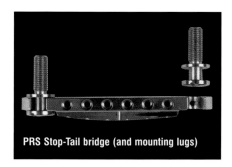

PRS Stop-Tail bridge (and mounting lugs)

The Limited Edition model appeared in 1989, the first production PRS to feature as standard a non-vibrato, tune-o-matic bridge and stud tailpiece. The guitar also featured hollow tone chambers, although the top was sealed without any f-holes. Along with curly maple, unusual but highly-figured woods for tops such as cedar and redwood created one of the most unusual PRS guitars from this period. Of Signature quality and price, the Limited Edition was only planned as a small 300-piece run, though fewer were actually made. Both the Signature and Limited Edition proved that there was a highly lucrative market for limited-edition PRS guitars.

By 1988 some dealers, not to mention new export markets like the UK, were calling for PRS to make a less expensive guitar. The result was the first PRS bolt-on-neck instrument, the Classic Electric (quickly abbreviated to CE after Peavey objected to the use of "their" word Classic). Originally the CE, with its alder body and maple neck and fingerboard, brought a more Fender-like style to the PRS line which up to that point had exclusively featured set-neck guitars. Initially the market was confused, and the company realized that players wanted a cheaper PRS Custom, not a different-sounding instrument. So a black-face headstock quickly followed, as did a maple-top option and, of course, the majority of PRS options such as bird inlays.

The CE evolved into a highly successful guitar. Its body changed to mahogany in 1995, a year after 22-fret versions had been added. It wasn't until 2000 that the standard, non-maple-top CE 22 and CE 24 were phased out, not for lack of popularity or sales, but for simple economic reasons. The start-up CE made little profit for the company and, with pressures on production space caused by increased demand, the CE was an obvious candidate for shelving.

Yet especially in the UK and Europe the CE didn't really satisfy the demand for a lower-priced PRS. This market pressure led the company to produce the bolt-on-neck EG, the first flat-fronted PRS guitar and the first with a 22-fret fingerboard. However, the company soon realized that they were losing money on every EG that was shipped. Smith has said in retrospect that he was unhappy with the sound of the original EGs.

In 1991 a new version appeared, again with a flat front but a rounder, more PRS-like outline. This new EG line was quite a departure. The bodies were crafted on computerized routers by a Baltimore engineering company, Excel, who would manufacture the majority of PRS's hardware parts during the 1990s. However, by 1995 the EG line was discontinued, and at the time of writing they mark the final attempt at a cheaper PRS guitar. There are rumored

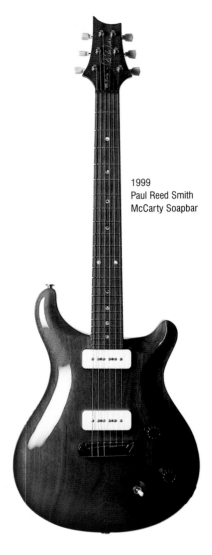

1999
Paul Reed Smith
McCarty Soapbar

1999 PRS McCarty Soapbar

BODY: double-cutaway body with offset horns, made from solid mahogany with a carved top; nitrocellulose finish.

NECK: set-neck of solid mahogany with unbound rosewood fingerboard, wide/fat profile, and elongated heel block; 22 medium nickel-silver frets; 10" fingerboard radius, 25" scale length.

HEADSTOCK: thinner and more steeply back-angled headstock; three-a-side lightweight Kluson-repro tuners.

BRIDGE: stud-mounted PRS wrapover style bridge.

ELECTRONICS: two PRS P-90-style single-coil pickups; three-way toggle switch for either pickup alone or both in parallel; master Volume, master Tone.

SOUND: full and round, with pronounced midrange emphasis and a slightly gritty-yet-snappy edge to higher-gain tones.

plans of a PRS guitar to be made outside the US ("offshore" in business-speak) as well as another attempt at a low-cost US-made electric.

Wood quality was paramount from the start of PRS Guitars, as it had been in Smith's "apprentice" days making one-off custom instruments. Early on, Smith had drawn the conclusion that the better the quality of the raw material, in terms of its weight and condition, the better the guitar would sound. Unlike many makers at the time, he believed that an electric guitar's tone was not all in its pickups and electronics, that it was an acoustic structure and the pickups and signal chain could not amplify what wasn't there in the first place.

This led Smith on a quest for the finest woods and timber suppliers, such as Michael Reid, whom Smith had first met in 1980. Reid became a valued part of PRS's production chain.

The fabulously curly and quilted maple tops were especially important to PRS Guitars. The company set up a grading system: the Classic grade, used for the CE Maple Top guitars, is about a "7" on the company's 1-to-10 rating system. The set-neck guitars use a Regular grade – now more commonly known as a Custom grade – of around 7 to 9. PRS's "10-tops" are an option on certain production guitars like the Custom, and are obviously 10 on that scale. The Signature series and subsequent limited-edition models use what Smith describes as "something spectacular."

In 1991 PRS announced the Artist I, which outwardly seemed a continuation of the Signature series. In fact, the Artist I signaled a fundamental change in the design of PRS guitars. Many of the top pros who'd been attracted to PRS guitars loved the look and feel of the instruments but felt there was room for tonal improvement. It seemed clear to some that PRS provided a natural progression beyond vintage Gibson Les Paul instruments – but the sound lacked the low-end associated with those classic guitars. So, along with its ultimate-grade timbers, the Artist I introduced a stronger neck construction and many different production techniques primarily intended to improve the "acoustic" tone of PRS guitars.

While the Artist got Smith closer to the sound he and his top-flight customers were looking for, it still wasn't close enough. Yet PRS's next sonic development was virtually missed by the guitar-playing public. When the Dragon I was launched in 1992 in a limited edition of just 50 pieces, the market was staggered by the exquisite computer-cut inlay down the fingerboard. But this feature, which brought the company a good deal of media interest, disguised the fact that the guitar featured a shorter 22-fret neck with a "wide-fat" profile, a new non-vibrato Stop-Tail bridge, and new pickups.

While the Dragon I was heading for guitar collections around the world, those lucky enough to own and play one realized the tonal improvement. This led the following year to the introduction of the PRS Custom 22, basically a Dragon without the inlay. Indeed, while 24-fret options still remain on the Custom, Standard and CE, the majority of future PRS guitars would follow the shorter and fatter neck concept. Smith says that a big neck equals big tone, and few players would disagree. As a consequence, PRS's other major models – the Standard and CE lines – were also offered in 22-fret formats from 1994.

These gradual changes in specification are typical of PRS. With a couple of exceptions the guitars have always used pickups designed and made by PRS. Originally, the Custom, Standard and Signature used what PRS called the Standard Treble and Standard Bass humbuckers. They looked like any other uncovered humbucker, but actually used magnetic "slug" polepieces in the non-adjustable inner coil, as well as a rear-placed feeder magnet, achieving a more accurate single-coil tone when split by the company's five-position rotary switch.

Catering for the more aggressive rock market, PRS developed pickups such as the Chainsaw, and the HFS ("Hot, Fat and Screams") as used initially on the Special.

1998
Paul Reed Smith
Archtop Artist

guitar facts

PRS vibrato (above) and an opened rear pocket showing vibrato block and springs

The Vintage Treble and Vintage Bass humbuckers first appeared on the Classic Electric, and the pairing of an HFS at bridge and Vintage Bass in neck position endures today on the 24-fret CE Maple Top, Standard and Custom. The first Dragon guitar featured the Dragon Treble and Dragon Bass pickups (which also appeared on the Custom 22), but since the McCarty Model and its new McCarty pickups the 22-fret PRSs have featured covered pickups which, tonally, chased a more "classic" sound.

In 1988 PRS launched the unique Electronics Upgrade Kit designed to improve the "fatness" and midrange definition of pre-1993 PRS instruments. It could have been called the "all we've learned since we started" kit as it reflected changes made over the years to minor components, such as lighter-weight tuner buttons and thumb screws, nickel-plated-brass screws for saddles and intonation, a simulated tone control for early switch-equipped guitars, and high-capacitance hook-up wire.

The Dragon I, meanwhile, had been a risk that worked. The Dragon II followed in 1993 (along with the 22-fret Artist II) and the Dragon III in 1994 (joined by the Artist Ltd). Both new Dragons were limited to just 100 pieces and each featured along the fingerboard a more flamboyant dragon inlay than the last. Announced in 1999, the most fabulous Dragon guitar was unleashed with a "three-dimensional" inlay, this time over the complex curves of the body. The Dragon 2000, limited to 50 pieces, may for some have been just another collectors' guitar, but it illustrates the desire of PRS to stretch the

boundaries of guitar-making in their ultra-high-end models.

Little known until 1994 was the involvement with PRS of Ted McCarty. He had been president of Gibson between 1950 and 1965, the period that many considered as the company's golden years. Smith says he "discovered" McCarty's name in the patent office. Just after starting his production company, Smith cold-called McCarty for advice. With great foresight, Smith subsequently enlisted him as a consultant. McCarty, meanwhile, "downloaded the hard disk" for Smith, explaining how Gibson made its instruments back in the 1950s.

But when it came to PRS's next landmark guitar, it was again player pressure that spurred the idea, notably from Texas guitar-slinger David Grissom. Leaving the opulence of the Dragon and Artist guitars behind, 1994's McCarty Model changed the formula in a seemingly subtle way, creating a PRS guitar that got closer still to the sound and feel of Gibson's classic late-1950s Les Paul.

PRS said the McCarty Model was essentially a Dragon with a thicker body, thinner headstock, lighter tuners and different pickups. In reality it was much more than that. It proved a turning point for PRS Guitars. The company had grown up and the McCarty Model quite quickly became the "player's PRS." Certainly when compared side-by-side with a mid-1980s Custom, the differences in sound and feel were startlingly obvious. Physically, the McCarty had a shorter, fatter neck, while the difference in body thickness, while subtle, is there: the McCarty feels slightly less petite. Generally

speaking, the McCarty has more of a Gibson-like, "vintage" vibe to it. It has a broader sound than an early Custom's typically aggressive, thinner tone, but still with plenty of PRS character, particularly a focussed midrange and a chunkier feel. The McCarty Model also featured for the first time on a major PRS guitar a three-way Gibson-style pickup-selecting toggle switch instead of PRS's unique five-way rotary switch. (Later, a pull/push switch was added to the tone control to coil-split the humbuckers.)

Mirroring the Custom/Standard relationship in the PRS line, the mahogany McCarty Standard without a maple cap was introduced at the same time as the maple-top McCarty Model. In 1998 the McCarty Model was offered with twin Seymour Duncan P-90-style "soapbar" single-coil pickups as the McCarty Soapbar, cashing in on the popularity of P-90s toward the end of the decade. In fact the all-mahogany McCarty Soapbar returns to the construction and style of Smith's early pre-factory pre-maple-top guitars which usually favored mahogany construction and P-90 pickups. Another "soapbar" guitar, the Custom 22 Soapbar model, appeared in 1998, unusually for a PRS featuring a maple set-neck and three soapbar pickups controlled

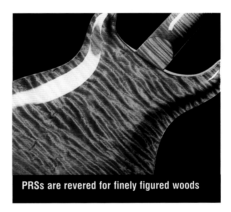

PRSs are revered for finely figured woods

by a five-way lever switch, giving a unique "hot" Strat-style tone.

Ten years old as a production company in 1995, PRS Guitars released the 10th Anniversary model which featured "scrimshaw" engraved bird inlays and headstock eagle. After many requests, PRS also started making that year a repro of the pre-factory Santana guitar, with its old-style double-cutaway outline, 24.5" (622mm) scale-length and flatter 11.5" (292mm) fingerboard radius. Ironically, although this seemed a backward design step, it was among the first PRS guitars made using the recently installed computer-assisted routing machines. These began to replace the innovative jigs and tools that had helped to fabricate PRS guitars for the previous decade.

Carlos Santana always liked his pre-factory PRS guitars, although Smith says

---

1998 PRS McCarty Hollowbody II

BODY: 1 ¾" deep PRS-shaped offset double-cutaway body made from hollowed out mahogany back with carved, arched solid two-piece figured maple top; natural maple binding top and back.

NECK: glued-in one-piece mahogany neck with paua-edged rosewood fingerboard with 10" radius, 1 ¹¹⁄₁₆" nut width; Artist Package paua bird inlays; wide-fat profile; 22 medium-jumbo neckel silver frets; 25" scale length.

HEADSTOCK: back-angled three-a-side PRS-shaped headstock with Artist Package rosewood facing, inlaid signature, and ebony tuner buttons; headstock end truss-rod access.

BRIDGE: two-post stud mounted PRS compensated wrapover tailpiece.

ELECTRONICS: two McCarty Archtop humbucking pickups (slightly lower output than standard McCarty humbuckers) constructed with a single alnico bar magnet each in the traditional PAF fashion, including gold-plated metal covers.

SOUND: thick, full, round and sweet, with an airy and slightly acoustic resonance, and good sustain.

---

that the guitarist tried "really hard" to like the new, modern PRS design. Eventually, PRS made Santana some replicas of his now well-used originals. PRS wanted to make its new Santana guitar a production model, and to use Santana's name. A deal was subsequently arranged, and a large percentage of Santana's royalties go to charity. Thus Santana became the first PRS signature artist, and remained so for some time, although Mark Tremonti, Dave Navarro and Johnny Hiland have been added to the endorsee roster in recent years.

By the mid 1990s PRS Guitars had become a major force in the rarefied atmosphere of high-end guitar producers. The once seemingly colossal Virginia Avenue factory was now outdated and overcrowded. In late 1995 the company moved across the Chesapeake bay to a new, purpose-built facility on Kent Island, at Stevensville.

Having invested in computer-assisted routing machines in 1995, more were installed at the new factory to bring a higher level of consistency to guitars that were already renowned for their craftsmanship. Pushing production efficiency further forward, robotic buffing machines appeared soon after the factory move. But even with these new tools, PRS guitars still felt "hand-made," comfortable instruments rather than sterile, machine-made items. Even with the high-tech equipment, there is more hand-work in the sanding, coloring and finishing of a PRS guitar than most other production instruments.

The first new models to come off the line in 1996 were the Rosewood Ltd and the Swamp Ash Special. The former continued Smith's pursuit of the ultimate tonewood for necks, featuring a solid East Indian rosewood neck with Brazilian rosewood fingerboard, the latter inlaid with a fantastically detailed tree-of-life design.

Although mahogany is used for the majority of PRS's set-neck guitars, there's little doubt that Paul Reed Smith would choose rosewood if the cost was not prohibitive. Smith's personal "number one" guitar – an amber-colored Dragon I – was the first PRS to feature a rosewood neck, and an Indian rosewood neck option was subsequently offered for the McCarty. In 1999 a limited run of McCartys with expensive Brazilian rosewood necks was made.

While the Rosewood Ltd was a limited edition of 100 pieces, it was dramatically different to the Swamp Ash Special, which was intended like the original Classic Electric and Studio to bring a more Fender-like tone to the PRS line. The 22-fret Swamp Ash Special, as its name implies, uses a lightweight ash body with bolt-on maple neck and fingerboard, and pairs two McCarty humbuckers with a centrally-placed single-coil-size humbucker. Also launched in

1996 were two more luxurious Artist models, the III and IV, which replaced the previous Artist II and Artist Limited.

In 1998 PRS launched a new line of hollowbody McCarty guitars, marking a company well into its stride. The Archtop looked like any other PRS, save for the twin f-holes and substantially deeper body. A guitar like this would not have been commercially possible if it wasn't for PRS's use of computer-assisted machinery. This hollows out the central mahogany block, leaving thin sides, a pocket for the neck and, importantly, a block under the bridge. Not only was the front carved but the back too and, like a violin, the top and back were carved on the inside as well.

Launched at the same time, the PRS Hollowbody used the same construction as the Archtop, except that the body was less deep: about three inches at its center as opposed to four inches. The majority of production-built semi-acoustic or fully hollow guitars use laminated maple tops, back and sides. PRS's use of solid timbers matches the kinds of specification usually limited to hand-carved (and very expensive) guitars.

The Archtop featured a new version of the PRS Stop-Tail tailpiece with adjustable saddles to cater for the larger string gauges used by the jazz players for whom the instrument was intended. Also, new pickups were developed for the guitar's more

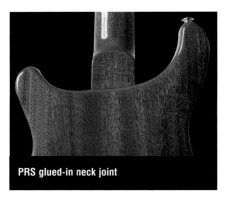

PRS glued-in neck joint

"classic" tones. The basic models came with spruce fronts and mahogany back and sides. The Archtop II and Hollowbody II added figured maple tops and backs, while the Archtop Artist was the top high-end model, what PRS called "a piece of art that doubles as a musical instrument."

This hollow guitar line had been developed by Joe Knaggs, PRS's master luthier who builds the majority of the company's custom one-off Private Stock line. The Archtop in particular was intended to enable PRS to offer a more jazz-oriented instrument. However, it quickly appeared that the more Gibson ES-335-like Hollowbody was the most popular of the new line, and by late 1998 it accounted for nearly half of PRS's total production.

All the Hollowbody and Archtop models are offered with an optional piezo-pickup bridge system, developed in conjunction with noted US acoustic pickup manufacturer L.R. Baggs. The extremely efficient piezo system allows these guitars to sound like amplified acoustic instruments as well as offering all the usual magnetic pickup tones. By 2000 the Hollowbody craze had settled, while the Archtop had become a minor part of PRS sales.

The introduction of left-handed PRS models came in 1999 for the McCarty and Custom 22 (with Stop-Tail or vibrato bridge). Typically, these were carefully detailed models with every feature properly left-handed, from the headstock logo to the control-knob labeling.

Some 25 years after Smith built his first proper electric – that single-cutaway flat-front Les Paul-alike – PRS launched the Singlecut, the closest the company had got to both the look and tone of those classic vintage Les Pauls. The company's first ads for the new model, which wasn't in the McCarty line, featured a profile picture of Ted McCarty and the caption, "Ted McCarty introduced the single cutaway, carved-top solidbody to the world in 1952. We learned a lot from Ted while we working on ours." This illustrated where PRS was heading.

Over the years many companies have either blatantly copied the Les Paul or used it as clear inspiration. Yet the PRS Singlecut will be seen by many as the closest anyone has come to the hallowed tone of Gibson's late-1950s Les Paul without actually breaching any trademarked design features.

Apart from the single-cutaway shape, the guitar follows the specification of PRS's McCarty model with, typically, many subtle changes. These include a slightly thicker body and new covered pickups, which are simply called PRS 7s. Smith believes these are the closest yet to the tone of original Gibson PAFs, but with modern-day performance standards.

On the Singlecut's launch early in 2000, initial sales proved immensely strong, but whether the Singlecut will prove as popular in the long term as the Custom and McCarty Model remains to be seen.

However, the launch of that new guitar was rather over-shadowed by the leading PRS player Carlos Santana, who simply refused to fade away. In February 2000, at the age of 52, Santana won a phenomenal eight Grammy Awards for his 1999 *Supernatural* album, equaling Michael Jackson's previous record for *Thriller* in 1983. At the time of writing, *Supernatural* had notched up sales in excess of 11 million copies. As the awards ceremony closed, there was Santana propelling his hallmark Latin-tinged music on his beautifully distinctive PRS guitar.

Paul Reed Smith is the first to acknowledge Santana's importance to the company. But the lanky, big-haired kid from Maryland, now in his early 50s, must have been extremely proud to witness Santana – some two decades after he'd first plucked a PRS – still making incredible music in front of the world's most important music-industry people on a guitar that was originally conceived in an impossibly small workshop in Annapolis. Maybe it was an accident of God after all.

In 2004 a US District Court in Tennessee upheld Gibson's claim that the Singlecut model infringed upon Gibson's patent for the Les Paul body shape, although in September 2005 a US Court Of Appeals reversed the decision and threw out an injunction prohibiting PRS from manufacturing and selling Singlecut guitars. Post-injunction, models such as the Singlecut Standard, Tremonti Singlecut, and Singlecut Trem Modern Eagle have proven themselves popular with players looking for an alternative to the original set-neck, single-cutaway solidbody. Meanwhile, PRS's imported SE range has also brought many of the Maryland maker's most popular models within reach of less well-heeled guitarists.

Rickenbacker

From the British Invasion of The Beatles, to the heavy Brit-rock of The Who, to classic West Coast janglepop, Rickenbacker electric guitar have established a distinctive but surprisingly versatile sonic signature that remains unequalled.

Rickenbacker is best known for great 1950s designs and its popularization of the electric 12-string guitar through prominent use by The Beatles and The Byrds in the 1960s. Adolph Rickenbacker was born near Basel, Switzerland, in 1886, but while still young was brought to the United States. Around 1918 he moved to Los Angeles, California, and in the 1920s established a successful tool-and-die operation there, stamping out metal and plastic parts. One especially enthusiastic customer for these was the National guitar company of Los Angeles.

At National, George Beauchamp and Paul Barth put together a basic magnetic pickup for guitar. Their experiments culminated in a pickup with a pair of horseshoe-shape magnets enclosing the pickup coil and surrounding the strings. Beauchamp and Barth had a working version in mid 1931. Another National man, Harry Watson, built a one-piece maple lap-steel guitar on which the prototype pickup could be mounted. This was the famous wooden "Frying Pan" guitar, so-called because of its small round body and long neck. It was the first guitar to feature an electro-magnetic pickup, and in that sense the basis for

virtually all modern electric guitars.

Beauchamp, Barth and Adolph Rickenbacker teamed up to put the ideas of this exciting prototype electric guitar into production. They formed the curiously named Ro-Pat-In company at the end of 1931 – just before Beauchamp and Barth were fired by National. In summer 1932 Ro-Pat-In started manufacturing cast aluminum production versions of the Frying Pan electric lap-steel guitar, complete with horseshoe electro-magnetic pickups. Ro-Pat-In's Frying Pans were effectively the first electric guitars with electro-magnetic pickups put into general production.

Early examples of the Frying Pan lap-steels tend to have the Electro brandname on the headstock, and so are usually referred to by players and collectors as the Electro Hawaiian models. By 1934 "Rickenbacker" (sometimes "Rickenbacher") had been added to the headstock logo. Also that year the name of the manufacturing company was changed from the bizarre Ro-Pat-In to the more logical Electro String Instrument Corporation.

Around this time Electro also produced some Spanish wood-body archtop electrics. The Electro Spanish appeared around 1932 – among the earliest of its kind – and the Ken Roberts model, named for a session guitarist, followed about three years later. Bakelite was the first synthetic plastic, and Electro started using it in 1935 for its Model B Hawaiian lap-steel and the Electro Spanish (also called the Model B). The latter was arguably the first "solidbody" electric guitar.

During World War II Electro worked for the government, extending the Los Angeles factory in the process. After the war Adolph Rickenbacker decided not to continue producing many of his musical instruments, including most of the poorly-received Spanish electrics. During 1946 he turned 60, and began to think about selling the musical instrument part of his business.

S1964 Rickenbacker 325S
BODY: double-cutaway semi-solid maple body.
NECK: set neck with 1 ⅝" nut width, 10" fingerboard radius, and 20 ¾" scale length.
BRIDGE: same as 360, with added Accent Vibrato.
ELECTRONICS: three single-coil toaster-top pickups; DC resistance of approximately 5k to 7k. Three-way toggle switch to select either the bridge pickup alone, all three pickups together, or neck and middle pickup together (no neck-pickup-only selection, although it can be tweaked with the…); Blend control for fine-tuning balance of neck pickup's input into other selections.
SOUND: bright, springy, slightly sizzling and somewhat loose.

1961 Rickenbacker 460:
BODY: solid maple body with flat face; top binding; deep double cutaways with easy access to the top fret. Semi-transparent cherry sunburst finish in nitrocellulose lacque.
NECK: maple 'through neck' (integral neck and central body block cut from one piece of wood); rosewood fingerboard; 10" fingerboard radius, 21 nickel-silver frets, and 1 ⅝" nut width; 24 ¾" scale length.
HEADSTOCK: back-angled asymmetrical headstock, with three-a-side Kluson tuners; synthetic nut.
BRIDGE: strings top-anchored in rear lip of sheet-steel base plate (forming bridge base/tail piece unit); one-piece die-cast compensated aluminum bridge, adjustable for height only (bridge stems from the design of the floating bridge of the Bigsby vibrato).
ELECTRONICS: dual single-coil pickups; early 'toaster tops' had quite low DC resistance readings in the 5k to 6k range, while those of the mid-1960s ranged widely between 7k and 8.5k. Three-way toggle switch to select either pickup alone or both together; two 250k potentiometers for individual Volume and two 500k pots for individual Tone for each pickup; 500k pot for 'Blend' control, which can add a little of the non-selected pickup to the sound of the one selected by the switch, or emphasize more of one or the other pickup in the middle switch position.
SOUND: generally bright, chimey and cutting, with a good blend of sparkle and tightness, and just a little sizzle. A classic rhythm guitar for British invasion or West Coast jangle sounds.

The eventual buyer was Francis Cary Hall, who had moved with his family to California when he was around 11 years old. He'd opened a radio repair store, Hall's Radio Service, in the 1920s. This led logically to a wholesale company distributing electronic parts, the Radio & Television Equipment Co (Radio-Tel), which F.C. Hall set up in Santa Ana, Orange County, in 1936. After distributing Fender guitars and amplifiers for a time, Hall began to see the potential for an instrument business where he not only distributed the product but also manufactured it. So in late 1953 Hall bought the Electro String Music Corporation from Adolph, with its guitar factory still at South Western Avenue, Los Angeles.

Around the beginning of 1954 German-born guitar-maker Roger Rossmeisl, previously at Gibson, was hired by Electro to come up with new designs for Rickenbacker electric guitars. That same year Electro launched its first "modern" electrics, the double-cutaway carved-top Rickenbacker Combo 600 and Combo 800. They were aptly named, combining the horseshoe pickup and almost square neck of the earlier Hawaiian lap-steels with the up-and-coming solidbody electric Spanish style. The first

George Harrison's 1964 Rickenabacker 360/12

BODY: routed-out double-cutaway maple body with single-ply top binding and recessed tail section; 21st fret neck join.

NECK: three-ply maple and rosewood neck, neck-through-body construction; bound and varnished rosewood fingerboard with a 10" radius, 21 narrow nickel-silver frets; 24 ¾" scale length.

HEADSTOCK: asymmetrical back-angled headstock, with six-a-side Kluson tuners (three mounted in standard fashion, three at right angles with buttons pointing to the back of the headstock); headstock-end truss-rod access.

BRIDGE: metal bridge with six individual saddles (slotted for two strings per saddle), adjustable for height and string-pair intonation; simple trapeze tailpiece inset in recessed body carve.

ELECTRONICS: two single-coil Rickenbacker 'toaster-top' pickups, with DC resistance of around 5k to 7k; three-way toggle for selecting pickups individually or together; independent Volume and Tone controls for each pickup; later models carried a fifth Blend control to add fine-tune the neck pickup's contribution to the overall sound.

SOUND: bright, snappy, round, with a crisp attack, a slightly sizzling front end, and decent sustain.

1993 Rickenbacker Tom Petty Model

BODY: solid maple body with flat face.

NECK: neck-through-body construction; maple neck with bound and varnished rosewood fingerboard with a 10" radius, 21 narrow nickel-silver frets; 24 ¾" scale length.

HEADSTOCK: asymmetrical back-angled headstock, with six-a-side Kluson-style tuners (three mounted in standard fashion, three at right angles with buttons pointing to the back of the headstock); headstock-end truss-rod access.

BRIDGE: metal bridge with six individual saddles (slotted for two strings per saddle), adjustable for height and string-pair intonation; simple trapeze tailpiece inset in recessed body carve.

ELECTRONICS: two modern single-coil Rickenbacker 'toaster-top' pickups, with DC resistance of around 7k to 9k; three-way toggle for selecting pickups individually or together; independent Volume and Tone controls for each pickup; later models carried a fifth Blend control to add fine-tune the neck pickup's contribution to the overall sound.

SOUND: bright, snappy, well-defined, with a crisp attack, a slightly sizzling front end, and good sustain.

Combo models began to feature on the headstocks a brand new "underlined" Rickenbacker logo of the type that is still in use today.

Electro's next move was to abandon the clumsy horseshoe pickup and apply a more suitable pickup to its Spanish electrics. First to receive the new pickup was the Combo 400, launched in 1956. Another first was its through-neck construction, a feature that would become a familiar aspect of many of Rickenbacker's solidbody instruments.

New Combo 650 and Combo 850 models appeared in 1957, introducing a body shape with a "sweeping crescent"-shape across the two cutaways. In various incarnations and dimensions this has been in continual use by Rickenbacker to the present day.

In 1958 a series of new models was introduced that formed the basis for Rickenbacker's success during the 1960s and onwards. The thin-hollow-body designs were largely the responsibility of Rossmeisl. For these new electric hollowbody Capri guitars he further developed an unusual "scooped-out" construction. Rather than make a hollow guitar in the traditional method he would start with a semi-solid block of wood – usually two halves of maple joined together – and cut it to a rough body shape, partially hollowing it out from the rear. A separate wooden back was added once all the electric fittings had been secured, and the neck was glued into place.

The first new Capri was the small-body short-scale three-pickup 325 model, a guitar

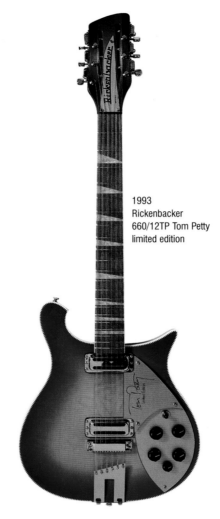

1993 Rickenbacker 660/12TP Tom Petty limited edition

that would have a great effect on the company's success when it was taken up a few years later by John Lennon. A full 12-model Capri line-up was launched during 1958, though the Capri name itself was soon dropped. There were four short-scale

1964 Rickenabacker 325S

BODY: double-cutaway semi-solid maple body.

NECK: set neck with 1 ⅝" 10" radius, 21 narrow nickel-silver frets; 20 ¾" scale length.

HEADSTOCK: asymmetrical back-angled headstock, with three-a-side kluson tuners; synthetic nut; headstock-end truss-rod access.

BRIDGE: metal bridge adjustable for height and individual string intonation; simple trapeze tailpiece inset in recessed body carve.

ELECTRONICS: three single-coil Rickenbacker 'toaster-top' pickups, with DC resistance of around 5k to 7k; three-way toggle to select either the bridge pickup alone, all three pickups together, or neck and middle pickup together (no neck-only selection, although it can be achieved with the blend control); blend control for fine-tuning balance of neck pickup's input into hter selections.

SOUND: bright, springy, sizzling and somewhat loose.

models: 310 (two pickups), 315 (plus vibrato), 320 (three pickups) and 325 (plus vibrato); four full-scale models: 330 (two pickups), 335 (plus vibrato), 340 (three pickups) and 345 (plus vibrato); and four "deluxe" full-scale models with triangle-shape fingerboard inlays: 360 (two pickups), 365 (plus vibrato), 370 (three pickups) and 375 (plus vibrato).

Two classic Rickenbacker design elements began to appear at this time. New "toaster-top" pickups were devised, nicknamed for their split chrome look, and unusual two-tier pickguards, made at first in an arresting gold-colored plastic. These comprised a base plate flush to the guitar's body carrying the controls, plus a second level raised on three short pillars, intended as a finger-rest. Another idiosyncratic touch was the shortlived "cooker" control knobs with distinctive diamond-shaped pointers on top.

In 1960 a new stereo feature called Rick-O-Sound was added to some guitars. The system simply separated the output from neck and bridge pickups so that a special split cord would feed the individual signals to two amplifiers (or two channels), made possible by a special double jack offering mono or stereo output from Rick-O-Sound-equipped Rickenbackers. In summer 1962

1968 Rickenbacker 360SF

the factory moved from South Western Avenue, Los Angeles, to Kilson Drive, Santa Ana, not far from the Radio-Tel HQ. Soon afterwards Roger Rossmeisl left to work for Fender.

During 1963 the company started to develop an electric 12-string guitar. Acoustic 12-strings had been around for some time, and the folk craze in the early 1960s had given a boost to their appeal. Electric 12s were far less common. The first had been made around 1955 by the small Stratosphere company, while Danelectro's Bellzouki model had been launched in 1961. The glorious electric 12-string sound derived from octave and unison doubling of paired strings to produce a wonderful "jangling" sound, almost as if two guitars were playing together.

Dick Burke came up with a brilliant headstock modification for the new Rickenbacker 12 that kept the existing six tuners where they normally were – three on each side – but added two parallel channels into the face, as if the slots of a classical guitar had been cut only half-way through. Burke attached the second set of six tuners at 90 degrees to the first set, the keys facing "backwards" – again, like a classical guitar, with strings attached into the tuners' spindles in the channels.

Rickenbacker made at least three experimental 12-string guitars in 1963. The first model went to showband singer, fiddle-player and guitarist Suzi Arden, whose Suzi Arden Show, a regular at the Golden Nugget in Las Vegas, was kitted out with Rickenbacker equipment.

Rickenbacker set up a special display at the Savoy Hilton hotel in New York City in February 1964 to show some equipment to The Beatles. The group's arrival in the US to play Ed Sullivan's TV show and three

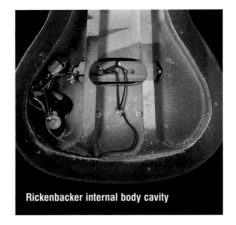

Rickenbacker internal body cavity

concerts had caused unrivalled scenes of fan mania. Despite missing the display due to illness, George Harrison ended up with a great prize, one of the company's experimental 12-string electrics, in model 360 style.

John Lennon also came away with a new guitar, a black 325 model with the new five-control layout, replacing the somewhat road-weary early-style 325 that he'd used for most of the group's early career. The company also promised to send Lennon a special one-off 12-string version of the 325, and Beatles manager Brian Epstein requested a second 360-style 12-string for another of his now famous charges, Gerry Marsden of Gerry & The Pacemakers.

For the two *Ed Sullivan Show* appearances in New York Lennon used his old 325, but for a further appearance, broadcast from Miami, Lennon gave his new five-knob 325 its public debut. The Sullivan shows were outrageously popular, each receiving an unprecedented American TV audience of some 70 million viewers. No doubt Rickenbacker boss F.C. Hall allowed himself a smile as he watched the group perform in the New York TV studio.

After their thoroughly successful invasion of the United States, The Beatles returned to Britain, and Harrison used his 12-string to great effect on some new recordings, including the distinctive opening chord of the title song from *A Hard Day's Night*, ringing out in typically jangling fashion. A rush for Rickenbacker 12-strings followed. Rickenbackers proved popular with other British pop guitarists during the second half of the 1960s, including Denny Laine, Hilton Valentine and, most notably, Pete Townshend.

During 1964 Rickenbacker officially added three 12-strings to its line, the 360/12 (two-pickup 360-style), 370/12 (three pickups) and 450/12 (two-pickup solidbody). The company also began at this time to supply export versions of certain models to distributor Rose-Morris in the UK, lasting until 1969. This would be unremarkable but for the fact that the British company requested instruments with real f-holes

rather than Rickenbacker's customary "slash"-shape soundholes, and models with this feature have since become collectable.

From 1964 Rickenbacker introduced an alternative body style for the "deluxe" models (360, 360/12, 365, 370, 370/12 and 375) with a streamlined, less angular look to the front of the body, as well as binding on the soundhole and, now, only on the back edge of the body. Designed to be more comfortable for the player, the new streamlined design was the main production style used for the models mentioned from 1964. Old-style versions (body bound front and back, "sharp" edges) remained available on special order. A year earlier Rickenbacker had also introduced a striking new tailpiece, in the shape of a large "R".

The name of the sales/distribution company was changed in 1965 from the old Radio & Television Equipment Co to the more appropriate Rickenbacker Inc, and the sales office moved within Santa Ana in 1966. The name of the manufacturing company remained as Electro String.

A "light-show" guitar was introduced in 1970 with a clear plastic top through which a psychedelic array of colored lights would shine, flashing in response to the frequencies of the notes being played. Roger McGuinn had a special 12-string light-show Rickenbacker built with slanted frets and three pickups, which he used for 'Eight Miles High' at the end of Byrds shows in the early 1970s. It was perhaps the most bizarre Rickenbacker ever made – a rare beast indeed, given the number of oddities that came from the Santa Ana factory.

Around this time demand for Rickenbackers began to decline. Fortunately for Rickenbacker, its bass guitars gained in popularity in the early 1970s and production began to pick up again at Santa Ana, concentrating on four-string models.

A new body shape appeared in 1973, although it was really only new to Rickenbacker's six-string guitar lines. The 480 used the body styling made famous by the company's basses, which had first appeared in 1957, with a distinctive elongated upper horn.

A few custom double-neck guitars had been made for individual Rickenbacker customers in the 1960s, but in 1975 the company's first production double-necks appeared. There were two types: the 4080 also used the electric bass body, while the 362 enlarged upon the familiar 360 style.

In 1983 Rickenbacker made a low-key attempt to recreate some of its older models, which the company noticed were increasingly popular among "vintage" collectors. A new generation of guitarists had also started to take up Rickenbackers, and this helped the company's climb back to popularity during the 1980s. Among the

Two Rickenbacker pickups: the 'toaster-top' (above) and a Hi-Gain unit

Rickenbacker stereo jack (and serial number)

most notable and visible players of Rickenbackers at the time were Peter Buck and Johnny Marr. The jangling, rhythmic thrust of Rickenbackers was once more to be heard at the heart of some of pop's most vibrant offerings.

The business operation of Rickenbacker was changed in 1984 when F.C. Hall's son John, who'd worked at Rickenbacker since 1969, officially took control. He formed a new company, Rickenbacker International Corporation (RIC), which purchased the guitar-related parts of his father's Rickenbacker Inc and Electro String companies. In 1989 Rickenbacker moved its factory from Kilson Drive after some 27 years, consolidating factory and offices at the corner of South Main and Stevens in Santa Ana.

A new idea during the late 1980s was the production of numbered limited-edition signature models. Rickenbacker made seven artist guitars in editions of between 250 and 1,000: Pete Townshend (1987), Roger McGuinn (1988), John Kay (1988); Susanna Hoffs (1988), John Lennon (1989); Tom Petty (1991); and Glenn Frey (1992). Also, a proper Rickenbacker vintage reissue program is underway; it began in 1984 with the 325V59, 325V63 and 360/12V64 models ("V59" etc indicates the vintage – 1959 in this example), and at the time of writing is up to eight models.

In 1992 Rickenbacker devised the new 24-fret 650 series. These share the body style of the earlier 400 and 600 "cresting wave" models, but have wider necks and high output pickups to compete with more mainstream instruments. Still in the line today, they complement Rickenbacker's continuing business with its set of classic and apparently timeless designs.

Silvertone
Whether stamped on a guitar made by Kay, Harmony or Danelectro, Silvertone is undoubtedly the brand that launched a thousand riffs.
It's likely that more American guitarists began on a Silvertone sold by Chicago's Sears, Roebuck & Co than any other beginner guitar. Supplanting the Supertone

brand when Sears divested itself of the Harmony guitar company in 1940, Silvertone (a former radio/record-player/record brand) was first applied to guitars in 1941, with a version of the Kay Thin Twin and Sears' first Les-Paul-style Harmony solidbody appearing in 1954. That same year the first Danelectro-made Silvertone solidbodies appeared, followed by masonite-and-vinyl hollowbodies in 1956.

The legendary single-pickup amp-in-case guitars debuted in 1962. "Silvertone" appeared through the 1960s on solidbodies by both Kay (such as the Vanguard) and Harmony (for example the Silhouette). By 1965 Sears was offering numerous Japanese Teisco-made Silvertones, although these were sold through stores rather than the catalog. The first catalog Japanese-made Silvertones, by Kawai, appeared in 1969. By the early 1970s the Silvertone name was dropped from guitars.

Squier
Begun as a means for Fender to combat imported competition, Squier has grown into one of the most prominent beginner and lower-mid-level brands in the guitar industry.
Beginning in the early 1980s, Japanese-made Fender instruments exported into Europe (and later elsewhere) bore the Squier brandname. The name was borrowed from a string-making company, V.C. Squier of Michigan, that Fender had acquired in the mid 1960s. Victor Carroll Squier had been born in 19th-century Boston, the son of an English immigrant. Later he became a violin-maker and moved to Battle Creek in Michigan, where he founded his string-making firm in 1890.

Fender's policy was that the new 1980s Squier guitar brandname should cater for lower pricepoints. That way the company could maintain its ever-expanding market coverage but, crucially, without cheapening the valuable Fender brandname itself. The Squier logo, supported by a small but important "by Fender" line, began to appear on an increasing number of models during the decade.

Fender had established its Fender Japan operation with two Japanese partners – distributors Kanda Shokai and Yamano Music – in March 1982. Fender Japan at first used the Fujigen factory, based in Matsumoto, some 130 miles north-west of Tokyo, to produce Fender instruments for the Japanese market, as well as Fender- and Squier-branded instruments for export. Fujigen made Fender's Japanese Vintage series instruments in the early 1980s, as well as the initially Europe-only Squier-brand versions.

However, escalating production costs meant a move to cheaper manufacturing sources for Squier guitars. Korea came on

line in 1985, and India made a brief contribution in the late 1980s for some early "Squier II" instruments (or Sunn equivalents – another borrowed brandname, this time from an amplifier company purchased by Fender). Fender's factory in Mexico, established in 1987, also came into the picture when it produced some Squier guitars in the early 1990s, and more recently China has become a new source of Squiers, providing entry-level electrics with the essential kudos of a Fender connection.

A return to Japanese production yielded impressive results with Squier's shortlived Vista series.

Hole guitarist Courtney Love's Rickenbacker-like design became the Vista-series Venus; the Jagmaster was prompted by Bush vocalist Gavin Rossdale's humbucker-modified Jazzmaster; and the Super-Sonic model was apparently inspired

by a photo of Jimi Hendrix unusually playing an upside-down Jaguar.

The more recent Squier Pro Tone line offered evidence of improving Korean quality, which has been echoed throughout the entire line, from the simple, workmanlike and super-affordable '51 model to the set-neck Master Series M80 and Esprit, which clearly aim to give Epiphone's Gibson-inspired guitars a run for their money. The continuing success of Squier makes it a fine "support" brand for Fender, often with a level of design and build quality that exceeds its apparent status as a secondary line.

Steinberger
While the minimalist, headless, rectangular-bodied bass and guitar seem an apt representative both of the styles and the music of the 1980s, Steinberger's designs have proven impressively enduring, and offer truly worthy instruments beneath the space-aged appointments.
Ned Steinberger proved that conventional materials are not essential to the production of a first-class instrument. Art-school graduate Steinberger moved to New York in

the 1970s, and designed the NS bass for maker Stuart Spector in 1977. Steinberger produced his own bass, the L-2, in 1981. It combined plastic materials with a radical new "body-less" and headless design.

A six-string Steinberger guitar, the GL, followed in 1983. As with the bass, the usual headstock was discarded, and tuners were moved to the end of the minimal body. The one-piece hollow neck and body was made of a fiber and resin composite, sealed initially with a removable "lid" on top to which the equally innovative active EMG pickups were mounted.

For a short time in the high-tech obsessed 1980s the Steinberger design seemed to be the future of the electric instrument. But despite use by many top players, including Eddie Van Halen and Allan Holdsworth, it proved too uncompromising for mainstream acceptance. Subsequently, wooden-body instruments appeared made both in the US and offshore, and in 1991 the conveniently-shaped Sceptre model appeared – with a headstock. It was the designer's last project for the now Gibson-owned Steinberger company.

In retrospect it is more likely to be Steinberger's hardware – notably the unique Transtrem body-end tuning system and the gear-less tuners – that are his lasting legacy to the modern guitar world. The 1990s saw some new popularity fueled by 1980s revivalists such as Warren Cuccurullo. The Steinberger brand has since been acquired by Gibson, and at the time of writing a broad range of both imported and US-made basses and six string models is once again available, featuring the classic Steinberger designs along with some newer shapes.

Supro

Although its existence was largely that of a budget support brand to one of the formative US makers in the history

1958
Supro Dual Tone

1958 Supro Dual Tone

BODY: plastic-covered solid body constructed from a softer hardwood; single cutaway.

NECK: bolt-on maple neck with rosewood fingerboard, 20 nickel-silver frets, and 1 ⅝" nut width; 24 ¾" scale length.

HEADSTOCK: three-per-side Kluson tuners; plastic nut.

BRIDGE: height-adjustable floating two-piece rosewood bridge; stairstep trapeze tailpiece.

ELECTRONICS: two identical single-coil pickups, each with single side-on alnico bar magnet and threaded steel pole pieces; three-way switch to select each pickup individually or bridge pickup with preset bright sound; individual Volume and Tone controls for each pickup.

SOUND: fat, clanky and bright, with a slightly gritty edge.

of the electric guitar, the Supro name has acquired the mantle of legend, and has earned its own moments in the spotlight.

As guitar manufacturers took their first tentative steps toward electric guitars in the 1930s, Supro emerged as the primarily electric budget-price line of Los Angeles-based National-Dobro. This was the recombined National and Dobro companies. The Supro brand first appeared on a cast aluminum "frying pan" Hawaiian lap-steel, a Spanish electric archtop and other instruments in 1935. It would also be the principal brandname used by National-Dobro on amplifiers through the 1960s.

Following a relocation in 1936 to Chicago, the Supro name was used on some of the earliest lap-steels with an amp-in-case design, such as the battery-powered Portable 70 – an idea that would return again briefly in 1955. Supro would appear on a variety of lap-steels through the 1960s, and was occasionally used on resonator guitars. The Supro Capitan electric archtop and Rio electric flat-top debuted in 1941, with more electric archtops such as the El Capitan and Ranchero picking up after World War II.

In 1942 Victor Smith, Al Frost and Louis Dopyera bought the company and changed the name to the Valco Manufacturing Company. In 1948 one of the brand's most distinctive features appeared, the under-bridge Bridge-Tone transducer pickup. It was usually used in conjunction with magnetic pickups.

Supro's first solidbody electrics debuted in 1952, the Spanish-shaped Ozark and single-cutaway Ozark Cut-Away Jet, both with small slab bodies, floating pickups attached to a large housing containing the wiring harness, and a characteristic bolt-on neck that sat very high on the body at the joint. The single-cutaway Supro Dual-Tone solidbody debuted in 1954, receiving top-mounted pickups the following year. Supro's first cutaway electric archtop also appeared in 1955. Beginning in 1957 the Bridge-Tone pickup was included on many solidbodys.

In 1962 the company modified its name to Valco Guitars Inc, and the guitar line changed from wood construction to fiberglass bodies in various colors with plastic-faced "Gumby" headstocks. Robert Engelhardt bought Valco in 1964, changed to a more Fender-style wood-bodied guitar design in 1965, and offered Supro's first double-cutaway thinlines in 1966.

The following year, with the guitar boom at full volume, Valco bought its competitor, the Kay Musical Instrument Company... and went bankrupt in 1968. At the end, the Supro logo was applied to a variety of Kay-made acoustic instruments. The Supro name was purchased at auction in 1969, but went unused until it resurfaced briefly on guitars assembled from old parts in the early 1980s. Recently, the name has also graced a "tribute" model from Eastwood Guitars, which has based its Supro DLX roughly on an old Res-O-Glas design, but instead uses a chambered mahogany body and dual humbucking pickups.

Teisco

Like so many kitsch designs, more interesting guitars in the quirky, often oddball Teisco range – low-budget alternatives at best when they first hit Western shores – have acquired a certain stylistic cachet in this retro-minded new millennium.

Emblematic of 1960s Japanese-made beginner guitars, Teisco was unusual in using mainly its own brandname. Atswo Kaneko and Doryu Matsuda introduced Teisco lap-steels in 1946, followed by Gibson-style guitars. By 1960 Jack Westheimer began importing Fender-like Teiscos to the US.

The Teisco Del Rey brand debuted in 1964, including the TRG-1 amp-in-guitar. In 1965 WMI also brought Teisco Del Reys into America, including 1966's flared-cutaway pushbutton Spectrum 5. Teisco was

guitar facts

1968
Tokai Humming Bird

Tokai's standards improved considerably during the 1970s, and the large Hamamatsu factory became responsible for much sub-contract work for other Japanese guitar brands. Tokai did not yet export its own-brand guitars, but this changed dramatically in the 1980s. The Tokai lines included over 100 models by then, many reproductions of popular instruments from the best American brands. Copy guitars were a well-established and commercial force in the world guitar market, but Tokai significantly increased the accuracy and quality.

Tokais began to arrive in Europe and the US around 1981 and were an immediate success. This was assisted in America by the dollar's soaring value compared to the yen, making Japanese instruments good value. The success triggered a fight from Fender, targeted most directly by the copying. Fender's answer in 1982 was to establish Fender Japan to produce "authorized copies." This proved a successful move which naturally dented the sales of Tokai and other Japanese copyists – although Japanese-made guitars continued to be popular.

Tokai catered for the Japanese market with a variety of models that ranged from the Triangle-X and Zero Fighter "reverse-body" originals to the Fender-influenced Versatile Sound selection. In the US the first line from the new Robin brand took advantage of Tokai's continuing sub-contract work. Prior to a change brought by legal challenges, Tokai used a very Fender-style logo. Other Tokai clones included recreations of Gibson's Les Paul, ES-series semis, Flying V and Explorer, plus various limited-production variations incorporating deluxe options.

Some Tokai originals appeared too: the 1985 Talbo had a distinctively designed aluminum body (Tokai ALuminum BOdy) while the same year's MAT series (Most Advanced Technology) was seemingly Fender-style, but with necks and bodies made from various combinations of fiberglass and carbon graphite.

By the mid 1990s Tokai had stopped exporting, and at home were limited to various synthetic-body Talbo models. In 1999 a revised version of conventional material appeared, the Talbo Woody. A full-range of Gibson- and Fender-inspired models was offered once again in the UK by the turn of the century, with plans afoot at the time of writing for Godlyke Distribution to handle sales of a broad Tokai line in the US.

Tom Anderson Guitarworks

The range of respected, independent "boutique" guitar-makers seems to grow every day, but Tom Anderson was at the front of the trend for the modern era, and remains one of the

F A C T   F I L E

Locking tuners are tuners (tuning keys, machineheads) that lock the strings in place within the posts, usually by means of a thumb screw or clamp threaded into the post from the top, in order to both increase the stability of the string's anchoring at the tuner and to make string loading quicker. Such tuners enable strings to be brought up to pitch without multiple wraps around the post, and thereby leave less string length to stretch – and, thereby, send the string out of tune – in the course of playing.

most respected designers and manufacturers in the field.

A small-scale operation making some of the most respected high-performance electric guitars, Tom Anderson Guitarworks was begun in 1984 by the ex-Schecter Anderson. It is currently based in Newbury Park, California, producing some 800 guitars a year. During the 1990s the brand became

1989
Tom Anderson
Guitarworks
Grand Lam T

purchased by Kawai in Japan in 1967. In 1969 WMI bought Kay, and by 1972 were using that brand rather than Teisco. Kawai revived the Teisco brand in the early 1990s.

Tokai
Its early designs were more inventive than those of many Japanese makers, and the company was notably late to the "copy game" when compared to Ibanez or Aria, but Tokai's "tributes" to major American makers earned the brand major kudos and genuine respect from players.

In the 1980s Tokai's blatant replicas of classic American guitars highlighted the threat posed to US makers by Japanese "copy" guitars. Tokai was based in Hamamatsu, Japan, and produced its first electrics in 1967, the Humming Bird models. Styling varied, but the "reverse-body" models were heavily influenced by Mosrite, though with savagely pointed horns. Tokai's quality at this time was adequate – better than some of the home competition, but not so good as makers like Yamaha.

As with many Japanese manufacturers,

synonymous with high quality. Their modernized Strat-style outline often employs a maple "drop top" (a method of laminating a thin maple top over the body's Strat-like contouring), with Anderson's own pickups and highly versatile switching, plus an option list that is wider than many custom shops.

Models include the Pro Am Classic, Grand Am Lam, Drop Top T, Hollow Drop Top and Cobra, all in a broadly Fender or superstrat style. Anderson was one of the first makers to embrace the Buzz Feiten tuning system, a standard fitting since 1996 (an attempt to "correct" the compromise of equal-tempered tuning using a clever compensated nut).

Nearly a decade later, Anderson took its first major step toward more overtly Gibson-inspired territory with the Atom, a single-cutaway, 24.75"-scale model employing a new two-bolt neck technology that Anderson calls the "A-Wedgie" neck joint. Anderson players include Vivian Campbell, Dann Huff, and Pete Anderson.

Travis Bean
Both revolutionary and of high quality, Travis Bean guitars nevertheless had some difficulty gaining mainstream acceptance.
Although not the first to feature aluminum necks, Travis Bean's guitars caused quite a stir in 1974. Based in Sun Valley, California, Bean decided he could solve stability problems and enhance sustain with the light metal necks.

The first and most famous Travis Bean was the equal-double-cutaway, two-humbucker TB1000, initially offered as the slab-bodied Standard but soon joined by the carved-top, block-inlaid Artist. The triangular-shaped Wedge looked and felt clumsy, but the "budget" TB500 was better.

With offset cutaways and pickguard-mounted controls, this slim-bodied solid offered Fender-like flavors, as did Bean's powerful single-coil pickups.

Jerry Garcia was a famous endorser, but many players didn't like the cold feel of aluminum. Business pressures made Bean himself shut up shop in 1979. Guitarists such as Stanley Jordan and Slash have since helped raise the brand's profile, and in 1998 Travis Bean returned to the fray with a remake of the TB1000, but high price tags in the $8,000 to $9,000 range appear to have limited sales of the instrument.

Valley Arts
From custom made in the US, to imported, this California company has provided guitars to cover a broad range of styles and requirements.
Valley Arts originated from a retail operation, expanding during the 1970s to build its own high-end Custom Pro instruments. These

mainly followed familiar Fender designs with variations determined by a comprehensive option list.

Larry Carlton was an early endorser resulting in a 1990s signature model; unusually for "Mr. 335" it was a small-bodied solid. It combined Tele and Strat styling, but hardware was Gibson-based. The Standard version came with a pickguard; the Custom had a carved top.

The Standard Pro series introduced in the late 1980s offered less expensive US instruments, while the same period saw the addition of Japanese-made models such as the M series. This lowered prices further, as has the involvement since 1993 of major Korean manufacturer Samick.

More recent lines include the California Pro and IML series, joined in 1996 by the Studio Pro series, along with signature models such as Ray Benson's oversized-Tele-style Texas T.

Veleno
Despite miniscule production numbers even by the standards of better-known independent guitar-makers, Valenos' outrageous looks attained the brand an enduring place in rock history.
The shiny chrome plating on these carved-aluminum hollowbody guitars was well suited to the glam tastes of early 1970s rockers – which is why they were owned by Marc Bolan, Eric Clapton, Gregg Allman, Pete Haycock, Alvin Lee, Ronnie Montrose, Martin Barre, Ace Frehley, Jeff Lynne, Lou Reed, Dave Peverett and Mark Farner. John Veleno was a St. Petersburg, Florida, engineer and guitar teacher who began hand-making his unusual aluminum guitars

around 1970, personally marketing them to touring guitarists who passed through Florida at the time.

By 1971 the early six-tuners-in-line headstock changed to the more common three-and-three V-shape with ruby insert, for the model known as the Original. Available in chrome, gold and other anodized colors (some with a black anodized neck), Veleno Originals primarily featured two humbuckers (by Guild, Gibson or DiMarzio) with coil-taps and phase-switching. Only between 145 and 185 Veleno Originals were made, probably until early 1977.

Inspired by a post-concert conversation with B.B. King and working with Mark Farner, Veleno also developed a mini-guitar known as the Traveller (two were made by Veleno, around ten by his son). Veleno made one bass, and built two Egyptian "ankh"-shaped guitars for Todd Rundgren in 1977 before abandoning the guitar business to become a wedding photographer.

Vox
Just a footnote in guitar history if not for their use by Brian Jones of the Rolling Stones and Tony Hicks of The Hollies, the better Vox guitars were nevertheless versatile and well-made instruments.
Vox amplifiers were a great British 1960s success, but the company's stylish guitars made less impact. Vox products were originally made by Jennings in Dartford, Kent, set up by Tom Jennings in the 1950s. The factory was not equipped at first to make guitars, so most early Vox electrics – aimed at beginners on a budget – came from other UK or Italian sources.

In 1962 the first Vox original appeared from Dartford. The Phantom had an unusual body styled by The Design Centre in London. Equipped with three single-coil pickups, a spear-shape headstock and a "Hank B. Marvin" vibrato tailpiece, the Phantom was without curves, making it a guitar to be played only while standing.

The second Vox design landmark came with the teardrop-shape Mark series, launched in 1964: Mk VI six-string and Mk XII 12-string. Marks and Phantoms were offered

---

1999 Tom Anderson Hollow Drop Top
BODY: semi-solid basswood body with quilted maple top with natural maple binding; offset double-cutaways.

NECK: bolt-on maple neck with rosewood fingerboard with compound (conical) 12" to 14" radius; 22 medium-jumbo nickel-silver frets, and 1 11/16" nut width; 25 ½" scale length.

HEADSTOCK: six-a-side sealed locking Grover tuners; Buzz Feiten Tempered Tuning system.

BRIDGE: dual-pole fulcrum vibrato bridge with six individually adjustable, piezo-equipped saddles.

ELECTRONICS: single Anderson H humbucker in bridge, two single-coil sized hum-canceling pickups; piezo pickups in bridge saddles; switching to achieve virtually all conceivable combinations.

SOUND: a myriad options and blends, from hot and singing bridge-position humbucker sounds to brighter, snappier single-coil sound, with faux-acoustic tones also available.

from 1967 with optional active circuits, controlled by six pushbuttons on the body. Alongside were more bargain models, better Fender-derivatives like the Soundcaster, a line of Italian-made semis, and an assortment of Vox oddities such as the mini-12-string Mando-Guitar (1965) and the unreliable Guitar Organ (1966).

Vox transferred guitar production to Eko in Italy from 1966, and now began to include many models made specifically for the US market. Mounting problems led to the demise of Vox guitars in 1969. The brand was revived on a number of occasions, including three unexciting oriental Vox-brand lines in the 1980s.

Interest continued to grow in the classic Phantom and Mark originals from the 1960s, and there were several low-key reintroductions. Phantom Guitarworks in the US made a higher-profile effort, but in 1998 electronic-music company Korg launched an impressive new line of US-made reproductions, including the Mk III BJ, a white two-pickup guitar offered in memory of the unusual Mk VI played by Brian Jones in the 1960s.

Washburn

One of the great names of the early days of the American guitar industry, Washburn has grown to be yet again a force in the mass market, although the maker has changed in all but name.

Washburn is a famous old US brandname that lives on thanks mainly to instruments of oriental origin. George Washburn Lyon was an associate in Chicago's big Lyon & Healy company, founded in 1864. Guitar-maker Patrick J. Healy was a founder of the American acoustic guitar industry, but it was Lyon's middle name that provided the brandname for a prodigious quantity of flat-top acoustics produced by Lyon & Healy.

By the 1920s competition had grown and business was down. Lyon & Healy sold the Washburn name to distribution company Tonk Bros in 1928. After World War II, Tonk did not revive the Washburn name, which went unused until a small company called Beckmen used it in the early 1970s. Beckmen soon sold the name to a Chicago-based importer, Fretted Industries Inc.

Fretted Industries was owned by guitar-maker Rudy Schlacher and musician Rick Johnstone. Both were experienced in retailing and realized the commercial potential in employing the Washburn name on reasonably-priced instruments. Japan was the obvious source for production.

The new line included electric guitars, the first to carry the Washburn brand. Launched in 1979, the Wing series employed high-waisted body styling with twin small-horned cutaways, through-neck construction, two humbuckers and a

conventional circuit with four controls plus selector. First models were the Hawk and Falcon, soon joined by the cheaper bolt-on-neck Raven and the high-end Eagle.

The following year brought the Stage solids which targeted the rock market in more overt fashion, shaped like a chopped-down Gibson Explorer and in various formats including a 12-string. By 1983 the electric line had increased considerably. Fender-influenced Force solids partnered 335-style HB hollowbodies and the Flying V-based Tour models. Various Stages continued, while Wings had withered to the Hawk, Falcon and Eagle plus the new T Bird. The headless-neck fashion hit in 1984 and Washburn responded with Bantam mini-body guitars, including a double-neck. Washburn also followed the trend for locking vibrato systems.

As the 1980s progressed a distinctly metal theme began to dominate Washburn's catalog. By 1986 the Wings had gone but the Stages remained. The Force models became more superstrat than Strat-like, and the Tour V now had an offset body like a Jackson Randy Rhoads. The new Heavy Metal models sported an overt, sharp-pointed body, while unsubtle graphics and the new Wonderbar heavy-duty vibrato were common features throughout the line. Artist-endorsed models were becoming increasingly common, including the strange angular form of the shortlived AF40V Ace Frehley guitar.

The first Korean-made Washburns were the Rebel series of cheap superstrats, debuting in 1986. Existing designs were also transferred to Korea, a source used by many brands at this time. Further models to originate from the new production base included the PRS-influenced RS8 and RS10, part of the Tour series. By now the catalog consisted of just the Tour and Force series, covering a variety of guitars where common model names had little to do with consistency of features or design.

Some Washburns continued to emanate from Japan, such as the Stephens Extended Cutaway T series introduced in 1987. Also known as Spitfires, these George Washburn-brand solids catered for players using the popular two-handed tapping technique of the time, their extreme carved cutaway allowing access to a 29- or 36-fret fingerboard. Through-neck construction and active circuitry were other features of this high-quality, US-designed super-superstrat. The late 1980s also brought the superstrat-style Chicago series, plus Les Paul-style models, marketed as the Classic series. Fretted Industries officially changed its name to Washburn International in 1987.

Increased prominence for Washburn in the early 1990s came with Nuno Bettencourt's signature model. It was a

popular move, prompting a succession of versions made in the US, Japan and Korea. At this time the G.W. Lyon brandname was employed on a line of ultra-cheap guitars and, plundering the more recent past, Washburn revived a reduced Wing series.

The Mercury solid series appeared in 1992, and this comprehensive line of guitars included models made in the US. It was revamped two years later and again in 1995. Other 1990s newcomers have included the Fender-style Silverado and Laredo, and the Steve Stevens signature six-string.

In 1996 the Dime series first appeared, as used by Dimebag Darrell and based on his previously favored Dean guitar. A number of variants have since been issued on to the market, including the Culprit of 1999, which seemed like a sliced-up Explorer.

Also in 1996 the US-made MG series was launched, designed by Grover Jackson, and the Peavey Wolfgang-like Billy T series appeared, evolving into 1997's Maverick series, some of which were made in Indonesia. Washburn's P series debuted in 1997, endorsed by Nuno Bettencourt, some made in the US, some in Korea. With such output from a variety of production sources the Washburn name remains prominent and continues to enjoy a credibly high profile worldwide – no mean achievement in today's increasingly competitive marketplace.

Yamaha

For much of its existence the Yamaha logo might have been more widely recognized as seen on the gas cap of a motorcycle's fuel tank, but those three crossed tuning forks reveal the company's deep roots in musical instrument manufacturing.

Although better known for a plethora of diverse products, the Japanese Yamaha company has produced some excellent electric guitars over the years, perhaps the most famous being the SG-2000, once favored by Carlos Santana. For a company with such a diverse product line, the standard and quality has been remarkably high throughout its history.

The company, started in the 1880s, began making acoustic guitars in 1946. Yamaha started to offer solidbody electric around 1964, but its first major line debuted in 1966. This consisted of the two-pickup S-201 and three-pickup S-302, later renamed the SG-2 and SG-3 (soon joined by a 12-string). These were bolt-on-neck models with pointed offset horns and Jazzmaster-style dual circuitry.

They were soon followed by the crescent-shape SG-2C and SG-3C, and what became the best-known of the early electrics, the SG-2A, SG-5A, SG-7A and SG-12A, known as "flying samurai" for their

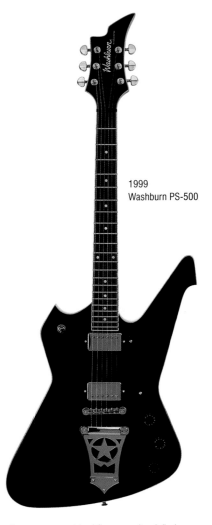

1999
Washburn PS-500

unique asymmetrical "reverse body" shape with dramatically extended lower horn.

The bolt-on-neck SA-15 semi-hollowbody adopted a similar outline, while several more such models, including the SA-50, employed more traditional double-cutaway styling. There were also full-size, single-pointed-cutaway archtop AE series electrics.

In 1972 Yamaha's solidbody line changed to a design with a single sloping cutaway. Still called SGs, these came with flat body or "German carve" edge relief. The following year these were joined by an equal-double-cutaway series employing a shape that would culminate in Yamaha's renowned SG-2000 solidbody.

By 1973 the semi-hollow line had been enhanced with the fancier SA-60 and SA-90 sporting more powerful humbuckers. Two new single-rounded-cutaway hollowbody guitars were offered, the AE-12 (sunburst) and AE-18 (natural). Around 1976 the shortlived SX-800 and SX-900 solidbodies joined the line. These had two equal almost flat cutaways and sharp pointed horns.

Yamaha achieved its first big success with the SG-2000, introduced in 1976 and endorsed by Carlos Santana. It represented a big leap forward for Yamaha, and was the guitar that at last reversed the impression

that Japan only produced cheap copies. It had a through-neck construction, carved top, twin humbuckers, and a bridge mounted on a brass block for added sustain.

Yamaha discovered that while their previous solidbody models had been of undisputedly high quality, they nevertheless had been too unconventional to provoke general popularity.

However, when Yamaha tried the equally high-quality but conservatively designed SG-2000 – in effect a double-cutaway Les Paul – they suddenly had a successful guitar. This was an important lesson for Yamaha and other Japanese makers.

Tracking the very many different Yamaha SG models that followed the 2000 is highly confusing. In America they were called SBGs to distinguish them from Gibsons. Furthermore, specifications on domestic Japanese models were quite different from those on export models with the same number. Yamaha stopped exporting the SBGs to the US in 1988, although the SBG-500 and 700 were reintroduced in 1998.

Demand for copies of American guitars picked up in Japan in 1977 just as one particular "copy era" wound down in the US. Yamaha obliged on its domestic market with high quality SR Strat-style models (SuperR'nroller) and SL Les Paul-alikes (Studio Lord). Also new in 1977 were the Strat-shape SC series, featuring blade-style single-coils, and Yamaha introduced the set-neck SF series (Super Flighter) with twin humbuckers and offset cutaways.

In 1982 Yamaha revised the SC series to reflect the old "reverse" SG body shape, now with three single-coil pickups in a Strat-style layout. Two years later Yamaha revamped its solidbody line again, adding more SGs and a number of Tele-style SJ-series models. There were also new Strat-based six-strings called the SE series as well as variations with twin humbuckers. New Yamaha endorsers included Cornell Dupree, Carlos Rios, and Barry Finnerty.

By 1984 costs of Japanese production had soared, and Yamaha moved most guitar-making to a new, modern factory in Kaohsiung, Taiwan, continuing to make only a few models in Japan. These included the evergreen SGs and 1985's EX-2 and VX-2

1994
Yamaha Pacific 604

guitar facts

1999
Yamaha AES-500

1999 Yamaha AES-500

BODY: single-cutaway body made from solid alder.

NECK: bolt-on maple neck with unbound rosewood fingerboard with 12" radius; 22 medium nickel-silver frets, and 1 $\frac{11}{16}$" nut width; 24 ¾" scale length.

HEADSTOCK: symmetrical back-angled headstock with three-a-side enclosed Yamaha tuners; synthetic nut.

BRIDGE: wrapover bridge with compensated saddle ridge.

ELECTRONICS: two Yamaha humbucking pickups; three-way switch to select either individually or both together, independent volume controls and master tone control with push-push coil tap switch.

SOUND: from thick, warm humbucking sounds to thinner, brighter pseudo-single-coil tones, all with some snap and ring.

Zemaitis
Metal front

Flying V-style model with carved-relief tops and locking vibratos.

Yamaha's new Taiwanese line was the Strat-style SE series, introduced in 1985, with bolt-on necks, locking or traditional vibrato systems and various pickups. In 1986 Yamaha briefly offered the minimalist G-10 synth guitar controller. By 1988 top-of-the-line, through-neck models came with either passive or active electronics.

Yamaha's RGX Series debuted in 1987, sleek offset-double-cutaway superstrats with scalloped, sharp, pointed cutaways, locking vibratos and a variety of pickups, with through-neck and active models. By 1988 the RGX Custom (through-neck and ash body) and Standard (flame-maple cap) topped the line.

A year later Yamaha introduced the flamed-top, set-neck Image series: Custom with LED position markers for playing in the dark; Deluxe with vibrato; and hardtail Standard. Designed at Yamaha's Kemble facility in the UK, these equal-double-cutaway solidbodies lasted only a couple years.

By 1990 Yamaha had opened a custom shop in Los Angeles, California. The SE series was history, and most RGX guitars were renamed RGZ, now joined by the new

Rich Lasner-designed Pacifica line and fancy Weddington series. The Pacifica instruments continued the enthusiasm for Fender styles, ranging from through-neck types with carved flamed maple top and internal sound chambers, to bolt-on-neck models with various pickups and vibratos, some offering excellent value and selling very well.

The Weddington Custom (carved quilt maple top), Classic (carved maple top) and Special (flat mahogany) were twin-humbucker Les-Paul-style solidbodies with an Aria PE-like sweeping curve down from the upper shoulder into the cutaway opposite. Most of the higher-end RGZ guitars and the Weddingtons were gone by 1995, replaced in 1996 by several American-made Pacifica USA models, using Warmoth bodies and necks.

By 1999 the Pacifica series included an ash-bodied Tele-style solid endorsed by Mike Stern. A new AES series of solidbodies and semi-hollowbodies appeared. These nodded to the neo-vintage revival with their exaggerated rounded single-cutaway and retro-shape pickguards, a generally 1960s image that brought Yamaha almost full circle. This continued in 2000 with the launch of SGV models, which were direct revivals of the "reverse"-body SGs from almost 35 years earlier.

Zemaitis
Extravagant and highly collectable, Zemaitis guitars have become emblematic of rock glitz and excess of the late 1960s and '70s.
Best known for his "metal front" and "pearl front" solidbodies built for players like Ron Wood, Tony Zemaitis made the highest-profile British guitars of the 20th century. He was based at Chatham, Kent, retiring in 2000 after 35 years as a professional guitar-maker. He first came to wide attention in the

early 1970s when Wood and Ronnie Lane began using his instruments, and from then on Zemaitis's list of acoustic and electric clients began to read like rock'n'roll royalty, including Hendrix, Clapton, Harrison, Richards, Gilmour, Honeyman-Scott and many others.

His electrics are flamboyant guitars for stage use, symbolizing glorious 1970s rock'n'roll decadence. They boast plenty of handwork, hand-made bridges, and engraved metal or mosaic-like pearl inlays. Some metal-front Zemaitis guitars featured work by shotgun engraver Danny O'Brien. The idea for the metal fronts started when Zemaitis shielded Strat pickups with metal foil and decided to take the idea further.

Most were custom-ordered, but there was a dalliance around 1980 with the shortlived Budget student model. Zemaitis instruments became desirable to later generations seeking 1970s styles; more recent players include Gilby Clark and Richie Robinson. They have become highly-prized and valuable electric guitars, and in Japan have reached almost mythical status. Unsurprisingly, Tony Zemaitis's death in 2002 served only to heighten the collectibility of his guitars.

acknowledgements

TOTALLY INTERACTIVE GUITAR BIBLE
Tutor Book; Guitar Facts Book; DVD; CD

The publishers would like to thank the following for their contributions to this project.

Guitar Facts:
Tony Bacon; Dave Burrluck; Paul Day; Dave Hunter; Michael Wright.

DVD:
Dave Gregory; Dave Hunter; Paul Balmer and Judy Caine of Music On Earth; Nick Squires; Tony Wass of Ninth Wave Audio; Ken Morse; Julian Ridgway of Redferns Music Picture Library; Matt Bristow of Cherry Red Records; Paul Riley and Toby Taylor of Proper Music Group; Dickie Goldberg; Sharon Angello; Neil Whitcher and all at Fender Musical Instruments (Europe); Joe Knaggs, Marc Quigley, Peter Wolf, and Tina Benson at Paul Reed Smith Guitars; Gavin Mortimer at Headline Music, Jeff Pumfrett at Machinehead Music; Jeremy Singer at Gibson UK; Bob and Cindy Benedetto; Ben Green and all at WD Music Products UK; Gibson Keddie of John Hornby Skewes & Co in Leeds; Mak Ogawa of Ivor Mairants Musicentre in London; Simon Law at SVL; Mark Brend; John Ryall.

Tutor Book and CD:
Deirdre Cartwright; Rod Fogg; Dave Hunter; Eric Thompson; Martin Goulding; Rikky Rooksby.

Design:
Paul Cooper Design; Balley Design Associates.